Skinheads Shaved for Battle

Skinheads Shaved for Battle:
A Cultural History of American Skinheads

Jack B. Moore

Bowling Green State University Popular Press
Bowling Green, OH 43403

Library of Congress Catalogue Card No.: 93-70440

ISBN: 0-87972-582-6 Clothbound
        0-87972-583-4 Paperback

Cover design by Gary Dumm and Laura Darnell-Dumm

For Mrs. Bowker, as promised.

Contents

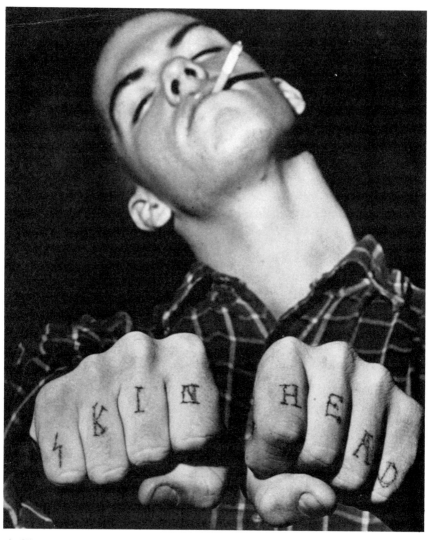

A 17-year-old St. Petersburg, Florida skinhead proudly declares his affiliation on tattooed kunckles in April 1988. Photograph by Bonnie Jo Mount, courtesy of the Tampa Tribune.

Introduction

This book began as a chapter in another book I was writing on a criminal case in Tampa, Florida, involving two young skinheads, 16 and 18 years old, brothers who were at first both accused of murdering a black man in December, 1987, on the balcony of the new Tampa Museum of Art. Eventually, the older brother's case was split off from the younger's, after he agreed to testify against his brother, whose idol he apparently had been. Attempting to describe as much about the cultural background of the case as I could, I wrote about the young men's lives, their parents' lives, the life of the man they were accused of killing. I wrote about the lawyers in the case, the jury, witnesses, I wrote about the local skinhead scene and about those who hung around that scene.

The presiding judge in the younger brother's trial ruled that information about the young man's affiliation with the skinheads could not be introduced into the proceedings because it would tend to prejudice the jury against him. So although the community was inundated with information about these skinhead links, the connections were not explored in any testimony. I decided that since the alleged killer identified himself so strongly as a skinhead at the time of his and his brother's murderous assault on a black man, I would need to set down precisely what skinhead meant. That need resulted in this book.

After establishing in a general way the violent history of skinheads in America and suggesting why they have come to exist as a frightening threat to civil peace, I thought it would be particularly helpful to American readers to review the English origins of the skinhead subculture, for although skinheads have disturbed society in most of the developed nations of Europe for some time, English skinheads set the style early for skinheads in America. It took me longer than I thought it would to set forth the outlines of skinhead activity in England, partly because I found that in doing so, I was often sometimes explicitly and sometimes inferentially suggesting what I hoped were illuminating differences between the English and American varieties, though

1

naturally there were many similarities for me to note also. And, frankly, the study of the evolution of the skinhead culture in England seemed fascinating to me, an American, who was far more familiar with the formation of hate groups at home than abroad. I also became interested in studying the academic and sometimes non-academic literature produced in England that studied skinheads, because in England (though to a lesser degree than in America, I think) what most people know about skinheads is what they read. Therefore their presentation became important as a part of their perceived image. What Americans wrote and thought about skinheads in part derived from their depiction in England. I was aided in my study of the English literature by some guidance from Stan Cohen and Dick Hebdige, and greatly helped by their books on the reception youth subcultures in the sixties received and the style of these subcultures, respectively. Though my own perspective is not necessarily theirs, I must thank them here for their collegial assistance and acknowledge the brilliance of their work which I have obviously found absolutely essential to my own youth subcultural analysis.

I would also like to acknowledge my great debt to a few of the many other people and organizations who truly made this book possible. The Anti-Defamation League of B'nai B'rith (my contact there was Gail Gans), and the Southern Poverty Law Center (my contact was Joseph T. Roy, Sr.), supplied me with much of the information about skinheads in America that I needed. These two organizations, along with the Center for Democratic Renewal, perform the invaluable service of keeping Americans informed of groups and individuals who commit hate crimes in America, and in different ways combat hate, prejudice, and discrimination in our country. Gail and Joe answered my questions, sent me materials, and let me know what they knew about skinheads. I hope I have used their wisdom wisely. B'nai B'rith not only let me use their archives, but agreed to let me adapt the title of one of their publications for my own use in a slightly different version as a title. Whatever worth my book possesses would have been greatly diminished without the help provided me by these organizations.

At critical junctures in my research, Ben Brown of *USA Today* and Elinor Langer came through with encouragement and facts, as did Claire Margolies and Cyma Horowitz at the Blaustein Library of the American Jewish Committee. Roger Adams, then on the staff of WUSF-FM in Tampa, kindly gave me some revealing interview tapes with skinheads and their leaders. Some skinheads and ex-skinheads also gave me revealing interviews but did not wish me to use their names. Steve Burcham, a filmmaker, helped me on an earlier project about skinheads that spilled over into this and gave me permission to use interviews with skinheads that he had taped. Jay Fuqua, Herman Dudley, Dean McKee (and his parents), Nicole Jacobson, and Phil Yost were helpful. Sean Moore supplied me with key musicological and (along with Tamsin Moore) punk/skinhead scene information. Karen Fain retyped my messy manuscripts into finished form while offering me encouragement and teaching me the rudiments of word processing. My wife lived uncomplainingly with the clutter of my research. The Institute on Black Life, at the University of South Florida, kept an eye on what I was doing and helped me feel my work could be important. My mistakes and opinions are my own.

Most of my book concerns who American skinheads are, how they have developed within larger youth group scenes, the world of their ideas and activities, how they are or are not organized, the role of music in their formation and development, how they have been perceived by the media in America, and what damage they have done in American society. I focus mainly although not exclusively on the cultural history of the skinheads in America during the 1980s, which is roughly the first decade of their development. I suggest that while they were originally in America a minor distraction on the punk scene, they have grown into a dangerous, far more politically engaged source of hate thought and crime in America. When I write of skinheads, unless I state otherwise, I mean racist skinheads. There are self-declared non-racist skinheads, and I deal with them briefly. I certainly recognize their existence, but they are not the subject of this book. While I wish to understand skinheads, I am appalled by them, and that is one angle from which this book was written. I believe that we can better understand the greater American culture that surrounds the skinheads, that incorporates them, if we understand them. But I do not write of their subculture as a completely disinterested anthropologist might.

Chapter One:
Obsessed with Violence:
The Skinhead Decade

The skinheads evolved in America during the 1980s from first being viewed as another counter-cultural component somehow connected to the punk music scene, to being recognized as a separate group outliving the reformulation or virtual death of that scene and developing a specifically political agenda drawing skinheads closer to right wing hate movements in the United States, England, and Europe. This transformation was accompanied by a growth throughout the decade in the number of skinheads but far more markedly in skinhead commission of hate crimes—bias crimes motivated by a spirit or ideology of hostility against victims because of their race, national origin, religion, or sexual orientation. By the end of the 1980s they achieved a reputation as the most violent extremist group in the country.

Throughout the 1980s the Klanwatch project of the Southern Poverty Law Center (SPLC) ordinarily listed nine varieties of hate crimes (the federal government as yet does not have a completely effective method for collecting, categorizing, and disseminating such statistics, although the Federal Hate Crimes Statistics Act signed by President Bush on April 23, 1990 is a greatly welcome step to those ends). These are murder, bombings, arson, shootings (non-lethal), assaults, cross burnings, threats, vandalism, and conspiracy. In the 1980s skinheads would be significantly involved in murders, shootings, assaults, threats, and vandalism. Rarely were they legally connected to incidents of bombing, arson, cross burnings, and conspiracies. Their absence from some of these categories may be misleading because these are areas in which, although crimes are often reported, frequently no one knows or can prove who committed them. Persons who are guilty of vandalism, for example, are frequently not apprehended. Who has spray-painted "Jews Die" on a synagogue wall is not easy to trace. The Anti-Defamation League of B'nai B'rith (ADL) concluded that "police are convinced that skinheads were responsible for burning a three-by-three-

4

foot cross on the front yard of a black family in Westminster, California," July 28, 1988, as they were for spray-painting swastikas and "SWP" (Supreme White Power) on neighborhood walls near Temple Beth David (ADL, *Young and Violent* 12). But no convictions for these acts were ever obtained, and no names of specific skinheads ever publicly connected to the crimes.

Nationally circulated reports of skinhead crime came late in the decade, considering the presence of skinheads in America at least since the waning years of the 1970s, but quickly accelerated. The first mention of skinheads in the Southern Poverty Law Center's Klanwatch "decade review" *Hate, Violence, and White Supremacy, 1980-1990* (though not the first time they were reported engaged in hate crime activity) lists two skinhead assaults occurring in April and May 1986, in Atlanta. Yet the SPLC publication *Klanwatch*'s annual (February 1989) report of hate crimes analyzing events of 1988 proclaimed, "Skinheads Blamed for Year's Worst Attacks," declaring that "not since the KKK of the 1950s has a white supremacist group been so obsessed with violence." The report continued, "The emergence of skinhead gangs represents a unique and frightening phenomenon in the history of white supremacy in America: for the first time, a nationwide racist movement is being initiated by teenagers who are not confined to any single geographic region or connected by any national network, but whose gangs sprang up spontaneously in cities throughout the country." *Klanwatch*'s annual (February issue) report for the following year added, "Skinhead Violence More Threatening in 1989." In less than a decade violence committed by skinheads catapulted them to perhaps the leading position among hate groups practicing violence in America. Klanwatch's "decade review" referred to them as the "New Revolutionaries" and treated them as one of the white supremacy movement's greatest rebuilding sources since the decline of the Klan in the late seventies and early eighties, and the destruction of the militant guerrilla group called "The Order" by late 1985. One of the final quotations included in the review's "Overview: 1980-1990" of white supremacy in the United States is longtime hate-monger Robert Miles's pleased remark that "If there's a future for the right wing, [skinheads] will be the first racial wave. They're what Nazi stormtroopers were in the early '20s."

Prior to the mid-1980s, crimes or more specifically hate crimes may have been committed by young men who were skinheads, but these seem not to have been reported on nationally and categorized as skinhead crimes. Thus, *Klanwatch* for example noted in February 1983 that "Youthful Racism is on the rise," that "Carolina Knights' Grand Dragon Glenn Miller has confirmed reports that his organization is actively recruiting members among high school children in Onslow County" and that in Kalamazoo, Michigan, a "dozen youths in Nazi uniforms, members of the SS Action Group from Dearborn" (where later skinhead activity would take place) stood guard at a rally at which Reverend Edward Warner waved a copy of *Gay Is Not Good* at the gathered crowd (4). But whether or not skinheads were among the youth involved was not recorded. Quite possibly skinheads were not part of either scene, or they simply went undescribed. It is also possible that among the young people who did participate in these hostile activities were later skinheads, or that the kind of young people who participated were like the kind who later became skinheads. Before there was skinhead crime there were young people who seemed willing to engage in some of the activities skinheads later became infamous for, but who were not part of the skinhead scene, or not identified within that scene.

That scene was certainly firmly in place by 1984 though not as peopled with young males, and to a lesser degree females, as it would later become. There was a skinhead audience in America aware of the political message English skinhead hero Ian Stuart sang about in his "Oi!" music, which he articulated plainly in anti-Semitic remarks to the anti-Jewish tabloid *The Spotlight* March 19, 1984 issue claiming that "the survival of our race is at stake." That some skinheads were not just aware of, but were receptive to the Englishman Stuart's message, is revealed by the Chicago Area Skinhead's (CASH) fascist iconography featuring young, jack-booted Nazi toughs in advertisements for a "Death's Head Muscle T-Shirt" that they were selling the same year. This does not mean that all skinheads in America at this time were fascist anti-minority homophobes, willing and eager to commit violence for one or another twisted political or social cause. But it does demonstrate that some skinheads had arrived at or accepted these positions. And *Spotlight*'s interest in the skinhead scene—in their January 6-13, 1986 issue they would claim the skins were "certainly prepared to do their part to bring a new social order to America"— demonstrates the continuing attempts by extremist groups to encourage them to join the political battles hate groups were waging. CASH's ugly solicitation would in retrospect become an early sign of things to come, but was not an event of national notice, and would not be spotlighted until the Anti-Defamation League's *Shaved for Battle* report issued in November 1987.

In the August-September 1986 *Klanwatch* the SPLC noted that "Greg Withrow of Sacramento" now led the White Student Union which was "the organizational offspring of the White American Resistance... and Tom Metzger" without identifying Withrow's skinhead links. Probably because skinheads in America were first viewed in the late 1970s and early 1980s as a group rooted in the youth music scene and not as a strongly politically oriented collection of young men, skinhead crimes until this time—as only later reported by the major monitoring organizations—were mainly associated with the music scenes they inhabited. But not always. In April 1986 at a political rally in Atlanta against aid for the Nicaraguan Contras, ten skinheads were arrested for assault, and in May three more Atlanta skins were accused of beating up a nightclub owner and trashing his club (Klanwatch's *Hate* 35). Atlanta was an early gathering place and spawning ground for skinheads. Since the 1960s it had been a magnet in the South for disaffected youth and runaways, and in addition supported a relatively large punk and new music scene. By the 1980s a predominantly black city (though one with several mixed neighborhoods), it was a business hub for extensive, mainly white suburbs surrounded by smaller towns that had traditionally been Klan territory: potentially a volatile mix. The Center for Democratic Renewal, based in Atlanta, published a page one article in its June 1986 issue of *The Monitor* relating how skinheads had been responsible for vicious, often racial crimes nation-wide, including recent incidents "reliably attributed to skins" in Atlanta including several murders, "three mob attacks, six other assaults and four" acts of "swastika vandalism." Atlanta skins wore t-shirts with the slogan "Sickle Cell Anemia: The Great White Hope" and openly avowed in publications such as *Maximumrocknroll* that they "joined the punk movement" because it "presented [them] with an aggressive, angry, stomping, fighting mad type of [Nazi] movement."

In its widely distributed and influential 1987 pamphlet *Shaved for Battle*, ADL reported that "Skinheads in Florida have disrupted rock concerts in St. Petersburg and Clearwater, and in October, 1986, five were arrested in nearby Ybor City," a skinhead hangout with at that time several new music establishments, "after allegedly clubbing a group of youths leaving a punk-rock club." The same publication described similar disruptions on the Pacific Coast. "In Portland's Old Town District" also in October 1986 a "gang of over 20 skinheads marched in formation toward a popular teen night spot armed with axes, pipes, knives, and baseball bats," but were interrupted by three dozen police before they could attack anyone. At least one of these skins hated enemies for more than their musical tastes, since he had "attended the 1986 Aryan Nations Conference."

Accelerating and expanding rapidly, by 1987 skinhead violence had far transgressed the borders of the new music scene, and had commenced what would seem an explosion of confrontations, assaults, and murders that derived at least in part from the ideas with which increasingly they associated themselves. *Klanwatch* for May-June 1987 reprinted a February 2 news release datelined Orlando which sounded distinctly alarming. "Authorities are worried by the presence of a number of youth gangs in central Florida, according to a report in the *Orlando Sentinel*. The only white gang is the skinheads, which models itself after the English neo-nazi [sic] youth. Two members have already been arrested; one for aggravated battery against two persons he believed were gay, the other for threatening a girl with a knife in a non-racial incident. Last fall, the skinheads were involved in several instances of racial violence in local high schools. After a crackdown by Orlando police, which included the thwarting of a plot to bomb a local gay bar, skinhead activity in the Orlando area dwindled. New reports of activity by the group are reported in the Sarasota and Tampa areas." An update in the August *Klanwatch* reported speculations in Tampa "that about 100 teenagers have affiliated with the skinheads" who "have attacked blacks, Jews, and gays in Florida and disrupted two punk rock concerts since 1985." The same issue told of an attack on Greg Withrow allegedly by disgruntled White Student Union members "upset over his renunciation of the white supremacist group," but strangely did not mention that Withrow also claimed the assailants who he said nailed him to a plank and slashed him with a razor were skinheads, a charge reported in ADL's 1987 *Shaved for Battle*. In this report the ADL was also able to list a number of skinhead gangs throughout the country, in Chicago, Cincinnati, Detroit, San Francisco Bay Area, central Florida, Portland, Los Angeles, Dallas, and Denver, and to quote the violent talk spoken by skinheads and their adherents, about smashing one minority power or another. What these truculent claims translated into in terms of action was revealed in an incident publicized by both the ADL in *Shaved for Battle* and the SPLC in Klanwatch's October 1987 *Intelligence Report*. In July, a 54-year-old black woman was confronted by four skinheads while trying to cross a bridge near a park in San Jose, California. The woman said one of the skinheads told her "niggers pay toll" and another said, "We're going to string you up in that tree." This was the kind of assault, *Klanwatch* indicated, that led to hate group organizer Dave Mazzella's declaration that "Skinheads are our front line warriors. They roam the streets and do what's necessary to protect the race."

Before 1987 ended, skinheads would commit far worse crimes. Skinheads in the Bay area putting up an anti-Semitic poster were confronted by a teenage boy whom they threw through a plate glass window (*Los Angeles Times*, November 30). In October, Michael Casey Martin's skinhead gang of Los Angeles area Reich Skins terrorized Hispanic families. On November 9, the anniversary of Nazi Germany's infamous *Reichskristallnacht* (often abbreviated to *Kristallnacht*) of 1938, when stormtroopers and fascist thugs throughout Germany attacked Jewish businesses and places of worship and beat up and killed Jewish citizens, skinheads in Chicago similarly desecrated a temple, smashed windows and spray-painted swastikas at two more synagogues, and for several hours systematically devastated identifiably Jewish properties including kosher markets, a bookstore and businesses owned or run by Jews.

The murder of black Isaiah Walker on December 20 in Tampa by skinhead Dean McKee following an assault upon Walker by McKee and his older skinhead brother Scott, seems the natural culmination of the violence skinheads had engaged in sporadically and to a great extent randomly since their appearance on the punk scene in New York and Los Angeles in the late 1970s, often implosive violence for a long time indistinguishable from the violence endemic to that scene. But now the violence was escalating, increasingly reported upon, and increasingly centered upon Jews, African Americans, Latinos, Asians, and homosexuals, although it was still in any meaningful political sense uncoordinated. The outbursts of violence, which can be seen partly as another strand joined to America's long history of homophobic, nativist, inter-ethnic hostility, and partly a recent manifestation of what the media and national human rights advocates saw as an increasingly tense period of racial and sexual tensions (caused by the AIDS predicament), was also a spontaneous phenomenon nationwide, whose regional incidents resulted from the neurotic hatreds of like-minded people not tightly joined together in any disciplined, formal sense. The repeated acts of violence seem more the deepest kind of unplanned social conspiracy, similar acts committed by separate people who did not have to consult closely or at all with each other because all operated from a roughly similar set of dangerous impulses.

Dean McKee's murder of Isaiah Walker was not known until late February or early March 1988. Rather than standing as a cathartic peak of skinhead frenzy, it was only a shocking prelude to a detonation of skinhead violence in 1988. Klanwatch's decade review *Hate, Violence, and White Supremacy* told of skinheads caught up in Satanism who murdered a convenience store clerk February 9 in Las Vegas; a skinhead who stabbed to death a white man attempting to protect a black man in San Jose on February 28; the murder of Mulegeta Seraw by three skinheads in Portland, November 13; three skinheads accused of murdering a black man in Reno, December 10. Skinheads in Dallas were arrested for shooting into and defacing a temple, and skinheads in Kenosha, Wisconsin, were charged with shooting at a predominately black church and at the house and car of a black family. Klanwatch listed for the year several dozen acts of criminal assault committed by skinheads against gays or minorities and almost a dozen acts of criminal vandalism against properties owned by or associated usually with minorities.

For 1989 Klanwatch's annual (February) review listed three murders connected to skinheads: a gay male stabbed to death in January in Hyde Park, Texas; a hairdresser shot and his car set afire in March in Denver; and a white male robbed and beaten to death in Pittsburgh in August. Skinheads raped and assaulted a lesbian in January 1989 in San Diego; in March in Vallejo, California, skinheads attacked a television news crew and in Silver Spring, Maryland, skinheads were convicted of beating an Asian man. Still in March, Richland County, South Carolina, skinheads attacked and cut a young black boy with a razor, and in April in Gainesville, Florida, three skinheads were sentenced for beating a black man. The same month skinheads in Auburn Hills, Michigan, assaulted a racially mixed group at a convenience store. Almost 30 assaults were noted in Klanwatch's hate crime summary for 1989 which was in no way an official nor necessarily a complete tabulation of crimes, since as the *Review* admitted, "no national system exists for tracking hate crimes" and there was currently "no way of knowing how many crimes are motivated by hate."

That Klanwatch's ten-year accounting is highly selective is demonstrated by comparing their hate-crime listings with information supplied elsewhere in their own publications. In their decade review *Hate* they noted 37 skinhead assaults nationally for 1988, while in their annual *Klanwatch Intelligence Report* February issue review for the year they state that "In Portland alone, where four skinhead gangs operate, police documented at least 40 serious crimes committed by skinheads in 1988. The crimes include 30 major assaults" (5). The Portland police, however, did not break down this information to indicate which crimes were hate crimes. Since Klanwatch's information base is compiled mainly from newspaper clippings and news releases, and not police blotters in individual cities across the nation, their statistics are inevitably affected. Moreover, the police themselves did not ordinarily distinguish the motivation of crimes in their records to indicate how many were a result of hostile political or social beliefs. Clearly, however, as the decade progressed, skinheads committed more and more hate crimes.

Increased skinhead activity in 1988 was also seen as a prime cause for the highest level in five years of anti-Semitic incidents (ADL, *Audit of Anti-Semitic Incidents* 1) in the United States. The first reason listed by the ADL for this escalation in the number of episodes of vandalism and desecration (823, or up 18.5 percent from 1987) and acts of harassment (458, or up 41.7 percent from 1987) was proliferation of skinhead gangs. Another reason for the increase was "an unusually large number of incidents" occurring in the South, including states having very small Jewish populations "but disproportionately large skinhead populations"— such as Florida, which accounted for a record 89 incidents, 64 more than in 1987. In 1989, the ADL noted in its annual audit 2,432 anti-Semitic crimes—the greatest outburst of anti-Semitic hate in 11 years. Skinhead crimes against Jews increased by 200 percent. Some of this increase should probably be attributed to advanced record-keeping and the greater attention given skinheads in the state and nationally. But it would be naive to assume that greater skinhead activity against Jews was not also a factor.

12   Skinheads Shaved for Battle

If murder is used as a measure to gauge the progress of skinhead violence, the conclusion is clear that in the last half of the eighties, skinhead hostility was increasingly directed towards (if not at heart caused by) political and social targets. That is, granted the violence and hostility pervading much skinhead behavior, more and more the victims of skinhead wrath were social or political enemies. In the earlier years of the eighties the skinheads were known if at all for their disruptive actions on the music performance scene. More and more, however, their murderous assaults upon minorities together with their ties to organized hate groups became a matter of public scrutiny and accelerated anxiety.

The prosecutor in Dean McKee's 1988 case, the first recorded skinhead racial murder case to be tried, was considerably limited in the facts of the 16-year-old boy's life that he could communicate to the jury in order to justify his demand for a first-degree conviction. He was not allowed even to mention that the boy (or young man) was a skinhead. Everyone who read about the case knew that, but the jury did not. That line of inquiry could not be pursued in court. The prosecutor established premeditation by proving to the jury that McKee was highly prejudiced, that he hated blacks, and that in some fashion, prior to McKee's alleged murder of Isaiah Walker, he recognized this was a black man, the man he wanted to kill. Though McKee's life revealed him as an extremely violent person who had engaged in—sought out—fights with a great many people, and though one suspects in personal battle, drunk as he was, he might have killed anyone who fought against him the night he and his brother found Walker sleeping on the balcony of the Tampa Museum of Art, his crime can be viewed as a political act carrying out his hatred of blacks and manifesting his feelings of their inferiority. Where formerly he had terrorized a variety of people with whom he came into contact in the music and punk scenes of Tampa and St. Petersburg, his ultimate act of violence was directed against a black man and presumably not simply because the man was vulnerable at a time McKee wanted to kick somebody's, anybody's ass. At the time of the murder, McKee was not part of any skinhead or hate group organization beyond his own local gang, a not particularly cohesive bunch called the Saints.

In February 1988, in San Jose, even before McKee's complicity in the Walker murder was discovered by police, a skinhead named Michael Elrod, 19, killed a white man during a violent interracial encounter.

Klanwatch's February annual review issue reported that Elrod had been taunting Fred Ross, a black man in the company of white Scott Vollmer, and telling fellow party-goers to "go get that nigger." Elrod, like the 16-year-old McKee drunk and also an alcoholic (which McKee too may have been), flashed a knife at Ross. His friend Vollmer intervened to stop what looked like an attack, and was stabbed to death. Premeditation could not be established in this murder, and again, the presiding judge disallowed allusions to Elrod's skinhead history in court, so a plea bargain was struck. Elrod pleaded guilty to and was convicted of voluntary manslaughter. Later in the year, three more teenaged skinheads drove the streets of Reno apparently "looking for a black person to kill," according to *Klanwatch* (February 1989). Seeing Tony Montgomery, a black man, standing outside his sister's house, one of them fired at and killed him. The criminal complaint against them "alleges they shot Montgomery solely because he was black."

One of the 1988 skinhead murders was not connected with race. Two Utah teenagers with extensive drug, theft, burglary, and robbery records shot in the face and killed a convenience store clerk "for no apparent reason" (*Klanwatch*, February 1989). The young killers like many skinheads had been part of their local punk music scene, playing in a band named "Rigor Mortis," and were also devotees of Satanism, and thus were linked to another anti-social (but not in any ordinary sense political), deviant practice. Their conviction resulted in great part from evidence obtained by an informant who attended a devil worship session "with about a dozen other Utah Valley Skinheads" where Edward Bennet, who fired the shot killing the clerk, confessed. The Southern Poverty Law Center's collection of skinhead materials contains a number of articles linking skinheads to Satanism, which is not an unusual connection considering the mild popularity (if not advocacy) of Satanism in the new music scene, where Satanic symbols are frequently played around with though not usually seriously believed in. Satanic and fascist imagery can be equally appealing to the bitterly alienated. Bennet and his partner Joseph Benson sported skinhead and Satanic tattoos. *Klanwatch* would report later in the year (August 1988, p. 4) that a skinhead arrested in Maryland "had burned a swastika into his chest with a coat hanger" and tattooed "666" (the mark of the beast, Revelations 13:16-18) on his shoulder. The encircled "A"—symbolic of anarchy—is another favorite skinhead sign. In general, the skinheads of the 1980s could be said to have lashed out violently compelled by anarchic impulses as much as fascistic or certainly Satanic ones.

Ken Mieske and his two skinhead companions' murder of Mulegeta Seraw on November 13, 1988, was the first skinhead homicide case investigators successfully linked to specific origins in extremist network organizations. While the earlier three racial murders may have been viewed as individual acts committed spontaneously but within the context of extremely prejudiced attitudes shared by skinheads generally, Mieske's bludgeoning of Seraw was presented by lawyers for the Southern Poverty Law Center and the Anti-Defamation League as part of a consciously planned strategy of destruction originating with Tom Metzger and White Aryan Resistance, communicated and encouraged purposefully by his designated representatives, including his son John, and carried out, even to the detail of employing the preferred skinhead weapon of a baseball bat, by Mieske and his buddies. Mieske embodies the "front line warrior" that extremists have claimed the skinheads to be, in a very real and not simply metaphoric fashion.

Ominously the skinhead scene was becoming increasingly political during the late 1980s, as skinheads were being actively courted and recruited by extremist hate groups to serve in some military fashion. Some skinheads themselves began for the first time actively recruiting new members from the ranks of high school students, consciously seeking out boys and young men, not simply to hang around some punk or new music performance or to hassle gays in parking lots or to shout obscenities at blacks peacefully walking city sidewalks or even to enjoy occasionally an evening of "the old ultra-violence" (a favorite sport of the McKee brothers), but to join at least loosely organized cadres supporting a specific political agenda. Tugged from above in the organized hierarchy of hate, skinheads tried to pull to themselves new warriors from the masses of young potential bigots close to them in age and, though perhaps only in a latent fashion, ideology. Selling not good times drinking beer or banging bodies in the punk dance pit but a chance to fight for the new order, skinhead recruiters were active in 1988-1989 in Waco, Texas; eastern Oregon; Orlando, Florida; Orange County, New York; Phoenix, Arizona; Austin and Houston, Texas; and McKeesport, Pennsylvania (ADL, *Skinheads Target the Schools*). The Anti-Defamation League review of these recruiting attempts does not suggest that they resulted in large numbers of new skinheads or, immediately, in any new members at all, but the directional shift in skinhead style is still significant.

Whatever the skinhead scene was early in the decade, it was joined voluntarily: nowhere were skinheads a major peer pressure group among the young able to force or achieve membership through the magnetic attraction of their size or social glamour. In fact part of their attraction lay in their small numbers and conscious lack of standard social allure. Some recent attempts to engineer a shift in skinhead image are remarkable. In Waco, Texas, letters were sent to "proud parents" by the Confederate Hammer Skins stoutly warning them of "the dangers posed by minority gangs and drug pushers" and resolutely declaring that "it is time that the common White Americans stand up and demand that their children attend schools not polluted with drugs, gangs, and anti-Christian immorality." Finally, the Hammer Skins offered the presumably concerned and anxious parents further information telling "what we are doing to help the White schoolchildren of America."

Underneath this melioristic rhetoric, however, skinhead behavior seemed to remain as violent and insulting as ever. David Lynch recruited in Orange County, New York, in 1988 and throughout Florida, particularly in Orlando, in 1989 for the American Front, a skinhead gang based in San Francisco. On June 2, 1989, a flag proclaiming "White Power" flew above the American flag at Oak Ridge High School in Orlando, along with American Front's insignia. Some of the school's portable classrooms were also spray-painted with swastikas. Lynch himself was ultimately arrested in Edgewater, Florida, for carrying concealed weapons and possessing drug paraphernalia. The new skinheads may be more politically harnessed for hate than the old, more sought after by their extremist elders, but they seem no less volatile, no less a sign of social breakdown and social rot, and of continuing human perversity.

Chapter Two
Last Year's Youth:
Skinhead Evolution in England

Early skinhead history outside America underscores through likeness and difference much about the later developing skinhead scene within America. The skinhead phenomenon in America had its origins in the phenomenon as it evolved in England, although the American variety is in many ways different and separate from its British step-brother. Probably neither phenomenon would have become precisely what it turned into were it not for the way each has been reported upon in the popular press and, curiously enough, in more academic sources, since like most collections of newsworthy and stereotyped individuals in our day, skinheads are influenced by what they read and hear about themselves. As they react in society, British or American, they may behave in consonance with or antagonistically to their images as these have been formulated in newspapers, who have relied frequently upon academic or other presumably authoritative scholars in determining their own conceptualizations of the phenomenon for popular audiences. Other popular media such as the television news industry also participate in this reification process. They are intrigued to report upon the skinhead phenomenon and in doing so transmit to both skinhead and non-skinhead audiences pictures of skinhead behavior revealing what the public should expect from these people, and supplying opportunities for skinheads themselves to learn expected behavior or to counter-attack expectations of them through offering counter-images, embracing the more acceptable sounding white pride instead of white power, for example.

American accounts about American skinheads that narrate skinhead history delight in discussing the British origins of what is frequently treated as a movement of possibly world-wide scope. This repetition is appropriate because it is in many ways historically valid. But the explanation also can function as a way for some Americans to see the racism that dominates native skinhead thought and behavior as a foreign import like the Mafia. At the same time it can provide the skinheads with a way of connecting themselves to a less localized, more extensive and yet still specifically Anglo-Saxon tradition.

Two striking features of these American accounts are the slender number of British reports used for information about the history and nature of skinheads in England, primarily Nick Knight's 1982 *Skinheads*, and the relatively few organizations in the United States that local newspaper reporters consult to determine local skinheads' pre-American roots (primarily the Anti-Defamation League in New York, the Southern Poverty Law Center in Montgomery, and sometimes the Center for Democratic Renewal in Atlanta, all of whom track American skinhead activities). Thus, while much is written about violent skinhead activities in America, information about their English backgrounds is derived from and distributed by very few sources. What Americans including American skinheads know about English skinheads, other than what they can read in random contemporary news reports, is largely what can be found in Knight, as filtered down through reports distributed by a few concerned agencies and as thereafter cannibalized in other newspaper articles. In some ways it is as though a current of information were being channeled through a funnel held backwards, with the details to be transmitted pouring from a narrow stream and then flooding out. Knight's book is a source pulling together in its pop and highly subjective narrative some excellent work by English scholars who dealt with the skinhead subject previously and intensely. It contains a brilliant section by Dick Hebdige, whose 1979 *Subculture, The Meaning of Style* was in part a decoding of early British skinhead fashion and ideology. By including Hebdige's essay "This is England! And They Don't Live Here," Knight's book was able to tap the important but highly academic and esoteric research performed by a network of English sociologists (Marxist anthropologists might be more accurate) and the truly seminal investigation of how British youth culture clashes in the 1960s were exploited by institutions of the dominant culture (including the press and government) in Stanley Cohen's 1972 *Folk Devils and Moral Panics, The Creation of the Mods and Rockers.*

Unlike the attitude of repugnance toward the skinheads that would later prevail immediately in American media responses, the stance toward them in the sometimes-skinhead Knight's book and in much of the more specialized academic literature Hebdige and Cohen deal with in their studies is fairly sympathetic. Pete McGuire, co-editor of one of the most revealing books about English skinheads, refused a publisher's request for an earlier work on the subject because he realized he would have been "happily taking part in a conspiracy to exploit our friends" (Daniel & McGuire, *The Paint House* 7). As Cohen says, the perspective viewing most (then) new theories of deviant cultures in England was Marxist. Delinquency was considered "a collective solution to a structurally imposed problem" that appeared in a "sour, post welfare state Britain which had patently not delivered the goods," and which "tended to be a dreary and colorless environment with little for the young except unimaginative dance halls" (Cohen, new preface to *Folk Devils*; Mike Brake, *Youth & Society* 180). The skinheads are depicted emerging possibly from the working class Cockney subculture of East London, a waste land in which they "were aware that they attended the worst schools, lived in the poorest districts, and had the worst jobs with the smallest wages. They perceived hippies in the same way as they viewed students, as idle layabouts living off the state. They drew on traditional working class values which admired those who worked hard, while despising those seen as lazy and dirty." They possessed "Puritan work ethics" (Brake 188, 190). An implicit attitude of the early investigators seemed to be "what is wrong with society that it has forced this behavior it defines as deviant upon these people?" Cohen refers to a new skepticism that when it saw concepts like "deviant," wanted to ask was not deviance often an appropriate response to a society that had itself deviated from humane norms? Much of this work was being carried on during the late 1960s when R.D. Laing was intellectually so popular and saying that what society called madness was often a reasonable response to impossible pressures exerted on individuals by society itself. Knight announced that he was writing his book "to do...justice" to the skinheads "of the 1967-72 period" who showed him "such a pride and passion for their style" (6). In his 1982 essay, Hebdige compares skinhead style to Rasta since "Both can be seen as genuine attempts at making something out of nothing, attempts at getting something even if it's only a laugh out of a life which, in many cases, by 16 has already run into a collection of brick walls labeled 'unemployment,' 'shit jobs,' and 'routine brushes with the Law' " (32).

Tracing the Growth of Youth Subcultures

These English accounts identify the skinheads as one of a succession of imbricating, interacting youth cultures originating with the Teddy Boys in the post-World War II, post-Churchill world of the 1950s. Groups of young males and the young females who associated with them overlapped with each other sometimes, brawling or coexisting, all with their own fiercely maintained style of appearance, their own tastes (especially musical), their own sense of belonging to their special scene, though often at various points of fashion, attitude, or desired music, they shared preferences. From the outside they were viewed variously with wonder, attraction, and sharp distaste; they were apples of Sodom, forbidden fruit, and sometimes to other yearning young seemed like manna. It was certainly easier to negotiate the differences between them from inside: they could tell each other apart easier than the older, better established populations could. They were invariably seen, whether in the United States (beatniks, hipsters, flower children) or England (Teddy Boys, Mods, Rockers, Greasers), as rebels outside the mainstream of society (though perhaps they would be there only temporarily, until they grew up). Cohen theorized that "In the gallery of types that society erects to show its members which roles should be avoided and which should be emulated, these groups have occupied a constant position as folk devils: visible reminders of what we should not be" (10). Often their ways and antics were focused upon in the press, pulpit, and government halls with harsh intensity (and perhaps wishful thinking), and in this reporting sometimes their nature and histories became distorted. Cohen documents and analyzes this process as it was demonstrated in the "creation of the mods and rockers" which he treats as an example of "moral panic," virtually mass hysteria manufactured mainly though by no means exclusively in the popular press, in response to a largely fabricated threat to society.

While England and America shared the experience of producing various youth groups characterized as rebellious during the 1950s and 1960s, and while common (and sometimes common counter) influences connected these groups that seemed to be constantly glancing at and borrowing from each other in terms of their heroes, music, and fashions, the grounds the American and English youth subcultures grew upon and fed off and sometimes reacted against were always different, because the history each country lived through was far from identical. Culturally and historically speaking, what would one day put Doc Marten boots on the feet of the English skinheads would not precisely be what put them on the feet of their American counterparts, although all might find the boots a handy weapon in fights they expected to engage in as skinheads.

In terms of recent history, the skinhead movement, or rather the skinhead scene (because movement implies an organization and planned evolution the early skinheads generally lacked) emerged in England from a series of almost unrelieved social and political disasters: the Depression of the 1930s; the devastation of World War II; and the continuing condition of deprivation—the endless fall from the old power and glory of the Imperial nation—in which the new welfare state seemed mired. England had helped thwart Nazi designs for the glorious thousand-year Reich, but in the decade or so that followed had not achieved the good times that appeared to mark America's post-war days. America too had lived through a wracking Depression and sacrificed many of its youth to defeat the perceived German and Japanese threats to democracy. After the war it would be gripped by wild anxiety over Communist Russia's threat—in the late 1940s and early 1950s it would even fight in Korea another cruel and this time indecisive but contained war. Yet compared to England's history following the Depression, America's had been a time of economic prosperity, high employment, the fattening of consuming classes. The growth of the economy, increased distribution of goods, and further educational and vocational opportunities in America after the war glossed over many intense inequities in the system, but speculation was common that ultimately the system would be able to satisfy nearly everyone. Ultimately the flow would water all fields so they could flower (some more profusely and beautifully than others, to be sure).

In England, the youth subcultures emerged from a time of want and dissatisfaction, in America from a time of apparent prosperity and achievement. Many English kids must have felt they were sailing on a rotten, sinking ship below whose deck they were performing—if they were working at all—drudge jobs. America was more like a cruise vessel heading for ports of call where some of the young passengers and deckhands did not want to go.

The British youth subcultures seemed, at first anyway, more focused, perhaps because their political and social agendas (when they had them) were more contained and identifiable, or because the geographic terrain on which they operated was so much more limited, tightening up their configurations, putting them into closer contact with each other, making their style and ideologies more identifiable. But there were always links between the English and American youth subcultures, for example in some of the heroes they shared. This was in England and America the age of Marlon Brando, James Dean, and their musical composite, Elvis Presley. All three were sexual threats more than political, though for different reasons. Brando was macho, swaggering, brutal, nihilistic. Social critics and the kids they develop their theories from studying always seem to remember the answer Brando gives in his war against the boondocks bar owner and his pretty daughter in *The Wild One* (1954) when he is asked what he was against, and Brando, bored but potentially very destructive, drawls offhandedly, "What have you got?" Kids didn't have to see the movie to know the attitude; they could just look at Brando's poster image as motorcycle anarchist. Dean was much softer, more vulnerable, yearning, androgynous yet very, very (young) male, and dead (and this was part of his allure) before anyone knew exactly how glorious he was. Brando might have become a storm trooper for disorder but Dean was apolitical. Brando had no parents, Dean had (*Rebel Without a Cause*, 1955) everybody's, dad a fumbling, bumbling, feckless Dagwood Bumstead, mom a fierce castrator with a whine that could cut marble like a buzz saw cuts plywood. In *Rebel Without a Cause* Dean and a couple of his sensitive friends would form their own family, become interchangeable mums and dads and little rascals. Presley merged the two teen icons and projected them through his manner (often tough, sneering) and his musical subject matter ("I wanna be your teddy bear"). He was soft and hard, scared parents witless but loved his mom, and unlike Brando and Dean, who were both loners, possessed qualities of both Peter Pan and the Pied Piper: he needed a crowd of good old boys around him as he led bands of kids away from home and through a highly sexualized adolescence. He was tender and tough, a troublesome performing star in the center of hordes of adolescents who seemed safer with him than they would have been with Brando or Dean, and not nearly as homeless as they pretended so theatrically to be.

The American boys and girls watching and listening to and idolizing Brando and Dean and Presley would live in an expanding economy of seeming plenty, but the English lads and lassies would not.

22 Skinheads Shaved for Battle

In England, the first youth subculture to achieve significant recognition in the media (mainly the press, but in television news and in films as well) was the Teddy Boys. As Stan Cohen has written: "The Teddy Boys were the first group to mark their symbolic innovation...with defiance, anger, or gestures of separation" (179) rebelling "not so much against 'adults' but the little that was offered in the fifties: the cafe, the desolate town, the pop culture of the dance halls" (183). Emerging in the early 1950s, the Teddy Boys were mainly working class young whose musical preference was for American rock and roll or as close to it as young British imitators could get. While America exported its musical style, the sound was grafted onto English fashion: the distinguishing visual sign of the Teddy Boys was their mode of dress which was doubly English, according to Knight (8), similar to that "worn by young men-about-town" (and therefore of a higher class) during the new look period of the late 1940s, and of course reminiscent of narrow, tightly fitting clothes that epitomized the much earlier Edwardian (again upper-class) style.

The Teddy Boy manner of dress never caught on among American youth as the skinhead mode later would with some, though it may have briefly tempted American high fashion producers and consumers. Whatever the style meant to young men and women in England, it did not translate to America. Britannia's Edwardian epoch was really too exotic for Yankee tastes, too filled in its own day with fin d'siecle "effete sophistication," in the *American Heritage Dictionary*'s phrase, and marking in retrospect for later generations a time of fading glory for the British empire, of nostalgia for an epoch of diminishing greatness, perhaps England's last as a dominating world force. In America the Edwardian age roughly coincided with Teddy Roosevelt's tenure in the White House, with the acquisition (not the disintegration) of America's empire, with the great growth of middle class force in America. The Edwardian Age in England was totally irrelevant to American teens as a symbol of something to emulate or mock. Furthermore, and this always complicates symbiotic relationships between American youth and English, the American class system, whatever it might be, is not like the English class system in its history, fixity, complexity, and consequences. There is at best only a negligibly self-aware American working class culture, compared to what existed in England, and this always affects the cultural relationships between youth movements in England and

America. In the fifties, for example, under-employment was not a major problem for great numbers of American youth, partly because, unlike their English age counterparts, instead of looking for jobs after public schooling, a majority (of white youth anyway) were looking for a suitable college to attend.

James McKenna's musical *The Scattering* exemplifies the difference between the late fifties' youth cultures of the two countries, although it is Irish (therefore even more extreme in the intensity of social and political problems it illustrates) and not English, and although it concerns "greasers" in Dublin, not Teddy Boys in London. Like the American musical comedy *Grease* it employs early rock and roll type songs as a happy musical background to its presentation of teen life and styles. In fact, it expropriates songs by Americans Gene Vincent, Eddie Cochran, and Elvis Presley. But its plot is completely depressing, focusing on the blighted, hopeless lives of working class boys in Dublin who assault a young woman and terrorize their neighborhood while aimlessly seeking to escape the social trap they have apparently been born into. One of them even kills a stereotypically brutal policeman. There is a strange—to an American—disjuncture between the energy and optimism and upbeat joy of the American rock music *The Scattering* employs, and the drab, violent, wasted lives of the street boys who sing most of its musical numbers. In sound the work is a musical comedy, but in plot the work is bleak kitchen-sink despair. Written in 1959 and first produced in Dublin in 1960, it combines the musical verve of *Grease* with the dark mood of Sidney Kingsley's depression melodrama about kids in urban slums during the Great Depression, *Dead End* (1935), only it is even more pessimistic than Kingsley's play.

A feature of youth cultures in both post-war Britain and the United States has been the uneven but generally rapid acceleration of self-conscious generations. By some older reckonings, a generation took perhaps 20 to 30 years to develop—the approximate time for the reproductive cycle to move through birth, sexual maturing, and the establishment of a new family as the individual progresses from infant to parent. Moreover, many developing youths prior to the fifties hardly thought of themselves as a member of any particular generation at all. If cohesive youth cultures existed, they scarcely seemed aware of their special anti-generational identity. The convergence of a great many changed institutions in addition to substantial historical watersheds such as World War II and the separateness, the distinctness it forced upon great numbers of people (you were old enough to fight or you weren't; you could be a block mother or work in a defense factory or you couldn't; the war knocked against you hard or brushed you or it didn't, it was only a game or a film or a fantasy) helped make possible this awareness. Television, the record and clothing industries, in the U.S. the drastically changed radio medium that played almost nothing but music for teenagers, harnessed by advertising organizations who realized a vast, exploitable consumer class in clannish batches of the young, all contributed to the development of the new generational march forward that moved often in quick step. As the British punk band Menace would sing in 1978, "Don't you know you're last year's youth?"

So now sometimes the young were not only against the government and their parents, they were also not so sure about their older (or younger) brothers and sisters. Whatever the modish word was, it got around quickly and over long distances through the telly or radio or on the latest recording, or wherever the young danced and listened to music. By the very early sixties the Teddy Boys were replaced as youth culture trend setters in England by the Mods, who pared down some of the excesses of Teddy Boy fashions while quickening their style, their pace. Professional academic observers in England often reported this change as a clarification of style. Stan Cohen commented that "The mods were to emerge in what [Jeff] Nuttall calls the *Classic* as opposed to the *Romantic* idiom. The Teddy Boy style—born in what was very much the traditional working-class areas of South London—ended up (as clothing styles often do in their last dying moments) in grotesque *extremes* which gave way to the more 'reformed' drape suit" (184). Nick Knight presents the Mods almost as a hermetic sect "who at first had been a very exclusive, almost secret underground working class movement. They wore immaculate clothes, regarded themselves as an elite and behaved like gods. [!] They bought the finest Italian suits and rode on Vespas and Lambrettas" (8). Hebdige (52), less ecstatically, treats the Mods as working class youth who affected dandyism, wore merely "conservative suits," and were "fastidiously neat and tidy" (a more frequently used and important word in England, where "Keep England Tidy" signs seem perennially popular. In America, "tidy" contains genteel womanly connotations, and traditionally most boys/men would reject the description). The Mods also kept their hair "short and clean" (the Teds were long-hairs) and actually "pushed neatness to the point of absurdity." Their sharp style seems to have achieved its point through being honed by mocking the manner of their elders and socio-economically their betters, but was also the tip-end of their own drive forward, their own hostilities, their own speeded-up, anxious behavior. Hebdige points out that they were "a little too smart, somewhat too alert," partly as a result of the amphetamines they used (and popularized) to keep them going, sometimes at work, sometimes at play (*Subculture* 52).

Americans whose image of "Swinging England" during the sixties was set by films such as *Georgy Girl* (1966) and *Blowup* (1966) may be surprised to discover that the affluence that seems to have been so much of the terrain from which American counter-cultural movements sprang was not at all a foundation of British youth protest at this time, though economic conditions in England improved during the decade over what they had been in the 1950s. English youth of the day—working class youth—who participated in identified "youth-revolt" groups still perceived a future of diminished expectations. The economy, while not as wizened as it had been during the 1950s, was still far from pouring plenty of goods for nearly everybody, as it seemed to be capable of accomplishing in the United States. Plays such as Arnold Wesker's *I'm Talking About Jerusalem* (1960: The play's action occurs 1946-1959) offered a more accurate picture of the still depressed England in which many working class youth lived, one that evoked ideological sympathy from a growing number of more highly educated, economically privileged young allies including writers, journalists, and academics:

Dave (angrily): Don't moan at me about visions. Don't you know they don't work? You child, you—visions don't work.

Ronnie (desperately): They *do* work! And even if they don't work then for God's sake let's try and behave as though they do—or else nothing will work.

Dave: Then nothing will work.

In Edward Bond's *Saved* (1965), a group of less melodic young toughs than those in McKenna's *The Scattering* stone to death an infant in a pram, out of boredom, self-hate, and anger at the state, presumably. The scene is bleak, not psychedelic. *Georgy Girl* and *Blowup* were popular in the U.S., the plays rarely seen.

26 Skinheads Shaved for Battle

Cohen feels that the "Mod era reached at least one of its peaks by 1963" (184), by which time Mods shared the youth culture stage with the Rockers, kids who seemed to Americans straight out of Brando's 1954 *The Wild Ones*, whose stylized uniform was dominated by a leather jacket and who drove motorbikes or sometimes heavier hog-like cycles—or who rode behind the more fortunate friend who could afford and repair some vaguely similar machine. Cohen calls them *"lumpen,"* a word whose wonderful Marxist ancestry and English connotations links them to masses of seemingly undifferentiated clots of undereducated, unskilled workers. Though in some ways the Rockers were similar to the Teddy Boys, Cohen says they "hadn't caught on to the new teenage image personified by the Mods; also, they were much more outgoing and direct, closer to the butch image of earlier years," young boys who "saw the Teds becoming too respectable." If the Mods refined the Teddy Boys, the Rockers purified them through their more common, some would say primitive gestures. Cohen notes they eschewed poncey "coffee bars" in the city for roadway "transport cafes" (165).

Americans knew best of the Mods and Rockers through their greatly publicized—Cohen demonstrates overpublicized and greatly distorted—squabbles at seaside resorts and along selected London streets. The English middle and upper class might have delighted in the mutual destruction wreaked by these two anti-establishment young mobs, but instead magnified their disputes through its own "moral panic" (Cohen's excellent term) into a kind of a war that undermined society—like fighting dogs that might bite owners during the turmoil of their bloody squabbling. Perhaps it was a small sign of increased prosperity that England could now accommodate two youth movements, even though—or perhaps because—they were antipathetic to each other. As Jeff Nuttall articulated the counter-images in *Bomb Culture* (333), " 'Mod' meant effeminate, stuck-up, emulating the middle classes, aspiring to a competitive sophistication, snobbish, phoney. 'Rocker' meant hopelessly naive, loutish, and above all betraying: for the Mods...wanted a good image for the rebel group, the polished, sharp image that would offset the adult patronization by which this increasingly self-aware world of the adolescent might be disarmed."

To the American outsider it might seem that the Rockers would be better equipped than the Mods to win a war fought with fists and brickbats and heaved-up cobblestones, and that ultimately the skinhead scene might emerge from their ranks, seemingly more indigenous to the working class landscape in which the skinheads would eventually aspire to root themselves. But according to English commentators this was not so. The war of the Mods and Rockers—at least the war for the hearts and minds of the succeeding generation of youth—was fought not so much on the cold, pebbly beaches of southeast England, but in newspapers and over the telly and (hard to gain scholarly information on) in school corridors or at dance halls or on street corners wherever kids gathered and talked about each other as opposed to the adult world. The real battle was the shadow battle of images of Mods and Rockers, and what the media and government halls and pulpit articulated about these shadow images was not necessarily what the kids heard and talked about. Younger kids, youth-rebels to be, could translate the negative media presentations into their own subversive idiom, the same way they translated church hymns into their own jokes: "Nearer my God to Thee" becomes "Nero, my dog, has fleas." Though the famous "rioting" at Clacton took place Easter Sunday, 1964, and the seaside fights—"days of terror" wallowed in by the press—stretched on into the mid sixties, Cohen claims "by 1963…the rockers were left out of the race: they were unfashionable and unglamorous just because they appeared to be more class-bound. The images of lout and yobbo which they had inherited from the Teds hardly made them marketable property" (185) and, though he does not say so, made their style less tempting to young English intellectuals. Some of these sympathized with the Rockers' rebellion against a sick, rotten-mouthed society. But surely they would not want to emulate in any fashion the tackiness of their yahoo mannerisms which appeared to possess no tolerance for the androgyny that tinted if it did not pervade the elite academic networks of young analysts who examined the youth cultures in conflict. (Cohen notes "in many ways Mod was a more female than a male phenomenon" [186].)

Finally, the Mods were more commercially exploitable. The veneer of their style could be more easily grafted onto the appearance of greater masses who would not fully emulate their rebellion, including both the privileged and secure wealthy and those who faced or endured a drabber, less cared-for existence. Both might enjoy aping elements of Mod style but would not or could not risk the consequences of total immersion in or commitment to a manner that seemed fairly openly, contemptuously disdainful of accepted public political and social standards.

Actually, as Cohen points out, already by the early 1960s there was no one "Mod style" in fashion, attitude, or music preferences. "Almost from the beginning there was a distinction between the more extravagant stream [the most marketable and consuming], attracted to the frothy world of the boutiques, the camp, the flotsam of the art school followers. They were very different from the sterner group, with their wide jeans, old army anoraks or combat jackets, canvas shoes" (187). Both groups, early on, apparently shared a liking for American black music (from James Brown's inspired, frenetic screeching to Motown's cooler, throbbing love beats) and West Indian sounds such as ska, listened to and performed by increasing numbers of Caribbean immigrants to England's fragmenting urban centers.

Emergence of British Skinhead Style

Victims of their own success (or is it excess?) by the mid 1960s (Hebdige suggests 1966 and Stan Cohen 1964-65), the Mods seem to have divided into at least two groups which Cohen designates as the hard Mods "wearing heavy boots, jeans with braces, short hair, the precursors of the skinheads, usually prowling in large groups with the appearance of being jumpy, unsure of themselves, on the paranoic edge, heavily involved in any disturbance," in other words violent and given to imagining or actually seeing conspiracies ranged against them; and "smooth Mods (usually older and better off, sharply dressed, moving in small groups and usually looking for a bird)" (187). Smooth Mods, then, seem to have been more grown up, more successful, more socially (and less politically) oriented. The hard Mods would have been more out of work, on the dole, felt they faced a bleaker future.

Nick Knight claims that "As early as 1964 one could recognize mods...who resembled skinheads in that they had short, cropped hair, wore Ben Sherman shirts and Levis. These styles can be seen in the pictures of mod rallies at seaside towns" (9-10). The formed style he suggests, however, did not coalesce until about 1966, nor become fairly fixed until 1967.

If the skinhead expression was nurtured within the youth counter culture development as it evolved in England in the 1950s and 1960s, a parallel phenomenon did not occur in America. While counterparts to England's "Smooth Mods" and later hippies certainly existed in America, the skinheads, except as perhaps an occasional freakish individual occurrence, did not. Why? Simply in terms of style—the tough look, the beatnik wandering, certainly the anti-social stance and to a degree what will be seen as a skinhead characteristic, a nostalgic yearning for some nation of the past peopled by solid, ordinary, peasant-like citizens of the sort in America one sees enshrined in socially conscious depression era posters and murals—there were intersecting correspondences. But in America the Beats (and there were never very many) were invariably college-trained middle-class kids or intellectuals who had the learning equivalent of something close to a college education. There was a pining for the working class (though not one's parents, if they had been workers) but definitely viewed from outside the experience of that class, and often paired with a yearning for oriental Eastern grace and insight: behaviors the English skinheads would have considered "poncey," oppressively intellectual and unmanly. Then, in the 1960s, American counter cultural youth movements were for a variety of reasons "into" long hair and—as the chorus of the tribal love-rock musical *Hair* sang—"beauty, happ-i-ness." Beauty and happ-i-ness were not what English skins were about. America seemed in the sixties a land of plenty, and even when the hippies rejected plenty they did so bounteously.

The anti-war movement attracted into its engulfing maelstrom hundreds of thousands, millions of American youth who exuberantly cried out against AmeriKKKa's bestiality in Vietnam, but again these were largely protests fermenting on college campuses where the truculent skinhead style as it developed would have been an ugly affectation without a source in the culture even as an anti-style. There were in America in the 1960s other kids against these anti-war kids, young men and women who supported the banner of Americanism and free enterprise, who had benefitted from the system as had most of the demonstrators (but as the skinheads would come to feel they had not), but the skinhead style would have been even less adaptable to their interests. The anti-hippies favored a standard, clean-cut, Coca-Cola advertisement image, apple-cheeked and clean-shirted as a high school student body president, young men who would have been, had they worn hats and overcoats, indistinguishable at an F.B.I. convention, women ready to leap high, back arched, dimple kneed, in a "T-E-A-M" yell. Also, perhaps as a result of an American history that for most of its early period found women a scarce and therefore special commodity and that has, for many reasons frequently remarked upon by foreign travelers and local commentators, made woman's path in the U.S. somewhat different from the one trod by her sisters in England and the Continent (though still American women were forced to follow men), the youth counter cultural movements in America seemed more sexually integrated, perhaps simply because more American women completed high school and went to college. The skinhead scene in England was rooted in heavily male-segregated activities like the pub and particularly football (soccer). Throughout the 1960s and early 1970s, currents of association between English and American youth movements would reveal a flow and counter flow of cultural detail. The *New Left Review* drifted across the Atlantic, the Beatles arrived by jet. From America C. Wright Mills' angry rhetoric castigated American entrepreneurial imperialism to the delight of young British leftists, and black musicians like Muddy Waters provided more artistically than just a name for the Rolling Stones. Very short skirts, Peter Max bell bottoms, Indian fringes (sexy fetishes and authentically minority-sprung) could tumble dry together in the laundromats of Berkeley or Soho. But the skinheads in the sixties would remain English. There was no cultural place in America for a youthful working class expression of discontent and open, ugly antagonism to the middle class.

In their 1976 essay "Beyond the Skinheads: Comments on the Emergence and Significance of the Glamrock Cult," Ian Taylor and Dave Wall stated that "Students of youth culture in Britain are agreed that the skinheads are dead." This was true of the first phase of the movement, which the authorities they refer to contend "emerged" as a distinct and recognizable phenomenon "in the East End of London sometime during 1968," though it was not greatly well known then. In 1969 skins were described in a report, but not identified, not labeled as skinheads, attending a soccer match August 11 in Portsmouth (a British Navy base city), looking like sailors "when they are on fatigue duty," and a month later combining the attire of "an ordinary English" working class laborer "and an American teenager of the fifties...untouched by psychedelia and...swinging London." They also at that time wore braces (suspenders) which were seen in England as "some sort of weird throwback to the Thirties" (107). They were style conscious and neat, unlike the hippies whom they viewed as too "scruffy" (Daniel and McGuire 34). Their braces were often brightly colored, their Levis loose around the waist, their "trouser legs turned up so as to expose the leg just above the ankle." Any shirt style other than a Ben Sherman "was usually sneered at" (6).

Most were young, in the 15 to 17 range, and in these early years seemed to lack any "authority structure, or defined leadership." Their "most striking aspect was" their conformity apparently "controlled by group pressure." Their main interest was fighting: "when it was the Mods, it was all clothes and fashion, when it was Rockers, it was all motorbikes, with skinheads it is fighting." They shaved their heads to make them look hard, the better to image the violence which was "one of the main means of relieving boredom and, in certain situations, frustrations" (Daniel and McGuire 116, 26, 25, 82).

Soccer was surely the designated sport of the skinheads. Nick Knight quotes Ian Walker's 1980 memory of having observed 4,000 skinheads at a match in 1968. Skinheads were soon fanatic and violent supporters of various London teams: Tottenham, West Ham, and Chelsea. Walker recollected the skin fans he saw "all wore bleached Levis, Dr. Martens [boots], a short scarf tied cravat style, cropped hair. They looked like an army and, after the game, went into action like one" (11). If Walker is correct in his estimation of the number of skinheads at the match, his remembrance suggests two more important differences between the early skinhead scene in England and its later manifestation in America. First, estimates of the total number of true skinheads in America still have not reached the mass who acted "like an army" in London in 1968. Were that many skins to assemble in the U.S. the extent of "moral panic" would be dizzying. Never have anywhere near that number of skins gathered in America for any event. The sheer size of the country and expense of necessary travel would work heavily against it. There is always possible in England a concentration of subcultural activity implausible in the U.S. Second, American football, a game parallel to England's soccer in its violence and popularity, has been preempted curiously enough as a function of American school systems at the public and college levels. Though Americans of all classes (however they might be designated) attend football games, the sport is rooted in the schools. Up until the professional level, if you do not attend school you do not play football in any major sense. Spectators are predominantly high school and college students or alumni. And since American education is heavily coeducational, simple observation demonstrates that American football audiences are gender mixed to a much greater extent than English soccer fans. Thus, a prime rallying point and opportunity for group action for the skinheads is absent from the American skinhead scene. In America the football stadium in effect walls them out, rather than collects and focuses them. From time to time black and white football players shave their skulls, but they do this as an extreme display of commitment to their team, not as a sign of allegiance with a counter-culture group.

The size of English skinhead groups and their intense (Knight says passionate) devotion to football teams suggests other differences from the skinhead scene that would ultimately develop in America. John Clarke and Tony Jefferson noted in 1976 that skinhead "support of a particular team provided a focus for the assertion of territorial loyalties, involving both a unified collective identity...and an assertion of territorial rights, not those of property ownership, but of community identification" (154). Knight adds that "Skins were extremely defensive of their own territory. Each gang, called a crew, had its own area which it defended against other skins and non-skins...some crews, such as those from large housing estates, had 200 or more members" (18). Since American skinheads have not attained the greater numbers the English skins achieved (though this is a threat groups who monitor skin activity in the U.S. fear, particularly if they are contemplating the English model of the movement, imagining thousands of brutish, bare-skulled white toughs marching through the streets or commandeering the underground after a football game) they seem to lack this territorial imperative: when operating in a city scene, American skins have nowhere attained anything like a critical mass necessary to dominate a neighborhood, though they might effectively control a building or part of a street or parking lot where they collect. Moreover, again as a result of the greater distance, generally, between American urban centers, interaction between groups of skins (for example British football fights) has little opportunity of occurring.

In the Florida region, for example, the few Tampa skins may be wary of groups of Orlando skins, but individual skinheads move rather easily from one locale to another in terms of skinhead acceptance. Atlanta, a scene of vigorous anti-skinhead police activity in the mid-eighties, was the original home of a number of skins who then traveled to Orlando or Tampa for what they hoped was a better scene. In areas such as Los Angeles or Chicago where gang fights are frequently the result of turf battles, skinheads still do not possess sufficient numbers to claim a home territory, or their way of life does not lead them to establish territorial protection as a high item on their agenda. In the Tampa Bay region, skinheads drift between the cities of Tampa, St. Petersburg, and Clearwater, depending on the night's activity, often determined by what band they like is playing at which music venue. Perhaps they are simply embodying American rootlessness. Essentially a middle-class phenomenon, the American skinhead is more familiar with the suburb than the public housing development, which was home to the English skin. In America, the public housing project is generally associated with black or minority dominance. The suburban street would be far more difficult to establish as a war zone to defend than a city block. American skinheads seem to live more on the surface of the land and sometimes to skitter across it, than to dig into and attempt to defend their neighborhood, in which they may be isolated or outcasts anyway.

The dominating elements of early skinhead style in England were almost instantaneously noted, and deemed by cultural analysts (and later by American tourists who must have mailed home thousands of postcards depicting them) highly noteworthy. There were deviations in wearing apparel—Knight says that at the start skinhead "clothes worn in the evening were well-tailored and expensive. Suits by Dormeuil, a petrol blue and red two-tone suit, or a fine mohair suit were clothes which every skinhead would aspire to" (11)—and there was incertitude about proper hair length. The earliest skins did not ordinarily shave their heads completely, apparently preferring what barbers called a number one or two cut (four would be the least severe) but the cut was usually even all the way around, not higher on top like "flat-tops" had been in the 1950s. The style, whatever details added up to its final created statement, projected self-declared toughness, maleness (certainly not the androgyny found in some 1960s American styles), and working class roots, but at first, not necessarily whiteness. It would have been difficult in England, however, to assemble a traditional working class style that incorporated maleness and toughness that was black. English commentators who analyze the origins of the skinhead movement frequently emphasize its early links to black youth cultures of the day, but it is hard to comprehend how these links could have been very strong and durable granted the prevailing whiteness of its elements of style.

Dick Hebdige characterizes these first, 1960s skinheads that Ian Walker had earlier described as "aggressively proletarian, puritanical, chauvinist" and says they were dressed like a "caricature of the model worker" with "cropped hair, braces, short, wide Levi jeans, Ben Sherman shirts and highly polished Doctor Marten boots" (*Subculture* 55). Nick Knight provided unintentionally hilarious illustrations of skinhead styles through the years worn by pleasant looking chaps drawn about as tough-looking as young boy models in a Sears, Roebuck catalogue. The sources of the styles according to Hebdige and most commentators after him were contradictory: white working class and West Indian immigrant cultures. Skins reportedly took their language from both groups, and congregated on all-white football fields or at West Indian youth clubs sometimes, listening to Jamaican ska and reggae music. British skinhead style was apparently—early on anyway—neat, as had been the Teddy Boy and Mod styles. Clarke and Jefferson report "The clothes, heavy denims, plain or striped button-down shirts, braces, and heavy boots, created an image which was clean cut, smart, and functional—a youthful version of working clothes. The haircuts completed the severe and puritanical self-image, a formalized and very 'hard' masculinity" (156). This description indicates another minor distinction between the early skinheads and their later American stylistic imitators: the American style is less formalized, its overall impression sloppier. Simon Frith has quoted a 14-year-old English girl who wrote in her 1971 school paper "true skinheads always look neat. Their clothes are smart and expensive. Their boots are always polished to perfection." Frith notes, "American observers have always been amazed by the detail of British youth cults...There is nothing in the USA to match the *precision* of white youth styles in Britain" (216).

English commentators write of skinhead style as though it were consciously selected for a calculated effect. Clarke and Jefferson declare that "This emphasis on overt masculinity was visible in the most obvious areas of skinhead symbolism, most importantly...the 'prison crop' hair style from which their name derived" (156). Nick Knight states that the cut was "associated in the public mind with convicts, prison camp inmates and the military. It was exactly this mean look which the skins wished to cultivate" (12). Simon Frith, mixing irony with satire, assigned meanings to the major items of skinhead sartorial style and appearance, claiming they "took on the look of the cartoonist lumpen-worker." The shaven head was a "sign of stupidity, workboots...a sign of drudgery, body moving clumsily...a sign of brute force, dumb surliness...a sign of menace. The whole ensemble was a proletarian caricature of a dumb joke" (219). The closely cut hair or shaved head style also recalled concentration camp inmates, a sick, parodic joke in light of the movement's later clear anti-Semitism; and chemotherapy patients, suggesting stigmatization and the masochism of those who are as the popular American tattoo declares "born to raise hell" mixed together with the death-wish latent in considering yourself a terminally ill victim of society.

If the English academics who first tracked the skinhead movement are correct, the bundle of allegiances constituting the skins' cultural baggage these first years was bound up with considerable confusion, an inevitable situation for groups of unruly, anti-authoritarian, localized gangs without a focal leader and not comprised of individuals familiar with hammering out rationally derived ideologies. Skins liked to think of themselves as embodying working class values and so they dressed somewhat like workers (certainly more like workers than the hippies dressed), but the worker's world they dramatized no longer existed as they presented it, if it ever did exist that way. Their representation was nostalgic, founded upon dream visions of the worker's world, since in fact in their current world they lived outside traditional workers' society. Thus Dick Hebdige disagrees with Stan Cohen for stressing too greatly "the fit between respectable working-class culture and the altogether more marginal forms with which we are concerned here. For example, the skinheads undoubtedly reasserted those values associated with the traditional working-class community, but they did so *in the fact of* the widespread renunciation of those values in the parent culture" (*Subculture* 78-79. The emphasis is Hebdige's).

Clarke and Jefferson assert "they were a reaction against the contamination of the parent culture by middle class values, and a reassertion of the integral values of working class culture through its most recessive traits: puritanism and chauvinism. The puritanism crystallized in opposition to the hedonistic greasers and hippies, and the chauvinism in 'queer bashing' and 'paki-bashing' " (151), which could include any male who was "not overtly masculine looking" (156) and dark-skinned peoples resembling Pakistani immigrants. Individual skinheads may have been supported (as they often claimed they were) by individual English mums and das, but as gangs or a loosely structured counter culture, they were not embraced by the standard working class organizations of the day. They were their own constituency. The working class they may have wanted to be or redramatize in their own image did not exist as they formulated it in their behavior.

To American audiences, their claimed relationship with black subcultures has always been a matter of greater interest than the precise extent to which they represented the English working class. And the English commentators have always presented the declared black connection with, it seems, greater awareness of its cultural surprise. Phil Cohen's claim that appears almost to champion the skinheads as back-to-basics heroes, that they were attempting "to retrieve some of the socially cohesive elements destroyed in the parent culture" (quoted in Clarke and Jefferson, *Working Class Youth Cultures* 150), would simply seem irrelevant to the American scene. Far more germane to Americans is the by now strongly accepted, nearly folkloric belief, first established by the English academics and then repeated by Knight, American mass media commentators and by domestic American skinheads themselves, in the English skinheads' black links: the development of bi-racially loyal "2-Tones" groups and "ska-skins" who championed black music, "ska, rocksteady and reggae" (Hebdige, *Subculture* 53; *Klanwatch*, February 1991, 14-15); their early adoption and utilization of the "protest music of the West Indian ghetto poor" (Clarke and Jefferson 151) that "the black communities in South East London had brought from their homeland and which was the popular music of the Rude Boys" (Knight 14), young, black Jamaican working class youths.

There is no doubt the skins and young West Indians, often from London's Lambeth or Brixton slums, both disaffected with and excluded from the social, political, and economic heartland of British society, shared hostilities and music, Prince Buster's song "Madness," blue beat, and for a time "mixed freely at dance halls and clubs" (Knight 10). In England and the U.S. from at least the late 1950s, white youth cultures had been attracted to the black world (or what they fantasized about the black world) in a variety of ways. Suggesting the strength of this desire for a kind of blackness, Hebdige quotes a revealing passage from Jack Kerouac's *On the Road* where the narrator laments he is not "a Negro, feeling that the best the white world has offered me was not enough ecstasy for me, not enough life, joy, kicks, darkness, music, not enough night." Hebdige says that in London "there existed a whole network of subterranean channels which had for years linked the fringes of the indigenous population to the equivalent West Indian subcultures. Originally opened up to the illicit traffic of weed and jazz, these internal channels provided the basis for broader cultural exchanges" (*Subculture* 39-40). In 1969, "The Skinhead Moonstep" had a reggae beat (Knight 15).

The pervasive cultural strength of these early mainly musical links is questionable, however, as is the extent to which the links were connected to meaningful racial or ethnic harmonies and the degree to which non-white youth felt reciprocal affinities to the skins: their parents appear to have experienced none. The English commentators who appear to share with each other, generally, an anti-establishment stance, tend to emphasize that clearly there were rotten conditions in England in the fifties and sixties that helped spawn the young skinheads and that these conditions were caused, beyond historic reasons such as World War II's devastation, by unfeeling and wrongheaded governmental administration. Thus, to an American outsider anyway, it appears that their academic investigations idealize this early young white and young black counter cultural relationship to contrast it with the strong racism of the tainted, dominant, mainstream culture and with later racial hostilities between the groups in some post-Edenic phase. In America too, the young counterculture of the sixties was fascinated with black life or what they imagined black life to be, but the cultural attraction remained largely unreciprocated. The "symbolic links" Hebdige (*Subculture* 44) and others write about connecting white youth cultures to black seem to an American not extraordinary at all, since the dominant white culture in the United States has traditionally borrowed so greatly from the black, particularly black musical forms such as ragtime, Dixieland, blues, and jazz. The musical connections however seem not generally to have been a sign of increasing racial acceptance or harmony. Ragtime, for example, was popular during what some consider the nadir of black-white relations in the United States around the start of the twentieth century. Thus, the ideological significance of the fact that early skinheads listened with Jamaicans to Jamaican-originated music seems questionable, and need not be interpreted to prove the existence of some fitful Golden Age of mutual support (seemingly a long-standing, longed-for fantasy among white intellectuals, British or American) between skinheads and rebellious young blacks. As Ian Taylor and Dave Wall say in "Beyond the Skinheads" (108), "the skinhead liked Motown music, not the Four Tops."

Even early on, there were "significant exceptions (violent [racial] disturbances in Nottingham and Notting Hill in 1958, Hoxton and parts of the East End in the '70s)" to the "pattern of relatively peaceful coexistence" that Hebdige (*Subculture* 39, 40) claims developed as the youth cultures, including skinheads, evolved. All along, though "colored," Pakistanis in England apparently lacked the glamour, or perhaps it was the accessible music, to elicit cultural admiration from the English youth groups. The May 25, 1970 *New York Times* reported that the day previous "Several hundred" of them "marched to the residence of Prime Minister Wilson to ask for protection from attacks by skinheads." Remarks in standard American sources maintaining that when skinheads "began appearing in London streets in the late 1960s, they were actually identified *with* black culture" (Ridgeway 164)[1] are at the very least misleading.

Though early skinhead gangs may have enjoyed some black music and included individual neighborhood blacks among their members, strong antipathy toward Africans as a race was also early part of their social outlook. The skinheads presented by Susie Daniel and Pete McGuire in *Paint House*, one of the first skinhead gangs, listed Jews, young blacks, Pakistanis, and hippies under their category of "People on our backs..." (66). One of the gang complained that "them blacks, them young blacks who we've grown up with, they'll pinch our birds and jobs like that." Just like an American racist, the young skinhead added, the "trouble is, they think they're as good as we are" (69). Prejudice and denial of prejudice are revealed in another exchange of dialogue reported in *Paint House*:

"We want white rule, we want white supremacy, right?"

"No, we want a white England. Do you want a black slave?"

"No, I just want 'em to go 'ome." (81)

It is not at all strange, then, that Daniel and McGuire report that " 'Reggae' was important" to the skinheads "for only a few months in 1969, but it was soon rejected as it was 'West Indian' music" (12). According to a West Indian disc jockey when he played a song called

"Young, Gifted and Black," local skinheads would sing "Young, Gifted and White," and would cut the electric wires leading to the speakers. Fights would break out, and then after a short time, fewer whites came to his club (Hebdige in Clarke and Jefferson 149). Clearly the skinhead-black link was never idyllic though it was brief.

If "By the early '60s...some kind of rapport between blacks and neighboring white groups had become possible" because "sizeable immigrant communities had been established in Britain's working-class areas" (Hebdige, *Subculture* 52), the increased black population also brought to the surface racial disharmony familiar to black and white Americans throughout whose history it had flared incessantly. The fact that English skins for a time enjoyed West Indian rhythms did not seem to affect the tensions observable in working class communities. While even as in America some older blacks in England continued to seek their rightful place in the society by appealing to standard avenues of fair play and equal treatment, others, particularly the young, moved into more black nationalistic postures. The music of the young blacks reflected this shift just as the youth music of the English or American sixties sang of the new sexuality and a refusal to follow the ways of the older generation. In England's working class black urban neighborhoods, "As reggae became increasingly preoccupied with its own blackness, it began to appeal less and less to the skinheads who were gradually edged out at a time when the cycle of obsolescence had, as far as the particular subculture was concerned, almost run its course" (Hebdige, *Subculture* 57). Taylor and Wall write, "A crucial date in the 'natural history' of the skinheads was the summer of 1972 and the attack with white Liverpudlians on second-generation blacks in the Toxteth area of Liverpool." Then in November 1973 "the death of 'inter-racial Reggae' and segregation of black culture in general, was symbolized" by the publication of " 'Black Music'...directed at the West Indian population in Britain" (107).

I have suggested that the "harmony" in England between the early skins and black youth cultures was less firm and more limited than the standard English sources for American information on the connection have implied. Whatever the nature of the link, it did not last long, nor did the first phase of the skinhead phenomenon, which Taylor and Wall in 1976 declared was dead. I have also suggested that, for a variety of reasons, there was during this phase little room for or attraction to the skinhead phenomenon among youth cultures in America. You could not, after all, travel to San Francisco for the summer of love "with a flower in your hair," as the popular 1967 song requested, if you had no hair, and would have manifested repugnance for the hippie's open embrace of love. The nearly bald head, a fashion focal point of the skinhead scene, was aesthetically against the grain of the dominant American youth style. Some bald youths were ambiguously associated with the protest movement: small bands of bell-tinkling Hare Krishnas wove and chanted through their dances, smelling oddly like bubble gum and collecting funds for themselves at many demonstrations. They were tolerated as camp followers might be, but somehow they resembled eunuchs and were at any rate disconnected from the magnetic sexual and political rebellions and music scene so integral to sixties youth movements. Young Americans who rebelled against the manner and politics of the youth protest movement that dominated in the media emphasized a clean-cut appearance and traditional middle-class life style that the rough English skins with their dreams of a working class never-never land would have found appalling. In America, perhaps only an isolated creep or two might be a skinhead.

Punk Prepares the American Way

During the 1970s, what was in effect the language of the youth cultures, the apex of youth style—music—changed in England and America. Both countries also underwent political shifts toward greater conservatism. From the late sixties to the late seventies the mass of young people who had protested the Vietnamese war dropped away from the radical movement (though some remained devoted to achieving basic human progress) so that by the end of the decade political expression by youth seemed quiet and often indistinguishable from that of older generations. In this time of transformation the nature of the skinhead scene in England appears to have become modified and for the first time to have achieved its own life in America.

The subcultural ground upon which the skinheads in England and America developed in the 1970s is the punk rock scene. The term punk, like most terms attempting to represent the ideas and modes of a cultural expression, such as Romantic or Victorian or New Wave, has been defined many ways, often as a reaction against earlier variously defined forms of cultural expression. Jay Saporita calls it an "open protest against the more established forms" of commercialized rock. "Punks are proud of their rough edges...enjoy the principle of dangerous, or at least potentially dangerous, behavior...show the worthlessness of all our values," like Dada (65). Dave Marsh agrees that as a counter movement, its "rebellion was necessary as an antidote to what rock had become: a stuffy institution." It "reasserted a version of the garage-rock aesthetic, which boils down to 'anybody can do this shit' " (237). Punk at once possessed "an aggressively lower-class style" (Willis 72) yet was "ultimately...in America ...a student-led music with all the collegiate population's biases against growing up" (Marsh 237). It seems to embody in America a pseudo-proletarian hip-anti-hip style that is exciting and despairing sometimes concurrently, and aggressive nearly always. Punk "is the amylnitrate of music" (Guiccione, Jr. 6). Again like most identifiable (or critically labeled) cultural movements its prehistory stretches back in time. To the world outside that of popular rock music fans, this might not be considered a very long time. But to musical chair playing generations anxious to exclude outsiders for whom the time between an older brother's or a sister's flowering of subcultural independence could be only a couple of semesters or so, this time would be long enough for dozens of musical trends to develop that the expert kids and rock critics inside would spot and love or hate, and use to disqualify outsiders.

Lou Reed, who jerked onto the music stage in the mid-1960s, has been called proto-punk, his Velvet Underground group—"the first band to make rock 'n roll truly dangerous" (McNeil, *Spin* 52)—termed pre-punk along with Iggy Pop (a.k.a. "Stooge"), glitter rock (in America) and glam rock and David Bowie (in England), Patti Smith (just before she became a performance artist) and the New York Dolls. Andy Warhol, who helped form Lou Reed's Exploding Plastic Inevitable group (1966-67) is sometimes considered another pioneer explorer. The Ramones, one of whose most popular songs was "I Wanna Sniff Some Glue," are often considered the first full-fledged punk band. Their records would also be popular later among skinhead Oi! music fans (in but one instance of reverent emulation, the Oi! group Accident would cover their "Blitzkrieg Bop"). They were formed and played their raw, by most standards technically deficient, but high energy music in the summer of 1974 and made their live debut at the now famous CBGB club in August that year. The legendary venue, whose full name (CBGB

OMFUG) supposedly meant "country, bluegrass, blues, and other music for uplifting gormandizers" had opened in December 1973 and soon became New York's center for punk music. Richard Hell and his Voidoids played there and Hell sang "we are all a blank generation" which he later said meant his people had wiped the canvas of their life clean and could start fresh, but which also could be interpreted as a lobotomized nihilistic bleat. Richard Hell concert t-shirts said "Please Kill Me" (Bangs 261). Punk followers were in America still largely the children of the middle class, affecting tough guy styles such as torn jeans, t-shirts, leather jackets, and after a while, sometimes technicolored, spiked haircuts, which took them a step beyond Brando's *Wild One* fifties image. This was a fashion both boys and girls sometimes affected. Other styles such as glitter rock also blurred gender distinctions, a trend even the male-dominated skinheads could not entirely stem. The boys were no longer cuddleable James Deans at all, at least not very obviously, though inside they might be mushy victims young girl rescuers could console. *Punk* magazine certified with its first issue in January 1976 the primacy of punk in New York's subcultural underworld.

Though probably as Dave Marsh has said "the idea of punk is an American one" (24) England was ready for it. The Ramones "electrified" young Brits during an English tour and their "three-night gig at the Roadhouse" in London July 3, 4, and 5 (ironically as part of the 1776 Revolution's bi-centennial celebration) was according to Eddie Legs McNeil "England's first punk-rock event" (52). Perhaps so, perhaps not. The Ramones tour certainly seems to have at least catalyzed elements already suspended in the English rock scene and the crystallized reaction was English punk. Nick Knight records that the "long, hot summer of 1976 saw the rise of an extraordinary new youth culture, the punks" (23).

However long punk had been around (Dave Marsh says he first used the word in a 1970 *Cream* article [239] though Legs McNeil claims he originated the term, having appropriated it from Telly Savalas' repeated usage on his *Kojak* show [Kozak 59] that began in 1973), by 1976 it dominated the new music scene in England and America in a number of incarnations. The variations were many to insiders or knowledgeable critics though to an outsider all might have appeared to possess the same rawness or musical iconoclasm. Insiders could identify scores of mutated versions—and this would be a mark of their being insiders under the same umbrella shielding them from the acid rain of polluting, slick commercialism and general popular acceptability. Just to read the names of some of the groups was enough to appall what in the sixties had been called "middle America," and sometimes these names were the most creative achievements of the performers: The Sic [sic] Fucks, Suicide, Suicidal Tendencies, Teen Age Lust, Day Old Bread, Nervous Eaters, Teenage Jesus and the Jerks, Vic Morrow's Head, Foetus (sometimes known as Scraping Foetus Off the Wheel), Dead Boys, Dead Kennedys, Dictators, Impotent Seasnakes.

Sometimes it seemed all the kids and young ungrown ups needed to produce a band was a garage or vacant store to practice in; knowledge of three chords or maybe only two—how about one anybody?—an aggressive attitude, an impolite stance, and a rudimentary sense of rhythm or synaptic spasms close to that. Some groups emerging from the scene transcended it musically while maintaining the attitude—the Talking Heads are probably the best known example, or Blondie. Some groups such as The Clash developed greater technical proficiency as they evolved, though still reacting against what many punks considered the pretentiousness of bands like Yes and Genesis. Generally the lumpen-punk scene (as the British commentators might call it) was raw. It accommodated a variety of ideologies, inchoate or developed. It possessed no one political ideal. The scene incorporated disparate jumble-sale racks of groups pledging allegiance to a muddle of political and social attitudes. Moreover, since the punks were largely kids, they were incessantly growing into or out of their musical tastes. Observing the scene is in many ways like watching the movements of a granulated amoeba whose edges remain intact but whose shape and insides are constantly shifting as the organism rolls over assimilable or rejected objects of its accidental attention.

Even within America the scene was not the same everywhere, and there existed marked differences between attitudes in England (where punk was always more class conscious and tended to speak or scream in working class accents) and America. For example, Legs McNeil claims that "the West Coast punks hated the New York scene's artsy-poetry aspects, exemplified by the Patti Smith Group, Television, and Talking Heads" (McNeil 52). Ellen Willis has stated that "American punk and its British counterpart are not only different but in a sense opposed" (72). In his history of CBGB, Roman Kozak contends that generally punk was more upbeat in the United States than England because of England's more depressed economic situation (67). English punk seems also to have been more self-consciously political from its start than American. Following the infamously prefabricated (but ultimately authentic) Sex Pistols, the next great English band to emerge in the wake of The Ramones' incendiary tour was The Clash, whose initial album (named after themselves) featured songs like "White Riot," and "I'm So Bored With the U.S.A.," attacking America's imperialistic political and social violence. In 1979 the title track of their "London Calling" sang of an impending apocalypse caused by Western oppression of third world countries.

One source of The Clash's appeal seems to have been their political commitment. According to Lester Bangs, "punk had repeated the very attitudes it copped (BOREDOM and INDIFFERENCE) and we were all waiting for a group to come along who at least went through the motions of GIVING A DAMN about SOMETHING. Ergo, The Clash" (225). Mick Jones, one of the chief members of the group, said "we play black music.... We have a common bond with these people," and attacked guitarist Eric Clapton who had supported England's reactionary Enoch Powell, whom Jones derided for wanting "to send blacks to Africa" (Frith, *Sound Effects* 170).

In England and then in America, skinheads were part of this mid-1970s scene, could be observed within it, though increasingly they did not consider themselves punks, and in America certainly by the time (the early 1980s) they were being reported as social problems they would be anti-punk. Even in Australia, if Richard Lowenstein's purportedly authentic cult movie *Dogs in Space* (1987) can be trusted, skinheads were an accepted part of the punk scene. One of the opening sequences in that film depicts skinheads, punks, and other young kids waiting in the streets for tickets the night before David Bowie's November 1978 concert in Melbourne. In America, being so few in number, the skinheads would not be able to support or sustain a commercially viable location whose tastes, political or musical, they could dominate, but they could mix in with crowds at the fringes, or sometimes concentrate their numbers and control the pit or dance floor, or rush the stage and fight with the performers or simply dive off into the eddies of skinheads below. In England, the punk scene revived this waning youth subculture that had crested by the early 1970s and was at low tide certainly in London when punk arrived, though some skinhead groups still congregated there and in nearby cities such as Reading. By 1977 when young punks fought Teds in King's Road of London's Chelsea section, Nick Knight says skinheads battled on both sides. According to Knight, the older skins "tended to side with the Teds, who were pro-British and for the Union Jack, whereas the punks were anti-Royalist and happy to stick safety pins into pictures of the Queen. The skins who sided with the punks were a new breed," Knight claims, "who wished to be seen as more anarchist and more shocking than the punks" (23). The older skins apparently saw the punks as modernized hippies, their old enemies.

However, it would be dangerous to interpret Knight's observations as establishing a clear-cut political division between two precisely distinctive youth groups both of whom looked to the general public like skinheads. The motives determining rambunctious and violent youths to fight would not be easy to ascertain. Territorial or other localized reasons might have played a part in choosing up sides and it is always possible that the skinheads who engaged in combat may have possessed confused social, political or personally psychological reasons for fighting. What is important to note is that if there were two in any way temporarily separate groups of skinheads, both were clearly and vigorously engaging in violent actions. And while becoming more apparent through the seventies in the punk scene, the skinheads do not seem in England to have achieved the numerical strength they sustained during the late 1960s. Other youth subcultures seemed to have more allure and although part of the skinheads' attraction had always been to some its masculine ferocity, that primal truculence could also be observed as a reactionary or more simply old-fashioned quality. The working class dream that some skinheads seem to have yearned for may have been imaginary, but it was certainly a dream of the past, while punk seems largely to have rejected the past imaginary or historical. Punk seemed a dystopian dream of the future that drew heavily from what was grotesque in the present.

The opportunities for wildness and assertion that punk brought with it reinvigorated the skinhead scene in England even though committed skins and punks did not always get along with each other. Selected venues for music became common hanging out places for both groups. Another of the better early English punk bands was Sham 69, and this group, more than The Clash, attracted a large skinhead following. Jimmy

Pursey of the band would shout "Skinheads are back!" to the delight of skins in the audience, but after a time Sham 69 became disenchanted with the "mob's" violence and right-wing ideology and disavowed the skins' support (Knight 24). "All of a sudden, they didn't want to know the skins," one of their fans said angrily. "And we were the ones who put them up there in the first place. The Sham Army" (Hebdige in Knight 29). The fan would become a guitarist with The Last Resort, a white power band that was later one of the skinheads' favorites.

Oi! Arrives: Music to Riot By

By the late 1970s, a variety of music called "Oi!" had appeared in England that the re-emerging skinheads were attracted to, supported, and helped to shape, that they distinguished from the many different varieties of punk music. Additionally, by this time the extreme right wing National Front political movement in England had realized the potential for attracting recruits to its fascist, racist party by working the new music scene. They "decided to attract young street fighting skins into the NF by offering them gigs that would be heavily racist and anti-Jewish but not too political in their message" ("Jailhouse Rock" 19, in Center for Democratic Renewal skinhead packet).

At any time not all skinheads were racists, and at this time not all bands the skinheads liked most were racist or even committed to any brand of political ideology, but by 1980 those skinheads in England who were racist could listen to a number of groups who did have a specific extreme right wing political agenda, anti-black, anti-immigrant generally, and anti-gay. The music most closely associated with the skinheads, that they appeared to have the most proprietary interest in, was "Oi!" music, and the favored band that over the years has developed into the most notorious group with National Front connections is Skrewdriver, whose driving force was and remains Ian Stuart .

"Oi!" is a Cockney greeting like "Hi." As a term appropriated to designate the music the skinheads on the new music scene in the late 1970s liked best, it has been described somewhat apocalyptically by Dick Hebdige as "a ritual purge on everything that doesn't sound like the voice of the [skinhead] Mob with its back against the wall. It aims to root out all the 'impurities' of 'soft,' 'pretentious' post-rock-artiness, 'weird,' spacy lyrics, a studio-dependent electronic sound, a flirtation with sexually ambiguous imagery." Oi!, according to Hebdige, "is performing a similar function to early punk—taking rock back to the basics...reviving the original rebel-delinquent cluster—the myth of Elvis-as-a-hub-cap-thief, a poor white loser up against the law" (Hebdige in Knight 29). Somewhat less mythopoetically, a publication distributed by one of the first American skinhead gangs, "Romantic Violence," declares that Oi! "refers to a British social and sound movement that has been characterized as music to riot by." The leaflet further maintains that "a leader is never elected but allways [sic] announces himself through action," and that "nobody ever gains respect without force to back them up—when attacked, lash out to wound or kill the attacker...stand on the side of truth and Aryan survival." The item's unnamed author concludes "Oi! is a strong part of my arsenal. I love the music religiously and fly it as a banner." Another Romantic Violence leaflet explains that "The music of the Skinhead is a most powerful, hard driving style of Rock N Roll we call 'Oi!' Oi! is nothing like Rock, Hardcore or Heavy Metal. Oi! stands alone in classification with its crisp beat and melodic tune variation. Oi! is for warriors" (ADL archives, undated). This would seem to project the meaning of Oi! far beyond that of music to steal hubcaps by.

To the outsider, detaching Oi! from punk music or establishing the development of a separate, pure branch of Oi! music from punk roots is probably not possible, and even for punk and skinhead music cognoscenti perhaps a greatly arguable matter. In an analysis suspect because of its racist bias, claims have been made that the style simply combines two-chord progression white New York punk with various traditional and recent working class British musical forms (Jewell 4). As the muddle of punk styles developed and often rapidly evaporated from the mid-1970s until the early 1980s, a number of bands such as Sham 69 acquired the reputation of communicating or attracting real trouble. Some of these bands were claimed by skinheads as expressing the particular anger that they felt belonged uniquely to them, and sang of that anger with the steady, unvarying beat and usually shouted, unmelodic forcefulness the skinheads usually preferred in their music. One extremist right wing magazine, *The Nationalist*, called the sound "rough and boisterous" but asserted that some of the bands producing it were "of high quality" ("Nationalist Youth Create New Rock Movement" 14). By 1981 a few small record companies were already grouping together many of these short-lived bands on collective, retrospective albums that doubtlessly mixed true punk and Oi! music together in ways that perhaps only professional new music critics or closely listening musicologists among the punk and skinhead fans could untangle. A few of the bands on these albums are The Gonads, Accident, Chron Gen, Blitz, The Ruts, Combat 84, The Angelic Upstarts, and Cock Sparrer (all of whom appear on the Link Records release, "Oi! Chartbusters Volume 3"). To illustrate what this music was like, I will refer mainly to cuts from records belonging to some American skinheads.

Slaughterhouse and The Dogs formed as a five-piece band in Manchester in 1975, and by 1976 they were playing with other English bands such as the Sex Pistols, the Buzzcocks, and the Nosebleeds. They were a typically tasteless, musically crude punk band: one of their LP releases was the album "Do It Dog Style." They were not popularly designated as an Oi! band but many skinheads who championed Oi! music liked their brand of outrage and affront. Like most Oi! performers, they sang in heavy working class accents with a harsh sound, and the songs they played were monotonous and melodically almost tuneless, but they played loudly and with the very heavy, very steady beat that dominates Oi! music. Some of their songs have standard rock and roll lyrics; for example, "Mystery Girls" from their album "The Slaughterhouse Tapes" declares, "I wanna talk about love/Love love love love love love" (and then repeats this basic desire many times). "Boston Babies" tells of a "Boston Baby, Boston Baby/Walkin' down the street/Boston Baby, Boston Baby/You knock me off my feet." Other lyrics on Oi! albums are exceptionally misogynist even for rock lyrics: Splodgeness Abounds sings in a crude parody of Roy Orbison's popular "Pretty Woman" of a "Wiffy [smelly] Woman, walkin' down the street/Wiffy woman/I wanna smell your meat/...Wiffy woman, you smell like Billingsgate" (a legendarily foul prison). Barfing sounds punctuate the song's narrative (from "Oi! Chartbusters 3").

A better example of the kind of music that gained Slaughterhouse and the Dogs their notoriety is their skinhead song (released around 1977) "Where Have All The Boot Boys Gone?": "Wearing boots and short haircuts/We will kick you in the guts./I don't know just what I've done,/I just know I'm having fun./Where's the bloody boys gone?/Gone, gone, gone, gone gone" (from "The Slaughterhouse Tapes"). If the song lamented the passing of one generation of boot boys, it was hailed by the generation that replaced them, and similar to the problems Sham 69 experienced, "landed Slaughter in trouble with gig after gig canceled as the band felt the full force of the backlash" (Gary Fielding, album jacket, "The Slaughterhouse Tapes").

"Skins 'n Punks (3)" is an undated LP released in England under the Oi! Records label, featuring The Glory and The Magnificent. The music, to the untutored ear anyway, sounds like that performed by Slaughterhouse and The Dogs. Young male working class voices yell loudly to the background beat beat beat beat of tunes sounding very much the same from song to song, independent of which of the two groups is performing. On the album's front cover boot boys scramble in blood-red almost abstract outline. On the back cover a cartoon skinhead wearing an Oi! Records shirt under his braces shouts, "...If you know wots good for you! TURN IT UP MATE," and brandishes his fists. A few of the songs are anybody's love songs—"When I woke up, the sun was shining/Your body next to mine was so exciting./This is my lucky day."—but many of the lyrics of both groups sing of anger, violence, betrayal, tough guy camaraderie, and threats of social warfare. The shouted energy and fighting spirit exhibited in many Oi! songs combats the sad despair of anthems such as the Sex Pistols's "No Future." "Uproar" by The Glory screams, "The streets are burning/With desire and hate,/Flames are rising.../On the streets we win or lose..../Youth are running each and every race,/Rising uproar, while the government waits./Always the questions, always the lies/Sick and tired 'cause you don't even try." "Clockwork Land" describes a country whose ghettoes (or gutters) and suburbs are filled with "violence, devotion, democracy," where "out of the street lights, in a subway in the night," presumably skinhead "troops stand together on a mission of delight."

Punk and skinhead songs often allude to *A Clockwork Orange*, either Anthony Burgess's depressing novel or more likely Stanley Kubrick's even more dispiriting film based on it. The skinhead McKee brothers arrested for killing Isaiah Walker often said they were going out for an evening of "the old ultra violence," a phrase used by the hoodlums in both novel and film, and also the title of a rock song. Scott McKee owned a copy of "Clockwork Land."[2]

The Glory's "United in Anger" seems typical in communicating a feeling of life slipping away, of traditional ways eroding in the absence of any strong central force to preserve them. Opening with a yell of rage, the song progresses from anguished, passive contemplation to an angry, confrontive threat. "Lookin' at a life through the hour glass,/Lookin' at a life as it seemed to pass./Lookin' at a life and a liberty,/Trying to take away your democracy,/United in anger, united in pain/United in anger, again and again./Lookin' at a life, what they done to us,/Watchin' everything that they took from us,/...Jumpin' down our throat at the slightest mistake,/All right, come on, let's see ya,/United we stand, divided we fall, the ruling class has us against the wall." In these songs, either the ruling class or the government as controlled by the ruling class is the enemy, more than minorities who seem an effect of democracy's decline and not so much a cause. "Violent World" declares that the "Country's corrupted by the people in power" causing "others" to move "in with a minute to shower." While the enemy is frequently nebulous in these songs, the sense of unity among the "lager lads" who live to drink is clear. The Magnificent ask, "Who are always drinking in the pub? Lager lads/Who are always ready to smash it up? Lager lads./Who are never sober, but always drunk? Lager lads." Boldly printed in red capital letters at the bottom of this album is the disclaimer, "OI! = A WORKING CLASS PROTEST (NOTHING MORE-NOTHING LESS). If this deceptively simple definition had ever been true, it still would have demanded additional explanation to clarify its meaning. But as Oi! became for a time commercially and then politically appropriated and exploited, its meaning became more a matter of who was interpreting it for what reason. Like punk once a social slogan, it was transformed into a political outcry. And even more than punk, Oi! was music for those who sought rejection from the mainstream society, who defiantly craved separateness and attention. But skinheads increasingly did not reject far right ideologues who sought alliance with them in their growing isolation.

In England and eventually on the Continent, the names of the bands that seem most to have appealed to the neo-fascist core of the developing skinhead scene reflect the violence that had always been endemic among skinhead groups, whether they were political in an extreme right wing fashion or not, or whether they were heavily anti-immigrant, anti-black, anti-gay or not: Brutal Attack, Skullhead, Prime Suspects (English); Brutal Combat (French); Bohse Onkelz (Evil Uncles, German). The names of some bands seem simply calculated to induce repugnance (a conventional, reflex desire shared by many punk groups) but a few would focus their tastelessness on more specifically political targets: White Pride, Final Solution, U.S. Chaos, Tulsa Boot Boys, New Glory, Hammer Head (American).

By the end of the 1970s, then, the skinheads, which as a youth subculture in England had been waning in the early part of the decade, experienced a resurgence, a revitalization greatly influenced by the larger punk scene of which it was a part, and by the politics of the National Front, which was greatly increasing its membership during the decade, mushrooming over four-fold from its inception in 1966 (Ridgeway 158). The punk scene provided a bounded climate of tolerance within its subcultural bubble for those who affronted and rejected traditional society and cultivated the bizarre, particularly if their style or manifestation signaled destructiveness. The punk link proved for a time fortunate for skinheads. Skins shared sometimes the important medium of popular music (or unpopular popular music), anti-authoritarianism, a penchant for violence (including self-violence) and the accepted, fairly heavy use of drugs (alcohol or other chemically addictive substances) with many of the punks. But they increasingly did not consider themselves punks, and other punks recognized their separateness. By the late 1970s in England, some skinheads, perhaps a majority now of the diminished movement, became more avowedly political. Many skinheads from the start of the scene had been racists, homophobes, anti-Semites, and sexually and politically chauvinistic. Skinheads had always spoken or acted violently in defense of what they considered white working class English objectives. Of course some non-racist skinheads had not always subscribed to all the items on this comprehensive agenda. Doubtless some had friendships with West Indians, Jews, and gays. Some few were West Indians themselves. However, by 1980 in England in a roughly organized fashion, most skinheads were part of a network of fascist sympathizers and extreme right wing activists. A variety of music had emerged called Oi! that was sometimes produced by skinhead bands and listened to with great enthusiasm by skinhead audiences, that frequently delivered fascist, extreme right wing messages.

The connection between American skinheads and English skinheads appears confused in the American press which has overwhelmingly treated skinheadism as a specifically political rather than a broadly cultural phenomenon. The American organizations that monitor native skinhead activity such as the Anti-Defamation League, the Center for Democratic Renewal, and the Southern Poverty Law Center invariably function to battle various kinds of prejudice and discrimination. These organizations are the source of much of the information American newspapers and magazines print about skinheads—they also cooperate with each other and share information directly or indirectly (they read and sometimes collect each other's press releases as reported in the newspaper, and thus there is a reification process at work here too). People who perform research for these organizations understandably tend not to be pop music critics. So certain supposed facts that are repeated in stories about skinhead origins seem questionable. For many American reporters, punk music began with the Sex Pistols, for example.[3] A writer for the Center for Democratic Renewal declared that "British rockers first introduced the music in 1976" (Sears, "Far Right Youth Recruitment Serious Long-Term Threat" 5).

Some of this confusion or misinformation is minor, except that it obscures the symbiotic nature of English and American punk and therefore the origins of skinheadism in America where the style finally became implanted in the seventies as it clearly had not been in the sixties, a product of homegrown bigotry germinating at last within a youth culture in America as it could not during the earlier period, when there was surely no absence of bigotry among many American youth. In the seventies the style finally flowered ugly as a poisonous weed in America where the racist beliefs so frequently connected to it had always been held by some Americans, young and old. But only the young would become skinheads.

Punk was a fertile territory for skinheadism in England or America, because it tolerated or even demanded displays of hostility to perceived middle and upper class standards, because it was often violent, and because generally it seemed at least in theory or observable stance to identify itself with lower or working class fashions and mannerisms, though frequently in America these were often assumed by fairly well-to-do, ultimately college-bound suburban white youth. Punk was in America anyway heavily middle class, and so its adoption of some working class styles would be a conventional form of rejecting traditional authority and standards. Punk in America also contained much that attracted skinheads ideologically, even while skinheads clearly distinguished themselves from punk's less politically focused and more socially nebulous musical orientation. *The Nationalist*, mentioned in the Anti-Defamation League's *Hate Groups in America* as a monthly issued by the white revolutionary National Democratic Front, claimed in March 1982 that although the skinhead movement paralleled the punk movement since "both represented young White radicalism and openly condemned the Establishment and hypocritical social norms," the "punk movement was nihilistic and directionless, and eventually drifted into the control of the System which it supposedly opposed" ("Nationalist Youth Create New Rock Movement" 14).

Punk was alluring and accommodating for a time to skinheads because it was so open to various strains of defiance. And as Jimmy Pursey of Sham 69 said, "If punks are about anarchy, then skinheads are the most anarchist going...They fight, run riot, don't give a fuck about anything" (Walker 345). But also some skinheads did "give a fuck" about race, just as some punks were racist despite the heavily publicized "Rock Against Racism" campaigns. Dick Hebdige mentions that "In 1977, the *New Musical Express* helped briefly to divert a lot of punks away from the nihilism of the Sex Pistols toward Rock Against Racism and the Anti-Nazi League" (Hebdige in Knight 29), suggesting that there had been and continued to be a punk drift toward fascism. There was no invariable dispute between skins and punks on the matter of race because some of each—though fairly clearly a greater percentage of skins—were racists.

Lester Bangs has stated in a 1979 article (*Village Voice*, April 30) titled "The White Noise Supremacists" that "around 1970 there was a carbuncle named Wayne McGuire who wrote for *Fusion* magazine that the Velvet Underground represented some kind of mystical milestone in the destiny of the Aryan Race." Bangs also remembered "Iggy [Pop] hollering" in 1974 at his fans on the recorded-live bootleg disk "Metallic K.O." that "Our next selection tonight for all you Hebrew ladies in the audience is entitled 'Rich Bitch'!"

Bangs further noted that punk or new wave music was overwhelmingly white music by white groups for white audiences, so it should not be surprising that sometimes racism would be part of the scene, for example in a punk girl's term "boons" (baboons) for troublesome black males (Bangs 272, 282). Fascist symbols were employed so often by performers in the punk scene they became a minor tradition. One of the "Great Moments in the History of Punk" celebrated in *Spin* magazine's "10th Anniversary of Punk" issue was Lou Reed's 1975 act of shaving an Iron Cross in his head and calling it "the ultimate statement" (Holstrom 63). Reed has been described looking at this time like an "upwardly-mobile member of the Hitler jugend" (Diana Clapton in Henry 37). One of David Bowie's many alter-egos was the Thin White Duke (in "Station to Station") who "appeared in magazine interviews to grant approval to aspects of Nazism" (Henry 36). Also in *Spin*'s commemorative issue, musician and writer Legs McNeil points out that "while his lyrics aren't exactly a rallying cry for another thousand-year Reich, Dee Dee [Ramone] has stated in some interviews that his message may have been misconstrued. Dee Dee spent his preteen years playing in the rubble in postwar Berlin, where he discovered old relics that his parents used to scold him for bringing home. These relics were Nazi artifacts" (53).

While some punk groups of the late seventies such as England's Sham 69 sought to escape their skinhead followers, the presence of relatively large numbers of skinheads on the punk scene in England and America seems understandable in light of the mixed messages sent out by the new music and its performers. That half of Sham 69's "fans are punks and half are skinhead neo-Nazis" as Lester Bangs reported late in 1979 (283) may partly have resulted from the skinheads' confusion about Sham's message, but the mix of messages punks and skinheads received from the bands they liked often swirled about in a highly charged, violent, attack-filled, destructive, and clearly not always politically liberal atmosphere. In America, it was no isolated occasion when a member of the popular Teenage Jesus and the Jerks could be heard "yelling, 'Hey, you bunch of fucking niggers' at a crowd of black kids in front of Hurrah one night." Legs McNeil himself when he played with his band "Shrapnel" and wore army surplus clothes as though reenacting the Vietnam War performed a song called "Hey Little Gook." He claimed the term meant nothing more (!) than "kraut" in World War II films, or " 'slants' and stuff like that' " (Bangs 279). Perhaps McNeil was employing the word satirically in a reflexive fashion, mocking those who employed the insulting epithet, but it seems unlikely that all the kids who yelled to hear "Hey Little Gook" were post-modern ironists.

The punk scene within which the skinheads were harbored in England and in America contained blatantly racist elements. It was a white scene and would have been extraordinary had it not. While some punk groups and their supporters were indifferent to partisan politics, and some such as The Clash sang lyrics of a liberal bent for a time, racism pervaded the punk scene in England and America though it did not in any overt or ordinary sense, dominate it. But it was there.

There has been sometimes what seems a wishful denial of this by new music critics, perhaps resulting from or anticipating the outside public's desire to brand various subcultures in as repugnant terms as possible. Lester Bangs writes, "A lot of outsiders, in fact, think punk *is* fascist, but that's only because they can't see beyond certain buzzwords, symbols, and pieces of regalia that (I think) really aren't that significant: Ron Ashton of the Stooges used to wear swastikas, Iron Crosses, and jackboots onstage, but I don't remember any right wing rants ever popping up in the music he did with Iggy [Stooge, or Pop] or his own later band, which many people were not exactly thrilled to hear was called the New Order." In other words, because Ashton did not write explicitly anti-Semitic lyrics, the trappings of his stage outfit and even the name of his band, so offensive to Jews and anyone antagonistic to the Nazis' murderously anti-Semitic behavior, should not be considered as advancing or fostering fascist actions and ideals. Bangs repeats a familiar claim here, that "swastikas in punk are basically another way for kids to get a rise out of their parents and maybe the press, both of whom deserve the irritation" (275). But do Holocaust Jews deserve the anguish this teenage rebellion causes?

Stan Cohen notes with skepticism this tendency to shift the ordinary symbolic meaning away from fascist icons worn as trinkets of style among youth subcultures when these items are being rationalized by some observer sympathetic to the subculture: "time and time again we are assured that though this symbol is 'on one level' intended to outrage and shock, it is really being employed in a meta-language: the wearers are ironically distancing themselves from the very message that the symbol is usually intended to convey." Greil Marcus claimed that when "punks toyed casually with Nazi imagery" it was "implying that Britain's victory over Hitler had simply led to fascism by a different route." Another critic states that swastikas "were not worn to indicate that punk was in agreement with fascist philosophy but rather to remind society of the atrocities it permits" (Henry 80). Thus the song lyric "Belsen was a gas" (Cohen, new preface, xvii) presumably is not, finally, tasteless in its insensitivity to Holocaust victims, but is supposedly a sign of its singer's or audiences' refusal to accept the taint of an old sickness endemic to the parent culture that only pretends to be offended by Jewish slaughter, but that has slaughtered through its own disdain and vacuity millions the world over. But there is no assurance that this is what the song really means, or that someone outside the subculture will always have a skilled explicator handy to explain what it means, that in fact it should be interpreted any differently from the bumper sticker reported in Portland, Oregon in early 1981 that said "Gas a Jew for Jesus" (*Klanwatch* Nov./Dec. 1981).

Certainly some young English or American punks and performers have worn Nazi paraphernalia through stupidity or insensitivity (just as some whites are occasionally reported to don blackface for entertainment purposes), or as a matter of apish fashion. But equally certain is that for others the displayed symbols represent a willingness to declare prejudiced beliefs. Bangs recollects that in Florida in 1977 he read in a "fanzine called *New Order*" an article declaring "I love the Ramones [because] this is the celebration of everything urban— everything teenaged and wonderful and white and urban." The same fanzine showed the article's author "and one of her little friends posing proudly with their leathers and shades and a pistol in front of the headquarters of the United White People's Party, under a sign bearing three flags: 'GOD' (a cross), 'COUNTRY' (the stars and stripes), 'RACE' (a swastika)" (278). This does not mean that punk rock was a fascist musical culture, but it is more evidence supporting the idea that the new phase of skinheadism—which in its racial intolerance, anti-Semitism, and homophobia maintained and fortified strains found in its older incarnation—did not find a necessarily hostile climate for its growth within the punk scene. To the contrary, the cultural soil of punk rock possessed fertile patches for the new spurt in skinhead growth during the late seventies and early 1980s. At this time in England, and then later in America, right wing political organizations began actively courting the racist skinheads, realizing their potential as bully boys for fascist movements and the value of their music as a way of spreading messages of hate among young audiences. A frequently restated idea appearing in *WAR* magazine and circulated in right wing extremist literature is that "music is one of the greatest propaganda tools around. You can influence more people with a song than with a speech."[4] Oi!

music lyrics mirrored and spread feelings of bitter antagonism in strident and obscene cries against a generalized, authoritarian foe. The English group Blitz sang "Don't tell me what you want me to do. I never wanted to be like you....Fuck you! Fuck you!" In the late 1970s and early 1980s, these unfocused attacks would also become aimed at specific political and social enemies.

Hate Rock

The best known performer of what might be called white power hate rock is Ian Stuart Donaldson, leader of Skrewdriver. Stuart (who has dropped the name Donaldson as a performer) was born in Blackpool, England, to a middle class family in 1958. A booklet written by Stuart's friend Joe Pearce, honoring Skrewdriver's tenth anniversary, says that Stuart's first band Tumbling Dice was formed in 1975 while he was in public school. In 1977 the group reformed as Skrewdriver after one of its original members left, and played for a time at some concerts with punk bands which Stuart found increasingly too far left for his extremist tastes. His story is that "he decided to build up a following of skins rather than a broader audience" but one critical observer claims that more probably "their standard was so awful that any audience other than one numbed by glue and lager was likely to force them off the stage."[5] In 1979 Stuart joined the fascistic National Front, and he would eventually become, according to *The Nationalist*, "a member of the 18-man National Directorate which rules the NF" ("Nationalist Youth Create New Rock Movement" 14). His band's success was at first minimal, and he returned to Blackpool to work in a factory. In 1981 Skrewdriver regrouped and began issuing a series of records that together with Stuart's openly political activities eventually made them perhaps the best internationally known hate rock group. Centering his London days near the Soldier of Fortune store around Charing Cross and at The Last Resort record shop in East London, Stuart became notorious for the aggressively militant white power fascism he expressed in Skrewdriver song lyrics and fanzines, and in National Front publications. In time, he would help create an "Instant Response Group" for the National Front, "designed to be called out at short notice to attack political rivals or defend NF meetings." The gang wore "black trousers, white power t-shirts and black bomber jackets with Nazi insignia." Four of its members would be convicted for wearing illegal "political uniforms." Stuart himself spent six months in jail for physically assaulting a Nigerian. His biographer Pearce was his jail mate for a time, while Pearce served a "second prison term for offenses committed while editing the notorious NF magazine *Bulldog*" (see Footnote 5).

Stuart and his violent friends lived what they sang. The racial violence he calls for on his records he sought opportunities to commit on the streets, and he has served time in jail for instigating racial fights he claims were provoked. He also charges he is a victim of England's warped, Jew-ridden judicial system. Jews, he declares, control the media, banking, and police in England and America. Jews tried to make whites feel guilty about "what happened in the past to black people: we shouldn't feel guilty at all. We gave black people a lot of advantages" merely by placing them "in contact with people from the white world" (Moore 28). In 1984 together with several far right wing friends (one of whom, Nicky Crane, wrote a song for Skrewdriver's first album with the German company Rock-o-Rama Records) he attacked two bands playing at the left wing Greater London Council's concert for the unemployed along the Thames River. The same year he was quoted in the March 19 issue of *Spotlight* (published according to the ADL by the anti-Jewish Liberty Lobby) declaring, "One must be honest to people about one's beliefs and especially when the survival of our race is at stake." As the leader of Blood and Honour, characterized by *Klanwatch* as "a British skinhead, neo-Nazi musical organization," he has also claimed contacts with the Invisible Empire and Tom Metzger's White Aryan Resistance (*Klanwatch*, December 1988).

One of the earliest American skinhead gangs, Chicago's Romantic Violence, publicized Skrewdriver in a leaflet as "an institution, a stance of courage, determination, loyalty, honor and a will to win." *Klanwatch* has stated that Stuart's early 45s bootlegged at one time for up to $100.00 around Los Angeles, one of the first skinhead centers (February 1991, 15). Among Skrewdriver's long-playing records distributed by Rock-o-Rama Records are "Hail the New Dawn," whose album jacket shows an army of what look like hairy Norsemen with swords drawn for battle, landing from a ship and planting their flag on new territory; "Blood and Honour"; and "White Rider," whose album cover portrays a hooded Klansman carrying a yellow flaming torch, astride a white-sheeted, prancing horse. The rider is emerging from or poised before a wall of sharp, red-tipped forks of yellow flames, suggesting a battle conflagration. Stuart's lyrics though not always distinguishable on records, are shockingly explicit in their hatred of blacks and Jews and immigrants generally, and frequently call for a battle to purify England—or it could be any country contaminated by non-white scum. Musically almost old-fashioned, basic rock, with little technical innovation though more skill than some of the truly terrible punk and Oi! bands, sometimes energetic and sometimes monotonous, with a driving beat and occasional simplicity that would be conducive to sing-along group performance in pubs or at concerts, the band's songs offer no technical surprises. The performances are neither significantly raw nor polished, and it is difficult to imagine audiences being attracted to Skrewdriver's sound apart from the message Stuart sings in song after song, a message delivered openly with few arcane symbols. "When the Boat Comes In" would be as meaningful to American racists as it was to its original British fans, and was in fact a favorite of skinhead Dean McKee's prior to his 1988 conviction for murdering a black man.

> Close down the borders
> They don't fit in
> In our new order.
> Nigger, nigger, get on that boat,

Another song attacks individual and group complacency in accepting the takeover of England by undesirables from outside, but its words would speak clearly to Americans who feared inundation by Latino or Asian immigrants as well.

> I stand and watch my country going down the drain,
> We are all at fault now, we are all to blame,
> We're letting them take over, we just let them come,
> Once we had an empire, and now we've got a slum.

Imagery of consuming flames and impending battle to the death fill Skrewdriver's songs. In "I Can See the Fire" the hoarse, almost off-key Stuart chants, "I can see the fire and I know it won't die." The fire will eventually eat away the evils pervading England, a country most of the songs assume has been captured by blacks, Jews, communists, liberals, all enemies of the true heartland English white stock. Though "we see corruption at all levels/There's thunder in the cities/Thunder in the towns/Thunder in the villages/Let the walls come tumbling down." The

New Order, which is really the very old (white working class English) order, will attempt to stop the nation's decline until the death. "We Fight for Freedom" sings that "Our destiny hangs by a thread"—Armageddon is always near in Stuart's songs—but the white warriors are "willing to die" to regain England's lost Aryan greatness. In the struggle, death seems imminent. When there is "fighting in the city/It's a matter of life and death/It's as easy as black and white/You'll fight till your last breath." But death will not stop the resurgent movement. "You are the warriors fighting for the people/And you fight because you are strong/And they'll never, never beat the warriors/White warriors, white warriors" ("White Warriors"). "For your flag and country you're willing to die/White Rider, White Rider, your strength is your pride" ("Pride of a Nation"). "The final fight is here/It's either life or death" ("Pride of a Nation").

The warriors are a beleaguered minority who will find little support from the Outsiders—"history tries to put them down" ("Pride of a Nation")—but paradoxically the tide of history is on the side of whiteness. "If they bother to take a look around, they'll see the writing is on the wall/A lot of young people are waking up/And answering the white man's call" ("White Warriors"). And somehow despite all the death that seems to dominate the life of the white warrior movement, through battle they will eventually be victorious. "The cattle are lowin'/The vultures are crowin'/The traitors are celebrating/They think they won the game/They can stop their clowning/For soon they'll be frowning/They think that they have beaten us/But we will not be tamed/New Nation, I pledge my life to you" ("New Nation"). The dominating elements of these songs appear to combine a sense of doom along with the need to fight to the death to win back lost white greatness. The belief seems aggressive and fatalistic at once.

I have noted that the skinhead style had apparently not taken root on American soil during the first phase of skinhead activity in England during the late 1960s and early 1970s. Both in its manner and ideology it would be highly unattractive to the hippie movement among the young, and anathema to the more intensely politically focused organizations such as the Students for a Democratic Society (SDS) and the myriad other so-called radical youth groups. Nor did there seem to be a place for it among right wing youth societies such as the college-based Young Americans for Freedom. Standard, older hate groups such as the Ku

Klux Klan might have fostered the transplantion of skinheadism, but the phenomenon has always been essentially an urban growth while the older hate cultures operated most strongly and openly (though certainly not uniquely) in rural or semi-rural areas. Furthermore, the skinheads were only one of many youth subcultures who were considered rebellious and opposed to the authority of older generations. Although sociologists might view the English skinheads as attempting "to recreate through the 'mob' the traditional working class community" (Clarke in Hall and Jefferson 99), it does not appear that they were viewed within working class communities as a redemptive force struggling to bring back days of working class glory, whenever that might have been. More frequently, outside British academic circles anyway, they were generally viewed as destructive, disorderly yobboes without a decent cause. And so while eventually hate groups would use skinheads in America (as they did in England) as bully boys to advance racist doctrines, and would court skinhead groups and approvingly publicize elements of their subculture, particularly their music at a time when skinhead music was openly racist, this would not occur during the very early years of the skinhead evolution in the United States.

However, in time, the American hate groups would become more sophisticated in their recruiting tactics, and more cynical in their willingness to tolerate (even to take advantage of) the skinheads' unruliness and kamikaze brutality, their socially oppositional image, and antagonism to older generations. Ugly, hard, crude, seemingly uncontrollable and anarchistic; racist, defiantly young and apparently utterly disdainful of conventional authority, the skinhead appearance and stance found no receptive space in America's youth scene until the mid to late 1970s, when the comparatively massive political involvement of young American rebels—fitful as it had been and in terms of numbers actually limited as it had been, despite the vast media attention focused upon it—dwindled and lost its sporadically sharp focus (on the war in Vietnam, on the draft, on simple, basic civil rights issues).

Notes

[1]Ridgeway's book, I should add, is generally very reliable and helpful.

[2]"The Ultra Violence" is mentioned in a list of songs of questionable taste in *The Boston Jewish Advocate* (19 Jan. 1989), in ADL files. A private party obtained some of

Scott McKee's old record collection and made it available to me.

[3]PBS, "All Things Considered" interview with Malcolm McLaren, 8 Nov. 1989.

[4]ADL archives quoting *WAR* magazine.

[5]No author given; *Searchlight*, p. 3, in CDR's "Skinhead Nazis and Youth Information Packet."

Chapter Three
White Warriors Emerge:
Skinheads in America

By the mid to late 1970s in America, the punk world provided a haven for young people who felt that they constituted a distinct generation, constantly separating themselves not simply from their parents but from their older brothers and sisters or from older generations of students. It gloried in a variety of rebellious attitudes which frequently but not always were just that, attitudes lacking in substance but flaunted for the moment, modes of distancing themselves from the life the punks thought their parents led, or less conflictually, drawing themselves more closely to their peers, people (in the early days of punk anyway) closer to them in age and style. This world was anti-authoritarian but beyond that politically nebulous. It was at least permissive about acts of destruction, drug taking, and, like most of the rest of America, sexual liberation. It was contemptuous of the parent culture, even when emulating it in its willingness to exploit itself.

In England, skinheads seem to have been part of the punk scene from its start, probably because skinheads predated punk in England. The same cultural swamp that provided a growing place for the various seemingly simultaneous and successive strains of punk already contained the skinheads, even though their style was vegetating comparatively slowly, while punk burst into flower quite rapidly. In America, there was not even a dormant skinhead movement to reinvigorate through its association with punk, and so the skinhead development was slower, and engaged in by far fewer participants, than in England.

But by the late 1970s skinheads were part of the punk scene in America, operating more as individuals or loosely connected clusters of individuals than skinheads in England, who typically were members of quite specific gangs, sometimes living together in the same dwellings or public housing projects. Precisely how the style was transmitted to the United States—as opposed to the music shared by skins and punkers (or new music fans generally)—is difficult to pinpoint, although the question why was the style *not* imported before this time is possibly more to be wondered at. An osmotic free flow existed in new popular music among youth between England and the United States since the early 1960s, and youth cultures in both countries seem symbiotic, first one influencing the other, in a constant reciprocity. Middle-class American youth traveling or going to school in England would have observed the local skinheads and been intrigued by them. Record album jackets showed skinheads in live performance audiences, tourists delighted in sending back to friends in the States post cards bought in London showing presumably picturesque skinheads sometimes grimacing wildly, sometimes mugging next to the staid guards at English government offices or military installations.

On Broadway, Jonathan Pryce played a skinhead in the English playwright Trevor Griffith's transplanted *Comedians* (1976). Sometimes touring bands such as Bad Brains (a black group, an early industrial band playing confrontive, abrasive, metallic sounding music) or Throbbing Gristle would possess one or more skinheaded (though not necessarily skinhead) members. By 1981 a documentary about the Los Angeles punk rock scene in the late 1970s showed skinheads mixing with other punks in concert crowds, thrash dancing and leaping off the stage occupied by bands such as the Alice Bag Band, Black Flag, Catholic Discipline, The Circle Jerks, Fear, and Germs. Titled *The Decline of Western Civilization* and directed by Penelope Spheeris, this music film soon became a cult favorite similar to though not nearly as generally popular as the *Rocky Horror Picture Show*, playing late at night at urban and suburban multiplex theatres after more standard Hollywood offerings finished their evening runs. The film would reveal and might extend the skinheads' small dominion, through supplying images of them in action which could induce imitation.

The Decline of Western Civilization was shot at apparently a time of transition in Los Angeles's punk and skinhead scenes, a down, dark side for punk and just prior to the political crystallization that brought greater ideological coherence to the skins, and also just before the time they became numerically significant on the punk scene. Skinheads are on the fringes of that scene here, visible briefly from time to time, like shapes beyond the fireglow of some evolving (or in this instance decaying) forest civilization. Most of the elements of the skinhead way are shown in the film but not identified yet with the skinheads themselves, who are fleeting and few in number. Many of the traditional fascist symbols are produced—a singer for The Germs wears an iron cross, boys in the pit pogo dancing (jumping up and down violently) wear shirts with swastikas on them, an appreciative member of Fear's audience wears a swastika armband. There is incessant homophobia, and occasionally an understandable line in a song that could be racist (in Catholic Discipline's "Barbie Doll Lust," a hymn to masturbation, the masturbator and his penis "sit by a window away from the black kids") or that could be mocking racism but whose racial stance is at last unclear. The audience is overwhelmingly young and white, the atmosphere thick with belligerence, with male hatreds, with sneers against anticipated and probably sought-for rejection.

A kind of Punk's Progress is revealed by posters in The Germs' apartment: the headline "Sid Vicious Faces Murder Count" and a "Sham 69" illustration. Skinheads are most apparent in the segment devoted to Fear, a band whose performers look almost too old to be punks, not to speak of skinheads, but who spit out contempt upon their audience, homosexuals, and women. "Really we just think you're a bunch of queers" their lead singer, who calls himself Lee Ving, shouts, "and we don't give a fuck if you like us or not!" Acting like boot boys without boots, Fear's stage attitude is chillingly, sourly male. "She just wants my beef bologna" Ving barks in one song. Young men jump on stage and are pummeled and shoved off. Another Fear performer sickly tells a harshly anti-female joke as though he were just a nasty little boy: "You know why chicks have their little holes so close together?—so you can carry them like a six pack of beer"—driving the logic of macho male fantasy beer commercials to their perverse extreme. Dancers in the pit flail crazily as Ving, always sneering, sings what he calls Fear's hit song, "I Love Livin' in the City":

> My house smells just like the zoo,
> It's chock full of shit and puke,
> Cockroaches on the walls,
> Crabs are crawling on my balls.

Punk insiders often speak of the energy generated within the punk scene, which is often a destructive energy, a fury or lashing out at whatever comes close to them, including other punks like themselves. In *The Decline of Western Civilization* Fear insults its audience, many of whom smash back at them or spit at them gleefully. Punk anger against parents, older generations, country, authority, against other punks who don't like the kind of music they like, is unfocused. Everything sucks. Punk sucks. The skinhead scene, here much smaller than the punk scene, much less popular, would become much better focused and give those who participated in it, eventually, more specific targets for hate, and a more extreme program for carrying out violent inclinations than spitting and shoving. The skinhead scene seems unformed in the time of *The Decline of Western Civilization* (filmed from December 1979 until May 1980, a note from the filmmaker pinpoints it) but skinheads are visible in the punk crowd. An interview with Eugene, a skinhead, is used to frame the documentary's footage of band performances, audience reactions, and more interviews with band members and scattered hangers on. Eugene is very young, a sort of larval skin, angry and ready he says to fight, to get his "aggression out...all this fucking pent up shit" against what makes him so despairing, which is "just seeing everything...all the ugly old people...the buses, the dirt" that constitutes for him his own "livin' in this city." He's on his own, says "I just hang around by myself" and "I don't know where my parents are." He gets hassled a lot, says "sometimes the niggers come up to me...they'll be chasing me." It's all inevitable to him.

In one of the most famous poems of the twentieth century—a poem intellectuals love to quote about how terrible life has become in our times—Yeats describes what happens when "Things fall apart" and "the center cannot hold;/Mere anarchy is loosed upon the world." This nightmare according to Yeats presaged a second coming, so ominous and ugly he wondered "what rough beast, its hour come round at last,/Slouches towards Bethlehem to be born?" Yeats may have been misled, seeking only one beast. The 1980s would provide many, and the force young men like Eugene grew into, the skinheads, was one.

Pink Floyd—The Wall, directed by Alan Parker with fascinating, politically corrosive animated sequences by Gerald Scarfe, was released in the United States in 1982. The film is almost grotesquely portentous, and muddled in its left wing critique of Margaret Thatcher's England. As self-indulgent in its direction as the rock scene the movie briefly depicts, *Pink Floyd—The Wall* exploits the vices and social sicknesses it ostentatiously attacks: oppression of the weak or sensitive or young by parents, community, and state; sexual excess; compulsive self-mutilation and sado-masochistic cruelty; fascistic state control. Along with *Clockwork Orange*, the film was a favorite among Dean and Scott McKee's Tampa skinhead gang, "The Saints." It must have reaffirmed their feelings of having been treated very badly by parents and teachers, who are depicted in the film much like ogres in fairy tales, ever ready to humiliate or deny the children in their charge. In one sequence a boy (the film's protagonist as a child) is discovered writing poetry in class and is frighteningly degraded by his male teacher. In another notorious episode what seems like thousands of school boys and girls shuffle in step through what appears to be a prison (or factory?) in single file, chanting in unison like aggressive zombies or the stupefied workers in Fritz Lang's *Metropolis*," "We don't need no education, we don't need no thought control, no dark sarcasm in the classroom, Teacher, leave us kids alone." It is difficult not to track down one source of the children's plight to the director's need to reaffirm his young audience's belief in their unfair, totalitarian dominance by society. But he also reflects of course a traditional plaint of punkers, skinheads, and critics of formal educational systems. Even before *The Wall* was playing in movie houses, the English Oi! band Angelic Upstarts were including teachers in their litany of those who should "Fuck off and leave me alone" ("Oi! Chartbusters," Volume 2.)

The movie's protagonist, a sometimes nearly catatonic and sometimes explosively violent rock star called "Pink," imagines himself a fascist leader much like Hitler, presiding over scaled-down Nurnberg-type rallies such as those Leni Riefenstahl depicted with obscene glory in *Triumph of the Will*. Skinheads serve as storm troopers terrorizing and beating up Jews and homosexuals ("queers") at these rallies. Parker is clearly attacking fascistic behavior here but he presents it in a potent, perversely attractive fashion, and the skinheads remain unpunished, facilitating real skinheads' idolization of the film. Like most zealots, they are capable of inverting even harsh criticism and transforming it into praise. In their eyes, *Pink Floyd—The Wall* would demonstrate skinhead triumph amid attempts to purify a deeply corrupt society. In the film, skinheads become an unleashed force dominating the herd of misfits and weaklings who ordinarily people if not run the world that the fascist Pink must set in order.

Similar to *The Decline of Western Civilization, Pink Floyd—The Wall* shows the prevalence of skinheads on the punk scene, and particularly in an age of videotape availability, suggests another source for spreading the skinhead image in the United States. By the early 1980s, that image was fairly fixed, though it is questionable that all nuances of skinhead style became familiar to American skinheads across the sweep of the country until the dissemination of Nick Knight's book after its publication, around 1982. One of the characters in the cult favorite *Repo Man* (1984) for example, looks like a skinhead—although ideologically he seems far more punk than skin. But in the early 1980s, outside the punk world, American skinheads were rarely heard about, and if they possessed strong anti-minority hostilities, the American public was ignorant of these. And inside the punk world, skinheads generally were simply part of the polyglot mix the alternative music scene tolerated or endured. Though their numbers were small, they were strongly part of that scene because of their minimalist, mean appearance, and because of their physical abandon. They were ever ready to crash into each other or anyone else who bumped around near them, to invade the stage and shove performers about or dive back into the mob, they were particularly more eager than many of the other punkers (and then new wavers) to fight. Perhaps in a curious way, the much greater majority of non-skinhead punkers saw the skins as hostile but necessary brethren, supplying an aggressive violence and danger to the punker's rebellious sub-world. Maybe it felt good, to have such mean motherfuckers within your ranks, if you could avoid their hostility yourself. They would show the outside society you were not just fooling around. The skinheads possessed iconic display value. Their acceptance seems obligatory. On the jacket of the 1982 album "Mommy's Little Monster" by a band called Social Distortion, a skinhead appears in the still-photographic montage providing a visual context for the group's musical performance, together with a dedication offering "many thanks to the punk scene who we helped build and who helped build us."

Social Distortion is not itself a band particularly noteworthy as a skinhead favorite. Its lyrics are however expressive of several recurrent themes common in the punk mode, strains that would particularly appeal to the skinhead element within or on the fringes of that mode: pride in substance (mainly alcohol) abuse; love of violence; feelings of oppression; disdain for society and concurrently the desire for revenge upon it; a glorying in their toughness and fearsomeness. Social Distortion's song "Moral Threat" announces to someone who "beat us up when we're alone" and inflicted "stitches in my head" just "cause you didn't like my looks," that he will be sorry later "when your head is rolling in all the SHIT!!" Since the "justice system is slow/...we'll have to take care of you,/Your only safety is suicide." The threat of suicide as a punishment seems appropriate in the mainly teenage punk/skinhead world that is filled with self-destruction and self-mutilation (two of the more popular groups of the 1980s were Suicide and Suicidal Tendencies).

The song "Telling Them" openly declares a love of destruction but links it with fear of (or is it desire for?) reprisal by straight society's guardians, parents and the police. "Well I love the sound when I smash the glass,/If I get caught they're gonna kick my ass,/My mommy is worried about the way I drink,/My daddy can't figure out the way I think./They wake up, tell me to 'Get to work,'/I slam the door, say, 'Shut up you jerk!' " The straight world may be stupid and cruel but the punk scene offers welcome haven: "I can't wait till the show tonight./When I'm with my friends everything's alright." But the show will not last forever, and when it's over, the young rebel cannot return home. "They say it costs $6 to get in this shack,/I'll go around and sneak in the back./I hope the police won't show up here,/Then we'll have to hide out of fear." This infantile, childlike pose is continued in "Mommy's Little Monster," which seeks sympathy for a 20-year-old who "dropped out of school,/Mommy's little monster broke all the rules./He loves to go out drinking with the boys,/He loves to go out and make some noise./He doesn't wanna be a doctor or a lawyer and get fat and rich." An outsider to his own middle class family, the monster's "brothers and sisters have tasted sweet success,/His parents condemn him, say 'His life's a mess!'/He's mommy's little monster, he's not afraid to admit it/...DON'T TAKE [HIS] LIFE AWAY."

Punk (and skinhead) lyrics often seem death-drawn while, paradoxically enough, they magically proclaim, for example in "All the Answers," that these kids in "colored hair and funny clothes" who "are the menace of today" represent a new order. "But don't forget that they're your future!/They're loud, they're obnoxious/They're proud...But don't forget that they're your future./These kids [who] are accused of all the violence." The song concludes with voices yelling at the straight auditor, "AND YOU THOUGHT YOU HAD ALL THE FUCKING ANSWERS!" Within the intellectual, emotional, and psychological climate these ordinary punk songs embody, the skinheads found a space as they took root in America. While the punk scene lacked the openly announced racist and anti-minority edge that would come to identify skinheads as a distinct group ideologically, the punk world offered skinhead types a harbor if not a haven no youth subculture in the sixties in America had provided.

From the time of the skinheads' first real transplantation to America in the second half of the 1970s decade, the racist agenda that developed as part of the skinhead ideology in England, not an ideology all English skinheads subscribed to, spread unevenly as the skinhead style and musical tastes drifted from city to city, even as individual skinheads moved about, for example from Atlanta to Tampa, or from New York to Chicago or Los Angeles. Throughout the 1980s decade there would continue to be skinheads connected to the punk or new wave or new music scene who were not avowed racists, and at the peak of the skinheads' notoriety as a crypto-movement around 1988, these skinheads would openly declare war upon their racist, anti-minority compatriots. However, it is clear that some organized skinhead gangs in America very early in the 1980s decade were aware of and subscribed to the grab-bag of xenophobic, nativist, racist, anti-Semitic, anti-gay, anti-welfare antagonisms bands such as Skrewdriver expressed in England and in some instances tried to enforce, for example by appearing at National Front political rallies, or by actually beating up targeted enemies. But surely the American youth who as skinheads listened to the clear messages of hate sung by some of the "Oi!" bands and those groups encouraged by the reactionary National Front did not learn bigotry by listening to records any more than they would they learn brutality and violence from watching cinematic images of skinhead belligerence. However, they could feel that they were linked to an international movement whose constituency subscribed to ideas the same as theirs, a scene far beyond the local scene whose participants felt as they did. Moreover, they could declare their sense of belonging to this greater national and international scene by adopting the visual style of the movement.

The Americans did not have to adopt the ideology or behavior of the racist skinheads—they already possessed these. The young Americans did not need to learn to imitate the fascist-anarchist manner of the British skins, since plenty of examples existed for emulation on the home scene, provided mainly by racist attitudes and responses to black Americans in the 1960s and 1970s, lingering, sporadic outbursts of anti-Semitism in thought and deed, and a long history of discriminatory or violent treatment of homosexuals ranging from stereotyping male gays as mincing child seducers to virtual sanctioning of beating up gays by police or ordinary bar drunks. What the skinheads needed to learn ideologically or behaviorally they could learn at home or in their own American communities, though it is true that thoughts or actions that might only have been vaguely formed or mildly simmering within them could be stiffened and more intensely concentrated through the reinforcement skinhead life—skinhead songs and skinhead style—could bring. The style may have sharpened and given an emotionally strengthening uniform to the skinhead manner but it did not create skinhead beliefs or actions in America. Many Americans in the late 1970s and early 1980s, and not all of them young, thought and behaved like skinheads though they did not adopt the skinhead style, did not enjoy skinhead music, and never hung around the new music scene.

The number of skinheads in America has never achieved anything like the concentrations or proportions of England's skinhead population. As late as February 1988, the ADL estimated the total at 1,000 or as an upper limit 1,500 (*The Skinheads—An Update* 1). In October 1988, this estimate was raised to 2,000 (*Young and Violent* 1) and in June 1989 was lifted again to 3,000 (*Skinheads Target the Schools* 1). These numbers seem low, and perhaps result from the ADL's occasionally stated method of estimating only "skinhead activists," and not taking into account shaven headed high school kids or young men who appeared at new music concerts or sometimes loitered around bar parking lots with "activist skinheads," however these are determined. Still, excluding "wannabe" skinheads, even though the total of young males and females who identify themselves in some basic way as skinheads or skinchicks would appear to exceed ADL's estimate, their numbers were relatively small compared to English counterparts who in 1968 according to Ian Walker's previously quoted report could assemble 4,000 adherents at one football match.

Gathered in cities and city suburbs but spread across all regions of the country, American skinheads have come to receive attention in the media disproportionate to their population if not their cultural significance. But until 1984 or so they seem to have been treated in America merely as another weird element on the punk or new music scene without too much attention paid to their politics or potential dangerousness, except in stray depictions such as *The Decline of Western Civilization* few Americans saw, in which their brutishness was captured along with what seemed their typical mindlessness. Until the mid or late 1980s the press, local and national, was not nearly as entranced with them as it had been with the numerically far greater number of hippies or flower children of the 1960s and early 1970s, nor as fixated upon their menace as it had been with radical youth organizations such as the Weathermen of that same period. Although in cities that were new music centers, such as New York and Los Angeles and Atlanta, their participation in the punk music scene of the late 1970s and early 1980s was common, skinheads were not at first the focus of media questioning about "what is wrong with our children?" as had been the similarly small number of members of the extreme left wing SDS and subsequent splinter organizations during the 1960s and 1970s. Possibly perceived damage from the left was less tolerable and more threatening in the United States than damage from the right.

Perhaps also because of the relatively small numbers of skinheads their activities were not the source of academic investigation to the degree they were subject to in England. When their racism became known, it was attacked by a variety of organizations, particularly the Anti-Defamation League, the Southern Poverty Law Center, and the Center for Democratic Renewal, all of whom shared the role of social guardians attacking racism and hostility to minorities, manifested by individuals or groups. Skinhead behavior was labeled unacceptable and deviant, but generally unaccompanied or unmitigated by the concept that appeared so often in treatments of the skinhead phenomenon presented by academics in England that "deviance was a social creation, a result of the power of some to label others" (Hall and Jefferson 5). Perhaps an unstated feeling of these and similar civil rights guardian groups was that for a long time racial and ethnic hate was virtually a standard and not an ideologically deviant practice in America, and now that prejudice and discrimination were being combatted in American life through legislation and social pressure, those who acted out the twin hostilities should not be excused as merely constituting the "result of the power of some to label others." Occasionally of course articles inimical to the skinheads would contain messages of palliation or extenuation. Leonard Zeskind, research director of the Center for Democratic Renewal, has said that "we now have the first generation of young white kids who don't expect to live better than their parents and [they] are looking for scapegoats" (Cooper 271), suggesting that the skinheads belong to a generation unique in American history who face—or think they face— conditions no other white kids have had to face before.

The *Utne Reader* appended to its abstract (May/June 1989) of an article attacking skinheads that originally appeared in *Rolling Stone* an insert explaining that "the recent spate of racial attacks by skinheads is widely attributed to the slipping economic position of many young white males." The insert also quotes extensively from an article in the leftist *Dollars and Sense* analyzing the "decline in young men's earnings result[ing] from a change in the types of jobs now available to them" (84). Also contained within the *Utne Reader* abstract is a brief article by Chris Gunderson chronicling the hopes of "Anti-racist skinheads ready to strike back at Neo-Nazis." During the height of national interest in (or publicity on) skinheads, newspaper articles often told of attempts by non-racist skinhead groups to fight both their racist image and other racist skinheads. Essentially, however, in America practically as soon as the skinheads became known outside punk or new music circles, they were slotted into categories of weird youth and hostile, dangerous, racist bigots. Most of the information published about them in the print media told of their violence, their destructiveness, their criminality, and did not deal to any great extent with what might have been their unfortunate social situation.

Skinhead (Dis)Organizations

One of the first skinhead groups to be reported on nationally was Chicago's Romantic Violence, whose name indicates the sick attitude characteristic of many skinheads toward violence: they are attracted to it, and admire it as a way of asserting authority or expressing strongly held beliefs. Often in interviews skinheads will say something like, "We don't look for violence, but if it comes to us we are ready for it." But it is clear that often they do look for violence, they seek it out, that some skinheads have a compulsion to commit violence. A Tampa skinhead talking about violence said, "On the most part, we fight only when we have to." He explained, "We might get drunk, or something, which we do a lot, we come over here [to a bar], we drink, get drunk, get a little rowdy, but we don't go out and start fights. Somebody will walk [by], we'll say something to them, and if they come up and say, 'What the fuck'd you say?' and they want to fight or whatever, then we'll fight. But [among] most of us, there's some that go out and beat people up for no reason, and that happens with everybody" (Roger Adams interview, February 1988).

The young skinhead is claiming that skinheads are not to blame if as a group they attack individual people whom they have provoked, and who have responded to them in an argumentative or verbally hostile fashion. They should not be blamed for the violence they commit on their victims. At best this seems like blaming a fish, say, for thrashing about after being hooked. But the skinhead also says that (other) skinheads may act violently against people without any provocation, simply because that is their nature. But this he claims is excusable because all groups contain these mindlessly violent people. In truth, skinheads seek out violence. Even the anti-racist skinheads adopt the mean, intimidating skinhead look and typically engage in violent behavior such as thrash dancing or stage diving. When they declare their intention to combat the racist skinheads, they often consider violent combat their chief strategy. Skinheads complain that violence seeks them out, but actually by their appearance and manner they draw violence onto themselves, when they do not create it directly by initiating violent acts.

In 1984, by which time skinheads were commonly observable though quite small in number in scores of American cities like New York, Atlanta, Tampa, Tulsa, Los Angeles and San Francisco, Romantic Violence promoted "from a post office box in Cicero," according to the ADL, a "Death's-Head Muscle T-Shirt" through promotional flyers which "included pictures of jack-booted Nazi youth." Thus they came under the surveillance of the League's Civil Rights Division. Romantic Violence was one of the very best-organized skinhead groups in the country at a time when most skinheads were either only loosely affiliated with gangs who had names but no real coherence or structure, or who were what might be called part-time skins, high school kids for example who enjoyed the new music scene, adopted the skinhead fashions when convenient, and congregated at musical events skinheads typically attended, but who did not wholly embrace the hardcore skinhead manner. This limited allegiance and reserved attitude would become more and more difficult as publicity about skinheads in various communities and nationally increased.

Romantic Violence was also one of the first white power groups in America to attempt to exploit commercially the growing interest in skinhead style. They sold Skrewdriver cassettes and tapes of a few American bands such as White Pride, U.S. Chaos, and Final Solution, whom they called 'a new breed of heroes [who] have sprung from the midwestern soil, brave skinhead warriors ready to fight for race and nation' " (*Shaved for Battle* 3). Romantic Violence's marketing and other more violent activities were led by Clark Reid Martell, older at 27 than most American skinheads, who were usually teenagers.[1] Since skinhead gangs are ordinarily informally structured, unlike more disciplined street gangs with their Mafia-like positions of power and specific function, they tend not to have clearly identifiable leaders who develop specific plans of action to be performed by a regulated skinhead membership. Skinhead groups are often gangs only in the very loosest sense, and often seem more a collection of individuals who frequently congregate with each other at some hangout not exclusively theirs but at which they can display some unity and fraternity. Further, skinheads are essentially anti-authoritarian. They may exhibit beliefs associated in the public's mind with fascism, but they often appear incapable of submitting for long to the kind of higher central authority that fascistic systems inevitably impose once they have somehow attained some turf or territory or constituency—perhaps only their own less powerful members—over which they can exert control. Of course, exceptionally bright or imaginative or creative or intimidating skinheads may dominate the plans and activities of their skinhead buddies at given moments, but sustained leadership so far has been rare among the widely-dispersed growth of skinhead groups in the United States. Young and unstable, the skinhead mass changes constantly, making organized regimes of skinheads extremely difficult.

Martell is one of the many skinheads who has established a career as a public menace. In 1979 he had been sentenced to four years in jail for "attempting to commit aggravated arson against an Hispanic person." He did not serve his full time and by 1984 he was arrested again "that September in Oak Park [Illinois] for painting swastikas on village property." A fascistic man for all seasons, he "was also active in local neo-Nazi activities and did cartoon work for the...Chicago based American Nazi party" and was constantly in trouble with the police. He would later "be arrested in Ann Arbor by police in March, 1987 at a rally in which youthful neo-Nazis belonging primarily to Detroit's small self-styled SS-Action Group brandished swastika shields" (*Shaved for Battle* 2).

In 1984 Martell and Romantic Violence saw to it that skinhead music fans could buy the hate messages of Ian Stuart and Skrewdriver on music tapes, providing an opportunity for the skinheads' politicization. In the late 1970s it may have been possible for skinheads to miss the pervasive hostility targeted toward minorities that was increasingly a major part of the skinhead mentality, but by 1984 this was no longer true. Outsiders such as suburbanite parents may have been troubled merely by the skinheads' ugly and weird appearance, and have been unaware of the violent racism by now endemic to what they could once have thought of as a fad but that now almost resembled a movement. But those closer to it could clearly see the skinhead scene was now saturated with racism that skinhead activities and not just words made clear. Ian Stuart could not be blamed for hypocrisy when he stated in the March 19, 1984 issue of the anti-Jewish *Spotlight* that "I am not the type of person to creep and crawl to a bunch of weak-kneed, pacifist lefties and two-faced Zionists." Romantic Violence praised Stuart's Skrewdriver as "an institution, a stance of courage, determination, loyalty, honor and a will to win." Martell has been as candid as Stuart in declaring that Romantic Violence "stands for war." He declared this in 1986 at a training camp run for right wing extremist hate groups by Robert Miles, once Grand Dragon of Michigan's United Klan chapters, and Imperial Kludd (Chaplain) for the national United Klan organization. In the 1970s Miles served time in prison for conspiring to bomb ten school buses in Pontiac, Michigan, and also conspiring to tar and feather the pro-integration principal of a local school. At Miles's camp, often attended by several hundred hate movement activists, Martell made a speech stating, "I am a violent person. I love the white race, and if you love something, you're the most vicious person on earth" (*Shaved for Battle* 2), a non-sequitur appalling in its implications and a sign of perverse, inverse skinhead thought.

Romantic Violence was apparently the first skinhead gang to gain the attention of private organizations in America functioning to track hate or extreme right wing or anti-minority activity in the country. The Anti-Defamation League, perhaps the best known nationally of these organizations, apparently first took careful note of skinheads and Romantic Violence when they sold their Death's Head t-shirts in 1984 and when they "took part in a 1985 national conference of white supremacists in Michigan. Promoting a hoped-for American tour of a British white-power band (which never materialized) members of this group displayed all the by-now familiar characteristics: shaven heads, neo-Nazi tattoos, Doc Marten work boots, and an outspokenly vulgar advocacy of racism and violence" (*Skinheads Target the Schools* 1). The highly unpleasant image of Romantic Violence can serve as a prototype for the images of nearly all skinhead gangs whose activities would be reported on in the public press for the next several years, images constructed, in fact, upon the collections of press clippings sent to the Anti-Defamation League and other hate activity monitoring institutions by their correspondents. Further reports about Romantic Violence, such as their participation in a June 1985 "march sponsored by the (Chicago based) American Nazi Party to protest the annual Gay and Lesbian Pride Day Rally" (*Shaved for Battle* 4) or Martell's arrest in 1988 "for an April, 1987 assault in Chicago on a 20-year-old female [skinhead] member who wanted to leave the group" (*Extremism on the Right* 124) augment but do not essentially modify that image.

As the number of skinheads increased though not greatly in absolute numbers throughout the 1980s and spread to more cities in the United States, their notoriety increased in the popular media, though as I have indicated they never received the kind of serious, academic study afforded them by English scholars during the previous decade, nor except rarely the guardedly sympathetic professional analysis given them by authorities such as Dick Hebdige or Susie Daniel and Pete McGuire, nor the almost open adulation of Nick Knight. In America, thanks to groups such as the Anti-Defamation League and the Southern Poverty Law Center, they have been presented almost always as a violent hate group in the tradition of the KKK, an organization they generally do not resemble except in their violence and some of their hatreds. Unlike Klan members, the skinheads do not typically blend in with the dominant culture in their ordinary activities, and they have little organization in any formally meaningful sense: a boy or young man can be a skinhead if he wishes, but he cannot officially join the skinheads since no formal organization exists. There is no standardized skinhead membership, no dues paying, no organized meetings, no official skinhead hierarchy, no formal schematic connection between skinheads in different areas. It is possible of course for a particular male to be rejected socially by other skinheads, possibly even attacked for appearing as a skinhead, or for dropping the skinhead stance, but it is also possible, particularly in large cities, to maintain a highly flexible status as a skinhead in relating to other skins who may or may not belong to gangs.

Women in the Skinhead Scene

Most of the publicity about skinheads has focused upon boys and young men in the scene, partly because literature on right wing extremism has traditionally presented such ultra-conservative movements as dominated by men, and partly because the violent criminal activities that constitute so much of the interest about skinheads has mainly (but by no means exclusively) been committed by males. But females—girls and young women—definitely function as skinheads, just as books like Kathleen M. Blee's recent *Women of the Klan* show that older women have played a played an important part in the history of that hate movement.

Young women have been associated in some fashion with skinhead gangs in America since individual young male skinheads began associating with each other at first in very loose, informal groups in the late 1970s and early 1980s. The young women naturally tended to share the general views of the men, their musical tastes and their ideas to the extent that the young men expressed these, though the women were very definitely secondary to the young men who viewed themselves clearly as the dominant sex. The males engaged in criminal violence far more frequently than the young women, and to judge by the skinheads around central Florida, often thought of the young women primarily as sex objects. Within the group the male skinheads were to honor what appeared to be prevailing sexual relationships, but as in the outside world did not always do so. The young male and female skinheads' primary social structure—beyond that of their own biological family— more greatly resembled in some ways a free-floating, amoeboid commune rather than a nuclear family.

The women sometimes referred to themselves as skinchicks, but more preferred to be known as skinheads though they did not ordinarily shave their skulls. Sometimes other young women who hung around the skinhead scene for a variety of reasons but who did not think of themselves as skinheads, referred to the girlfriends of the skinheads somewhat derisively as skinchicks. By late in the eighties, the term appears not to have been greatly used.

When newspapers started interviewing skinheads, though they found that leaders of skinhead gangs were invariably young men, the young women on the skinhead scene sounded precisely like the men in their attitudes. In a story about local skinheads the *St. Petersburg Times* printed 21 June, 1987, 15-year-old Dean McKee's attraction to white power fascism and that of a 15-year-old young woman seemed the same. Declaring that Europe's Jews "must have done something" wrong "to make" Hitler "want to kill them," she was photographed together with three young girlfriends aged 15, 16, and 18 in front of The Ritz, one of the main punk and skinhead hangouts at that time for the young boys and the young girls on the Tampa Bay area's new music scene. Autumn Chapman's remark in the *News* of Camarillo, California, March 21, 1989, that "I don't have anything against blacks, but I hate niggers" tried to make a distinction for the public that young male skins also employed to mask their prejudices.

There is some indication that young women did more than just echo male skinhead dogma. Behind the scenes, a few were more than simply camp followers attracted by the power the skinhead image developed or that they thought skinheads developed. According to an article in the *Milwaukee* magazine for October, 1988, when 17-year-old male Pat O'Malley tried to reorganize a local non-racist skinhead gang into a more racist organization with ties to other similar groups in the midwest, he was greatly aided in the plan by Jane Rhodes, who continued to help him even after his release from jail and virtual exile to Madison, Wisconsin (Romenesko 3-7). Rhodes seemed an organizer as much as O'Malley.

By the end of the decade women were as common on the politically militant skinhead scene as men, though fewer in number and still generally not in positions of highest authority. Tom Metzger helped make Monique Wolfing's Aryan Women's League more visible. Founded in 1988 by the wife of skinhead Baxter the Pagan (Harry

Vaccaro), the League treads tenderly the thorny path extremist women must travel between declaring the strength of women and condemning feminism. Wolfing along with Metzger opposes "Jew-dykes" like Bella Abzug, helps raise money for so-called political prisoners (usually in jail for hate crimes), and says women should "help Mother Nature" by taking up the cause of wolves, who like Aryan woman "are pure...do not mix with other species...protect each other's welfare to the bitter end;...[and] are strong, proud warriors." One reporter has claimed that skinhead "women are more committed to racial purity...than the men" (Wolfing 6; Zia 25).

A crudely drawn cartoon in *WAR* (8:2, 1989, 9) by 12-year-old Kris shows a pleasant looking young male skinhead holding hands with a skirted young woman who could be a cheerleader. But skinhead women prove the veracity of Tom Metzger's remark that they "are tough." They are also violently criminal. In 1988 an 18-year-old skinhead woman was arrested along with her 20-year-old skinhead brother and Clark Martell for beating an ex-skinhead woman who had black friends. *Klanwatch* ("Cookbooks and Combat Boots" 7-9) has noted that in recent years, female skinheads have been arrested for beating another skinhead who was Jewish, murdering a black man in Reno, Nevada, attacking minorities in Tulsa, and vandalizing a synagogue in Tennessee. A 14-year-old skinhead girl was sentenced in Vancouver, Washington, to four years in a juvenile institution for her part in the murder of an ex-skinhead, and a young skinhead woman in San Antonio, Texas, was sentenced to a 15-year term for murdering another teenaged girl. Women are definitely on the skinhead bus, though perhaps toward the back and rarely as drivers.

Skinhead Communication

Communication between skinhead groups has been, particularly during the formative years of the scene through the early 1980s, usually random and localized. From time to time regional skinhead groups such as Chicago's Romantic Violence or the Grand Rapids, Michigan Pitbull Boys have issued publications—fanzines, brief newspapers, leaflets—that eventually are circulated beyond the local territory. For example these publications will be sold or given away at alternative music stores or distributed where school age youth congregate or sometimes at stores specializing in hate literature. Of course within local communities the availability of typing and duplicating (and recently, word processing) machines made relatively easy the creation and limited distribution of sometimes highly imaginative and often corrosive and obscene underground publications written (or compiled) by junior high and high school students. These publications sometimes attack skinheads and skinheadism but even so spread the word about the skinhead style. More conventionally produced and distributed publications such as Tom Metzger's *WAR* regularly feature approving news about skinhead achievements—for example Dean McKee's murder of Isaiah Walker—or events like skinhead gatherings and concerts. The local publications are usually short-lived and poorly disseminated, though any one paper or fanzine may travel far and be read by many including non-skinheads.

Calls for skinheads to organize at higher levels were not uncommon in the late 1980s. The *Oklahoma Separatist*, a segregationist magazine, announced in April 1988 that "WAR organizer Brad Robarge wants all you Boot-boys out there to contact him at P.O. box 65, Fallbrook, CA, 92028 [the address of Tom Metzger's *WAR*]. The American Skinhead Army is bigger and better than ever. Brad says 'It's time for W.A.R.'! Don't wait, 88!" Obviously the larger, more stable hate publications had readers in various distant communities feeding them information and in this way some reciprocal relationships may have been set up. The pictures of Dean McKee and his stepfather that appeared in the California-based *WAR* (2:4, 7) were first published in newspapers in the Tampa Bay region, and Metzger credits no national (or any other) agency for them.

Much of the long distance communication informing skinheads about other skinhead activities was also random though common. Conventional newspapers and wire services provided skinheads with a great deal of information about themselves. Paradoxically, Tom Metzger has praised the ADL for their focus on skinhead activities which he claims has helped popularize skinhead objectives and increased skinhead growth: "Two years ago WAR felt the skinhead movement was a short fad and was fading away. Presto! The Anti-Defamation League of B'nai B'rith to the rescue!" The League issued *Shaved for Battle* and distributed it to police agencies, political figures, and the media, focusing greater attention according to Metzger upon the skinheads, and intensifying attacks on them. "And you guessed it! The skinheads have grown like mad" (transcript, *WAR* hate message, Nov. 28, 1988).

Metzger did not mention in this pronouncement his own attempts, in addition to those of other established, organized hate groups, to organize and build up the ranks of skinhead groups to enlist them as warriors for various fascistic causes.

Skinhead ways were transmitted from American city to city in films such as the previously mentioned *The Decline of Western Civilization* and *Pink Floyd—The Wall* and through the appearances late in the 1980s of skinhead groups on television talk shows and radio interview programs that I will discuss shortly. Skinheads in Omaha (interviewed in the January 8, 1989 *Omaha World Herald*) said that they learned of skinhead activities elsewhere by talking with visiting skinheads passing through their city. Skinheads are fairly mobile, and seem constantly on the lookout for a more exciting or friendlier scene. Skinheads drifting down from Atlanta to Tampa or Orlando, from Tampa to Miami, or coming up from Miami to Tampa and Orlando seek, they say, a better music scene, or less "harassing" by authorities, or move because they are dissatisfied with their local skinhead friends. In 1988 skinheads in San Diego said they communicated with other skinhead compatriots through letters (though this seems rare) and at rallies (clipping by Bruce Canlen in San Diego newspaper, ADL archives). Skinheads new to a region generally appear to find an initially easy, open attitude from other local skinheads ready to befriend them, as if they were fellow outcasts traveling an underground railroad, though they may not immediately admit them as intimate insiders to the new skinhead group or gang. Skinheads also gather regionally at hate rallies sponsored by other organizations such as the different Klans, and occasionally attend conferences set up by these groups, thereby contacting skins from cities sometimes distant from their own local sphere. This last phenomenon is still unusual, but increased during the 1980s.

Skinhead Beliefs

If the skinheads lack organization and coherence on the national level, systems of communication do exist between skinheads and skinhead groups from various regions of the country. It seems increasingly apparent that there has developed a general set of basic beliefs and attitudes among them, binding them together and giving them a general unity of activity. It would seem strange to speak of a skinhead ideology, if by that term is meant a consciously fashioned, well developed, intricately worked out set of social and political stances. However, in their communications to each other and to the press, a remarkable unanimity of expression is apparent that discloses a few essential skinhead concepts. Particularly since their shaved heads and common mode of dress tends to drain individual skins of their physical individuality, and since they either assume for the press certain repeated postures during occasional picture-taking sessions, or editors carefully cull those shots of them that most adhere to the way the press feels readers expect to see skinheads portrayed (all over the country, skinheads tend to look and sound the same), skinheads often resemble clones of some standard model, like the robotic figures often depicted in music videos, all moving exactly the same frantic way to the same beat. This is ironic, since many skinheads avow that the course they have taken was set upon to protect their unique identity in a world generally populated by mindless, deindividualized followers of some enemy dictatorship.

This sameness of belief—at least of a few political and social beliefs of paramount significance that dominate manifold other beliefs that individual skinheads might not necessarily hold in common—did not develop overnight, but has grown unevenly, precisely because of the widespread and decentralized development of skinhead groups. Diffuse and lacking a centrally planned or coordinated communications system, skinheadism seems to have spread in the 1980s more like a fad than an ideology, by word of mouth and imitation rather than by orchestrated controls. As late as the summer of 1985, for example, skinheads in San Francisco—some of them—still "hadn't yet broken from the political mainstream" in their own estimation anyway, according to Eric Anderson, an anthropology professor at Yakima State College, who spent the summer with them while gathering information for his master's thesis (Frolik). He concluded that "most were refugees from the punk scene hooked on to violence...Oi!, available on bootleg tapes, was shaping their world view." These skinheads thought of themselves as Republicans, though it is doubtful that the organized Republican constituency would have agreed, just as it is questionable that the skinheads needed Oi! music's hostilities to teach them to be violent, though it may have reinforced and targeted or (in their own minds) given sanction to the violence already within them. They would beat up homosexuals and also sometimes shout, "Heil Reagan!" and chant

"Reagan, Reagan, he's our man, If he can't do it, no one can." This could be interpreted as corroborating the commonly made liberal claim that the Reagan administration was responsible for creating a social climate that made attacks on minorities more legitimate. The hypothesis seems difficult to prove and simplistic, particularly since so-called "queer-bashing" has never been an uncommon occurrence in America, and since skinheads among others in England also have typically engaged in the practice unencouraged by President Reagan (for whom minority rights however seemed no high priority).

A classic statement of skinhead homophobia appears in a pamphlet distributed by Chicago skinheads in 1987. "Skinheads worldwide are warriors. We never run away, back down, or sell out. We despise the traitors, the cowards, the apathetic and the limpwristed queers. We will fight forever to defend our people and our land. Our heads are shaved for battle" (ADL archives). Openly bellicose and claiming to be a part of a far larger contingent of warriors, the skinhead stance here sets up a clear and simple them/us split. But though it declares the skinhead intention to fight, it does not strongly suggest the fight will be victorious ("We will fight forever"). In fact, the advent of victory is not as strong a theme in skinhead declarations as calls to war. Homosexuals are usually tritely stereotyped in skinhead publications, though surprisingly enough are not ordinarily depicted in a strongly pornographic manner. Their offense seems almost more political than sexual. In general, when dealing with sexual matters (such as the corruptness of interracial sex), skinhead iconography is more politically than sexually obsessive—skinheads seem angry more for political than sexual reasons.

When publicly proselytizing, skinheads may affect a veneer of civility. The rhetorical harshness of this 1987 pamphlet is curiously enough complemented by a neat drawing demonstrating proper skinhead clothes (remarkably similar to illustrations in Nick Knight's *Skinhead*) that shows a pleasant looking young model skinhead wearing the proper attire for white warriors, including items labeled "flight jacket...Red Tag levi jacket...braces...Red Tag levi jeans...stay press (original) black, white, claret, blue, grey, Dog Tooth, Prince of Wales check." Knight's book devotes an entire section to the evolution of skinhead attire, depicting young skinheads who look clean cut as the "after" heroes of pimple medicine advertisements. Not exactly a best seller, *Skinheads* is a popular and in a way influential book among skinheads who generally treat it as definitive in matters of history and style. The few copies offered periodically are quickly bought, to judge from sales in alternative music and book shops in central Florida. In Milwaukee, police investigating a 1988 dispute between warring racist and anti-racist skinheads found a copy in the house that served as a skinhead hangout (Romenesko 3-7).

Often, skinhead homophobia is linked with a standard litany of hated opponents. Another flyer distributed by San Francisco skinheads ironically describes liberal, moral imperatives in the "Great Democracy": "enforce your right to Blow Dope; turn Queer; Marry a Nigger; Kill the Unborn; and do anything else to destroy America." The anti-abortion, anti-drug stances espoused here are common in skinhead declarations of belief, but among many skinheads these do not appear to be high priority issues. In fact, drug use among skinheads in England and America is very common (see for example Burr's "Ideologies of Despair").

Anti-Semitism is a another strong skinhead belief. The Anti-Defamation League has claimed that this element of skinhead ideology is stronger in the United States than it was in England, and that the belief has led to a greater proportion of anti-Semitic incidents in the United States involving skinheads, though a great many variables would have to be examined first to determine if this were valid (*Shaved for Battle* 1). Certainly in cities where relatively large Jewish populations exist, or where Jewish communities or congregations are visible, such as New York or Miami, skinhead attacks are common, and anti-Semitism is a recurrent strain in skinhead talk and commentary. A Chicago skinhead leaflet (1987) declared "the parasitic Jewish race is at the heart of our problem." The same year in Cincinnati other skinheads announced "we would prefer to smash the present anti-white, Zionist (Jew), puppet-run government" and replace it "with a healthy, new white man's order!" (ADL archives).

This declaration suggests a problem with conflicting publicly stated skinhead objectives, for while skinheads enjoy advocating an old-time patriotic support of America in the face of what they consider internal attacks by liberal or radical scum who now pervert its Americanist greatness, they do not ordinarily express support for any American government of recent years (despite as noted some occasional praise for Ronald Reagan's work), for they consider these governments in thrall to pro-black, Jewish, gay powers. The Uprise, a Philadelphia skinhead band, sings in "Land of the Free" that if you "Don't like our country, don't like what we say, then you can fucking leave today, U.S.A." Matt Andrews, one of the band's members, was once arrested for beating up on a train platform in Philadelphia a white man who said he objected to the racial slurs Andrews and two mates were making (Malshire 126). But in supporting America, skinheads like Andrews appear to be dreaming of some mythical nation of the legendary past, when America existed in a racially, ethnically, heterosexually pristine state. Though throughout American history elements within our governments and their constituencies have certainly been harshly inimical in thought and deed towards the very groups the skinheads in their publicly distributed statements state they violently oppose, it is doubtful that any one period or regime was pure enough in its openly stated doctrines and consistently brutal enough in its actions to qualify as a realistic model for the land skinheads say they seek to re-establish. The America they seek to return to is their own nostalgic creation.

Racist skinhead ideology is pervasively if not preeminently Caucasian in addition to being anti-Semitic, anti-gay, and chauvinistic. A poem printed along with a picture of three skinheads in *Pitbull Boy* 7 (1988), a "Journal of the Patriotic Skinhead," describes response to a skinhead parade:

> They all say you're nothing but scum,
> But some day soon
> The shoe'll be on the other foot!!
> White power today and forever.

The same issue contains an article titled "Weapons in Review" describing how canes and boots can be used for fighting, and a positive review of the album "White Warrior" by Skullhead, thus linking three important skinhead interests: white supremacy, fighting, and the music encouraging both.

The National Association for the Advancement of White People *News*, established by ex-Klan leader David Duke in the early 1980s, published a letter (No. 53, 1988, 3) defending skinheads and attacking "DRN," who in a previous issue called them "Fence-sitters...tattooed loners, high school dropouts, born losers, children estranged from their parents." To the contrary, NAAWP members were informed that the skinheads considered themselves "White warriors similar to the pilgrims" (!) who were "not afraid of Jew lies" and proudly cried for "White Pride! White Passion!" On the same page is a photograph— meant to be viewed with disgust—of a poster advertising Loyola University Opera Theater's performance of Verdi's *La Traviata* showing the opera's black male tenor lead about to kiss the white soprano playing Violetta's role.

A skinhead pamphlet distributed in 1988 that seems like a recruiting statement indoctrinating new or potential skins into skin ways combines more basic fashion information with a few essentials of skinhead ideology. "Skin hair is either zero-zero cut" on the barber's clippers, or can go as high as "up to number three." Skinhead girls are told they can wear the same regalia as the boys, "but even more feminine is the kilt skirt, preferably wool, and mini skirts. These skirts are worn with fishnet stockings and DM [Doc Marten] boots or DM shoes." Both girls and boys are reminded that "skinheads are the All American white youth, they love mom and dad and love thier [sic] flag." Skinheads should know the music that best reinforces their basic (racist) skinhead concepts. Oi! "is a battle rhythm for young youth and old who are fed up with regular race-mix type tunes we hear on the radio all the time." Skinheads should believe that ignorant, lazy, drug-ridden, sexually hyperactive blacks, linked with Jews or members of other "mud" races or with gays, are responsible for much of America's present sorry, decadent state, as though they are part of a pestilence visited on the land because of white passivity and failure to perceive the crisis in American life. In Tampa and elsewhere, some skinheads link black Americans with AIDS as a real plague, a feeling articulated in a 1987 issue of Tom Metzger's *WAR* (6:3) under the title "Nigger Plague": "Consider, too, that this is not a 'Gay Plague,' but rather a 'Gay/Black Plague.' In almost every corner of the world, it is Blacks, almost as much as homosexuals, who, by their substandard behavior, are effectively spreading the disease to Whites."

In their own literature and that published by other hate groups friendly to them, the skinheads are presented as a political movement with revolutionary objectives. The extent to which ordinary skinheads can be considered political is questionable, however. In any formal sense they are not, though they may sometimes be the tools or supporters of other organizations more politically organized than they. A great number of skinheads are simply too young to vote, and it is doubtful that many others are registered, partly because skins move around a great deal within and between urban communities: their way of life does not incline them toward voter registration, and their numbers are so relatively few that their vote would be negligible anyway. So orthodox political involvement seems at best irrelevant or perhaps even a joke to the ordinary skinhead, though this situation may vary from area to area, and some skins may be more politically sophisticated than others: *The Wall Street Journal* reported March 29, 1989 that some skinheads were supporting William Daniel Johnson's candidacy for Richard Cheney's vacated seat as a Representative from Wyoming. Johnson, under the pseudonym of "James O. Pace," is perhaps best known for advocating the "Pace Amendment" to the Constitution, which would reserve citizenship and residency in the United States to some whites while expelling all other ethnic groups. This kind of direct involvement with standard politics was rare for skinheads in the 1980s.

Skinheads as a Revolutionary Force
The public posture skinhead literature presents—which by its nature tends to be stated by the better organized skinhead groups and by a few of their more politically committed and articulate spokesmen—sets forth a revolutionary ideal which has been reinforced by calls to action by supporters of skinheads among larger and better funded hate groups, whose agendas are more clearly and predominantly political. Both the skinhead literature and the comforting words of their advocates describe this revolutionary group as working class, which is highly problematic. The working class attribution may result from the earlier skinhead tradition in England: adopting the appearance of their British predecessors and espousing some of their attitudes and ideas, American skins may have liked to think of themselves as also originating in the same class, to which some anti-authoritarian glamour may have clung. Those skinheads who were more ideologically inclined, or their mentors, may have reasoned that the working class in America, whomever that might include, was less tainted by the dominant culture's decadence, that the working class had escaped somehow the stains of liberalism infecting the state. Possibly the American skinheads, because they are so young and ordinarily have not yet advanced far into the social and economic systems, could be termed working class. The generalization

seems doubtful, however, particularly when youth of clearly middle class suburban origins heavily fill the skinhead scene. On this matter as on so many others, the thinness and breadth of the skinhead scene makes easy generalization difficult.

Though nearly all skinheads are young, even in one locality their demographics often vary greatly. In Tampa, for example, some few might be drifters in their late teens and early twenties who randomly work at low level jobs, others are more regularly employed at positions—counterman at a hot dog or ice cream stand—that are not very high paying. These might be considered working class jobs, though most of those who hold them, often high school or college students who are working only part-time, would ordinarily be surprised to hear themselves described as members of the working class, particularly since they may be occupying these positions while preparing themselves for higher-paying employment, and living in standard suburban homes. In the words of Robert Miles, ex-Grand Dragon of the United Klans of America, skinheads are "tuned in on the ghetto conditions where white youths find themselves nowadays" (*Shaved for Battle* 3). In Tampa, most skinheads are the children of roughly middle-class parents, live with their parents, and many have not yet really entered the work force in any socially meaningful sense. Still, the phrases "working class" and "ghetto" possess a resonant, populist ring for skinheads and their admirers. The same 1987 leaflet distributed by skinheads in Chicago declaring that "our heads are shaved for battle" claims that the "Skinheads of America, like the dynamic skinheads in Europe, are working class Aryan youth. We oppose the capitalist and communist scum that are destroying our Aryan race." What seems a nostalgic longing for association with the working class is one of the few themes the skinheads in America share with youth subcultures of the 1960s when the link appeared equally tenuous though it was often claimed. Another recruitment leaflet distributed in 1987 by skinheads in Cincinnati described skins as "working class youth proud of our racial heritage...part of a world-wide white nationalist movement of youth."

A few of the skinheads who have surfaced nationally as apparent spokesmen for skinheadism—though in reality they would possess this status only in the very loosest sense, sometimes only because they have been so designated by some reporter or journalist—have presented the skinheads as a uniquely gifted force for achieving a new order in the

United States. Again, the extent to which ordinary skinheads of varying degrees of commitment to the scene accept this advanced guard role, or are even aware of it, is questionable. It seems reasonable to assume, however, that just as the racist agenda of skinheads became more pronounced or pervasive as more skinheads were able from a variety of sources to discover the ideological drift of the national skinhead scene, more skinheads would become conscious of the idea of their special mission. Clark Martell was one of the first skinheads to articulate this high calling, to formulate it in resoundingly apocalyptic language. Commenting in 1988 on the claims of Odinists and Christian Identity members (right wing hate groups with perversely religious orientations) that skinheads were a "divine gift" from "the Gods," Martell proclaimed that the skins were "the saving and avenging Angels in Doctor Marten boots." Sounding greatly like a Nazi drunk on myths of Teutonic world domination or a Marvel comic book narration about the exploits of some post-Prince Valiant, Thor-like hero, Martell wrote that "we must throw ourselves, blood, bone, sinew, and soul, behind the skinhead battering ram as it rolls with the splitting of wood through the gates of power, into the evil one's domain" (*WAR* 7:5, 14).

Martell's spiritual war cry echoes an earlier 1988 outburst about "Aryan Skinheads" by Wyatt Kaldenberg (*WAR* 7:3, 5) also employing the religiously oriented language or paranoia heralding skinheads as the White Power movement's hope for the future. "Miracles are very rare. They seldom come twice in a lifetime," Kaldenberg asserted. "The race movement was blessed with a miracle in the late '70s but we let it slip between our fingers." The first miracle was the punk rock movement according to Kaldenberg. The skinheads are the second, "and if we blow this miracle we don't deserve to survive." The thread of Kaldenberg's argument is difficult to follow as he proceeds to describe the first lost chance for white racists to gain the support of and effectively use a popular force for advancing their ideas and achieving their goals, but his narration is informative in describing the music scene he considers a sadly lost opportunity for spreading neo-fascist gospel. A member in the early 1980s of the Los Angeles based Odinist Fellowship, which he describes as "a white racist pagan group," he admits that this organization failed because it "didn't appeal to women." The punk scene offered better opportunities for proselytizing. A fellow Odinist named Chicken Head owned a nightclub called Gonzillas (sic) that he decorated with Nazi flags and painted with slogans such as "The Holocaust is Bull Shit." According to Kaldenberg the venue attracted some of the leading punk bands who he says "all claimed to be White Power," such as X, Fear, The Circle Jerks, Black Flag, The Germs, and the Dead Kennedys. But Chicken Head lost his club to opportunistic Jews, and even Jello Biafra, whom Kaldenberg terms the "most outspoken 'Nazi' " of the Dead Kennedys, sold out to the ubiquitous Jews (in the early 1990s Biafra often spoke at college campuses on the perils of censorship). Kaldenberg implies that the skinheads would not be so easily bought off, and advises that the most powerful propaganda tool to attract potential young recruits to white racist organizations is the music to which they listen.

By the late 1980s, the significance of popular music as a propaganda medium for achieving the revolution was well recognized by several hate groups. *Frontline*, a publication brought out by a Maryland-based neo-Nazi group called the National Democratic Front, noted that skinhead and other white power band song lyrics "promote White nationalism in a form that young people like and understand" (*Shaved for Battle* 5). At the decade's end, white supremacist leaders vied with each other in praising the revolutionary hope that they claimed skinheads brought to hate movements through the ideas expressed in the songs skinheads thrash danced to, and through their violent attacks upon the host of enemies besetting white power organizations and presumably white society itself. *From The Mountain* is a publication of the racist Mountain Church and before he died in August, 1992 was the mouthpiece of Robert Miles, indicted in 1987 for seditious conspiracy but found not guilty in a tainted verdict. At least one juror subscribed to "anti-black opinions similar to those held by the defendants." Further, two female jurors later developed intimate relationships with two of the accused (SPLC, *Law Report*, January 1989, 3). In his magazine Miles explained why liberals feared the skinheads so greatly by proclaiming that "Now, with a new generation twice as mean and twice as lean, with nothing to lose but everything to gain, riding in out of the West, the age of the true barbarians may be coming back at last! And that is about the worst nightmare that ZOG [the purported Zionist Occupation Government controlling American life] and Zionism could have ever dreamed come to the post."

The attack on "capitalist and communist scum" in the Chicago skinhead leaflet previously noted indicates that some skinheads, doubtless a small minority, opposed both economic systems, presumably appealing to a revolutionary "third way" based upon race (white) and class (working), advocated by a few extremist leaders such as Tom Metzger. Both communism and capitalism represented authoritarian institutions to rebel against, and in the perverted and historically irrational world of hate groups also crazily reflected the declared Jewish conspiracy ruling the globe. Whether or not they subscribed to this theory of twin enemies, skinheads do seem to have embraced capitalistic consumerism at least to a limited extent.

Selling Skinhead Icons

Consumerism is another means of bonding skinheads into more cohesive groups. Like football fans or followers of a particular rock band, they are sold various symbols of belonging, beyond their fashionable Doc Martens and suspenders. The items they may feel compelled to purchase further reflect their iconography and become symbols of their beliefs. The first phase of skinheadism in England was not in this manner so commercialized, but as the skinhead scene developed during the 1970s, more and more skinheads in Britain and America were asked to buy a greater number of objects declaring their allegiance.

Record albums were the first items to spread the skinhead message and be commercially exploitable. Not only were the lyrics of Skrewdriver or Last Resort songs explicitly racist, but their album jackets and record sleeves also presented further opportunities for advertising skinhead ways or objects for sale that would enable skinheads to declare their musical and ideological preferences. Album jackets were placed like posters or paintings on walls where skinheads lived or at their meeting places. The No Remorse album titled "This Time The World" (echoing the Nazi claim "*Heute Deutschland, Morgen die Ganze Welt*": Today Germany, Tomorrow the World) depicts on its cover three generations of white warriors, a Viking, a stormtrooper, and a skinhead. The message is clear that skinheads have inherited the role of Nordic (or Aryan) fascist soldiers. No Remorse t-shirts, flags and patches were also made available for purchase showing a picture of Hitler imposed upon a swastika. In a small way skinhead images are marketed like Rolling Stones or Fleetwood Mac or Madonna paraphernalia. Reproducing images for display on decorative buttons, the clothing or bodies of rock group fans is an easy matter than can be performed locally, and thus even very minor, regional groups can hawk their own bumper stickers. What can be reproduced will be sold. Strips of tattoos declaring symbols of one's musical tastes (and thereby, frequently, one's political beliefs) are mass produced and easily available. No pain results from application to the skin, no teenager need fear parental objection to them. They are impermanent and some are soap-and-water soluble, though real looking as the tatoos legendarily drunken sailors receive that last longer than a lifetime.

The messages these sold images contain are quite clear and the context in which they frequently appear further ignites their meaning like a flare. The extremist English magazine *Blood and Honour* (according to Jim Mencarelli a logo-like phrase skinheads revere because it was inscribed on Hitler Youth Corps daggers), which offered No Remorse t-shirts for sale, also advertised a "Rock Against Communism" t-shirt showing a crossed hammer and sickle emblazoned with a skull. Distributed in the United States, the paper contains an "In Memoriam" dedicated to the skinhead hero Rudolf Hess stating "His Pride Was His Loyalty" and predicting he will be "Always Remembered." Admonishing readers that "WE TAKE OUR IDEALS FROM HEROES," the issue notes proudly that six representatives from national magazines and newspapers attended a recent Ian Stuart and Skrewdriver concert in Croyden (outside London). In this manner skinhead heroes are identified and praised. Allegiance and loyalty to them would be displayable through the items the magazine listed for sale which skinheads in America could purchase, sometimes in bulk for resale.

Skinhead stickers sometimes present simple images of racist force such as an eagle perched on a boldly drawn swastika with the words "White" and "Power" on either side of the swastika, under the eagle's wings, underlined by the words "White Aryan Resistance." The eagle is a frequently used skinhead icon, because it can represent both Nazi Germany and the United States of America. San Diego's War Skins, one of the earliest violent skinhead groups to maintain some organizational identity, produced a variety of illustrations and stickers in addition to the one just described, containing calls for hostile action in the war against ZOG (Zionist Occupation Government) and the mud races. One of their leaflets features an outline map of the United States stamped with an arm holding a gun. The injunction "Make 'Em Scared" is printed over the map, and underneath, the declaration that "White Revolution is the Only Solution" together with the order to "ACT NOW!" The gun in this drawing has a silencer on it, suggesting covert intimidation and stealth (in another War Skin sticker, a hooded man holds a semi-automatic rifle). The United States map is lined with barbed wire, and a Jewish star is formed by barbed wire. The obvious symbology here is that the country is a prison controlled by Jews or followers of ZOG. But the imagery would also threaten Jews with a return to the concentration camps of the Holocaust (which orthodox anti-Semites paradoxically deny ever took place: rationality and logic are not necessarily firmly set in skinhead thinking). Another anti-Semitic War Skin sticker shows a brick wall with the words "TRASH EM! SMASH EM! MAKE EM DIE!" printed as though exploding from the bricks. "DIE!" is underlined, and to the left of the message—outlined in (bullet?) pocks shaped like a boot—a hand holds a pistol.

More frightening because it makes greater use of human shapes to deliver its message in addition to letter graphics and overt statement, is a White Aryan Resistance skinhead sticker from California with large block letters demanding "GET OUT! JEW PIG!" "Pig" is an especially insulting term here since orthodox Jews consider pork unclean meat they are forbidden to eat. The human figures that create a special terror in this sticker are the figure of a capped, silhouetted man perhaps wearing a paramilitary uniform, who is aiming a telescopic rifle at the image across from him of a stereotypically large-nosed Jewish man (or possibly woman) whose silhouetted head in profile appears as it would be seen through the crosshairs of a rifle's telescope. The sticker clearly threatens —get out or we will murder you (ADL archives; *Young and Violent* 6-8).

Skinheads themselves are drawn as young, muscular, and typically blonde (when not completely bald) in skinhead illustrations. A "White Power" leaflet advertising "rock music and speeches" in a Chicago park where "all Whites [are] welcome" (ADL Special Edition, February 1988) features a booted, shirtless young man with a swastika tattooed on his back, standing over the words "SKIN HEADS." He is with a tough-looking, unsmiling blonde skinchick who wears Doc Martens, fishnet stockings and a thick looking miniskirt. The young woman is not drawn in a sexually provocative manner, though she is full breasted under her tank top. An American flag waves to the bottom right of the couple, and a swastika appears to their left, surrounded by the motto "for race and nation." Skinhead art is filled with patriotic references. One cartoon (ADL archives) shows skinheads duplicating the positions of Marines in their famous World War II flag-raising photograph taken at Iwo Jima. Sexual-political allusions are also common. A cartoon appearing in San Diego (ADL archives) captioned, "Is she worth fighting over?" presents an attractive, young blonde woman wearing a Viking helmet as an example of the type of woman skinheads are battling to preserve.

Narrative sequences of drawings similar to those in comic books or underground "comix" are popular features of extremist publications sold, traded, and sometimes given away to demonstrate skinhead objectives and ideology. Some "strips" teach the violent measures skinheads may have to follow to redirect corrupt and decadent America on a new, right (wing) course, purged of racial impurities and mealy-mouthed, liberal policies. The *Oklahoma Separatist* (March 1988) in an issue calling for an "Hour of Reckoning" contains a cartoon comic sequence, "The Adventures of Boot Boy." This extremist hero is a skinhead whose weapon of choice is a baseball bat, traditionally a symbol of America's "national pastime" but for American skinheads more typically a potent sign and instrument of violence. I have already noted that Mulegeta Seraw would be clubbed to death by bat wielding skinheads. Among the enemies Boot Boy will attack are blacks shown demonstrating for "equal rights," who will "make...the liberal government very happy," and Jews. One black demonstrator wears a t-shirt emblazoned with the phrase "Nigger Power." Standing outside a CIA office, "Senator Rosenburg" says to "Senator Rabinowitz," "Going precisely as planned." Rabinowitz is seeking the black vote "next November" by supporting the stupid looking demonstrators. "And I promise a watermelon in [sic] every plate."

The drawing and message of the cartoon are very basic and crude, with none of the flamboyance of style common to popular newsstand comic books of the 1980s such as the Marvel Comics, and seem more related to earlier hate-group art work, pornographic comics (though again, the skinhead illustrations do not emphasize sexually explicit or erotic drawing) and the consciously unsophisticated style practiced by some (but by no means all) underground comix cartoonists. The childish drawing and lettering in skinhead cartoon sequences seems appropriate to the tradition of hate art to which it belongs ideologically. When Boot Boy is shown smacking a baseball bat into the palm of his hand, the artistically basic, almost two-dimensional illustration seems correctly complementary to the ominous caption, "Boot Boy is very angry, and has vowed to stop the power hungry Jew." His course of action—and the course for all his true followers—is obvious.

The *Separatist*'s 24-year-old "Racist of the Month" Billy Wayne Worl might have been inspired by Boot Boy's vengeful intentions. Honored for his work as security guard at an Arkansas Klan rally in the same issue Boot Boy cleaned up his school, later in 1988 Worl would be convicted of attempted second-degree murder and malicious assault for his knife attack upon a black man. Seventeen-year-old James Carver was convicted along with him for participating in the assault. Carver, who claimed his Hispanic father "killed my mother's genes…by race mixing, by garbaging," had the letters "S-K-I-N-H-E-A-D" tattooed on his fingers (Morlin B1).

Another sequence of illustrations—skinhead comics rarely exceed a page or two in length—in a leaflet urging high school students to join a "White Student Union" (ADL archives) fuses simply drawn comic book figures with a message promising protection and ideological brotherhood to students plagued by black crime when "White Power Comes to Midvale." Like Charles Bronson in *Death Wish* or Clint Eastwood in his *Dirty Harry* series, dispatching—extra-legally—vicious enemies of mankind if not the ZOG controlled state, a skinhead "new student" violently routs blacks who steal lunch money from cowed and oppressed white high schoolers and then sternly lectures their stupidly liberal school principal. Playing upon white fears of black on white crime and disorder in the schools supposedly brought about by integration, and attacking liberalism for coddling vicious black hoodlums, the sequence is packed with white racist propaganda presented simply and forcefully. Possibly only one already convinced of the skinhead formula for retaliatory action would be influenced by it, or one already inclined to accept a racist depiction of America's pressing social problems. The production is conceptually and in execution at a level with most extremist presentations of the skinhead view.

Skinhead Duplicity

Examining skinhead beliefs through their written statements in publications they or some supportive group issue can be misleading. The publications generally emanate from the better organized gatherings of skinheads (or other hate groups) whose political purposes would be more imperative and better focused than those of ordinary skinheads, many of whom simply enjoy the music or attention or violence they can experience on the skinhead scene. Those skinheads who are less politically motivated will find little need to publish their political ideas. And, while skinhead literature is not among the world's most profound expressions of subcultural thinking, skinhead commentary that appears in skinhead publications or those of their supporters, usually conforms to minimal standards of writing and reasoning. Repugnant as their message is, shaky their sense of history, deficient their mastery of logic, skinhead writers and artists who are committed to their cause may constitute an intellectual elite among their own group anyway. They have refined their ideology and targeted their goals with relative precision, although they are not necessarily superior intellectually to skinheads whose voices are only heard on local scenes, who may not feel the clear drives that fuel the rhetoric and graphics of the elite spokesmen.

However, one of the main similarities among the ordinary and elite skinheads is that both employ double-talk in explaining their beliefs. One example is the claim common among skinheads that they do not go looking for trouble, but if trouble finds them they will not flinch from it. Repeatedly, skinhead actions disprove this. By their style and behavior they often provoke trouble, or actually instigate it. They dance so that they are destined to crash into someone also dancing or only standing in the "pit," thus they are causing trouble. They attack defenseless persons thus causing trouble. Sometimes the phrase white pride will be given as a skinhead belief, instead of the more generally objectionable "white power," but it is clear that when skinheads say white pride they mean white power. The glorification of one's own race is invariably accompanied by the denigration of other "mud" races, including the Jewish "race," which even if one accepts the generally outmoded and scientifically discredited concept of race (Gossett *passim*) is anthropologically not a race at all. Skinheads frequently claim to be aggressively patriotic Americans, but their twisted concept of what constitutes an American is extremely limited, ruling out as it does ordinarily blacks, Jews, people on welfare, homosexuals, even liberals and orthodox conservatives who remain under the domination of ZOG.

Sometimes the difference between elite and ordinary skinheads seems illusory, and caused by either an inability for some in the latter group to articulate what they believe with precision, or by the knowledge—when skinheads are being interviewed by traditional media sources such as local newspapers—that they are speaking to a generalized local audience whose disapproval they do not entirely seek to foment. Thus, during a period of agitation in July 1986, when Jacksonville, Florida skinheads were accused of anti-Semitic activities directed against the Jewish War Veteran's Post 199, and skinheads and surfers were clashing periodically following arrests made at the dance club "Einstein A Go-Go," one skinhead stated, "We're not Nazis as far as Hitler is concerned" (*Florida Times-Union*, 19 July 1986). The skinhead tried to explain what he meant by claiming a sanitized, de-Hitlerized Nazi status, suggesting that "Nazi means to us, that we're better than other club people...better than Communists. Every skinhead is pro-American. America is better than anybody [sic] else. We don't hate every colored person." Seemingly corroborating this skinhead's protestations, Dave Hart, owner of Hart's Weber House Surf Shop, who made and sold the area skinheads' t-shirts printed with "Nazi Skinhead" and swastikas on the front and back, asserted that the swastikas were ancient Mayan symbols signifying "well being to all." Hart, by no means an anthropologist, was correct in stating that the twisted cross had sometime in ancient days been a symbol of well being or good luck, but failed to mention that the sign was accompanied on his t-shirts with the letters "W" and "A" which stood variously for White Americans or American Warriors.

Similar linguistic masking or distortion can be seen in the statement by a spokesman for the Orlando skinhead band Bully Boys (advocates of "American Pride") who told the press that when the band shouted "Sieg Heil Sieg Heil Sieg Heil" they meant merely, "My Honor My Loyalty My Pride," and that "the swastika is only an adopted symbol of nationalism" (ADL archives). Admiration for Hitler and the murderously racist and ethnocentric policies he instituted with the help of other Nazis and many ordinary German (or for that matter other European) citizens is often more open among skinheads, even when they are speaking to the public press. The previously noted sentiment expressed by a 15-year-old girl in Tampa that the Holocaust Jews "must have done something to make [Hitler] want to kill them. And he did a damn good job" (*St. Petersburg Times*, 21 June 1987, 1B) would be echoed in Grand Rapids by the Pitbull Boys who considered Hitler a great man, and by "Matt" who led the War Skins in San Diego, who thought he could not really condemn Hitler for his attacks on Jews because "I think what he did was right at the time." Matt's historical analysis told him that "Jews were a real threat to the German people. [Hitler] didn't have the time to deport them all." Matt came from the punk scene, but he complained that "punks didn't have any answers except anarchy and smoking pot." Matt "wanted to take a stand," and the skinheads were the group for that (*Grand Rapids Press*, 24 July 1988; article from San Diego newspaper, ADL archives).

In Support of Hate

Although individual clusters or groups of skinheads throughout the country are often organized among themselves only in the most informal manner, and at least in the early years of the scene planned, systematic communication between these pockets of skinheads was negligible, when skinheads act or "take a stand" they behave with considerable similarity. They support other ultra right-wing, fascist, hate organizations, or engage in what might be considered, were it part of some overall plan and not simply random, individually conceived and carried out pathological acts, a form of sporadic guerilla warfare against their enemies, principally gays, Jews, blacks, and liberals. Even before Clark Martell's Chicago-based Romantic Violence triggered attention from the Anti-Defamation League in 1985 by participating in the American Nazi Party march objecting to Gay and Lesbian Pride Day, random news reports had claimed that skinheads unaffiliated with known gangs had been seen at Klan rallies in Florida and Georgia. Links between skinheads and the fortunately fragmented Klan organizations in different regions would grow during the last half of the 1980s. Increasingly and typically the role they performed for the Klan was as security force.

According to a Southern Poverty Law Center *Klanwatch* report (October 1988), Roy Frankhauser, a member of the Invisible Empire, claimed such a guard had been set up in 1988 comprised of "a number of very hand chosen Klansmen and a large group of Skinheads." Given the

100 Skinheads Shaved for Battle

Hooded Empire's predilection for exaggeration, this probably means at least some skins were mixed in with a few Klan members. The *Klanwatch* also noted that skinheads were active as security guards in Oklahoma's KKK rallies. Courted mainly for their muscle and attraction to violence, skinheads have also served as rabble-rousers at Klan rallies. The *Klansman* for March-April 1989, in describing a recent Klan rally ("KLUCKIN' SEASON STARTS") at Reidsville, North Carolina, supplied details of a speech by Bill Herrick of "Old Glory Skinheads" lamenting problems caused by the black racial oppression that white kids had to face in the cities, and promising the aid of "Old Glory" skins to other white power or pride groups.

The Anti-Defamation League concluded in 1988 that "Skinheads have joined forces with various Klan factions in every section of the country, rallying in Arkansas, Florida, Georgia, Illinois, Pennsylvania, Tennessee and Texas." Roy Frankhauser declared after a Klan march in Parkside, Pennsylvania that "The Skinheads stood like rocks right with us and we had a successful rally." After several paragraphs chronicling skinhead involvement with a number of Klan activities nationally, including bloody confrontations with police, the League noted "The KKK, whose ranks have been thinned in recent years, regards Skinheads as useful recruits, not only to help fill the void which has been left but also because the appearance of the shaven-haired swastika-bedecked youngsters brings the Klan additional publicity and visibility." A KKK literature distribution on October 2, 1988 in McKinney, north of Dallas, attracted more skinheads than Klansmen. But, the League added in an important apostrophe to its brief history of skinhead-Klan mutual attraction, "How devoted these youngsters will ultimately be to helping build Klan organizations on a day-to-day basis remains to be seen" (*Young and Violent* 1).

Though the various Klan memberships themselves contain a variety of Americans exhibiting different character types, Klan members have generally tended to be more mainstream, in-the-grain Americans, frequently—in past times—tolerated or at least accommodated by many other Americans who would not publicly condone their violence but who sympathized with many of their racial, nativist, and religious beliefs. Klan members were sometimes businessmen, police, civic officials. Skinheads have been since the public knew anything at all about them, viewed as deviants, even when merely parading along with other punkers in the late seventies in the new music scene, as a sign of something gone wrong in American life. Part of the attraction of skinheadism to skinheads is the feeling that they are recognized as social pariahs. If the Klan personality is sometimes greatly capable of sadistic behavior, the skinheads seem more masochists, behaving so they will be vituperated or punished or attacked. The skinhead subculture is preeminently a youth culture, rebellious, anti-authoritarian, inimical to older ways and hostile to domination by older persons, whether parents or agents of the community. Skins do not appear to compartmentalize their racial hostilities, their life-style. Even those—perhaps a majority of them—who retreat into ordinary social and communal life when they are not congregating with a few or larger groups of their brethren, are identifiable—and must wish to be—as skinheads. Many Klan members, for most of their lives, are not easily identifiable. It is not easily possible to ascertain much of the time if a known racist is a Klan member. Klansmen are often integrated members of the community.

Like Klansmen, skinheads are often fascists, but their style is also frequently nihilistic. Skinhead rituals, such as thrash dancing or diving off the stage, or even the repeated ceremony of breaking up concerts or dances, are explosive, planned chaos. Klan rites typically ape orthodox or even Christian conventions. In their search for national purity, the Klan would seek national order; tightening up; proper hierarchies of submission. Skinheads appear to favor disorder. They are lords of misrule. Many seem not to have progressed much beyond the desire to break up society, without much desire to restructure it. The skins of the 1980s were young, very young. Skins like to brag about "fucking around" sexually. Klan members are older as their institution is older. However, often their claims of attending secret meetings mask a desire to "fool around" covertly...on the sly...like good old boys are allowed to: but openly Klansmen support the traditional family. They have customarily claimed as one of their functions militant opposition to those who would tear the fabric of the family through infidelity (female more than male). Skinheads, if they want a family, want a family of other skinheads, other young, mostly male peers, aggressively heterosexual skinheads. A skinhead might grow into a Klan member, but it would be unusual for a Klansman to regress to the skinhead stage, except that he might privately long for what he perceived as the skinhead's freedom from social ties.

Robert Miles, an ex-Klan official originally from New York, who established his own racist Mountain Church on a 70-acre farm in Choctah, Michigan, near Lansing, attempted to place skinheads into closer contact with other right wing hate organizations as part of his efforts to produce greater unity among the splintered groups who possess similar ideas of white supremacy, Jewish conspiracy, black inferiority, and gay decadence. His belief that "Our nation is the nation of our race, under a white God for a white people...We are in a war for our race's survival" could stand as a gloss for the theory behind many of Skrewdriver's songs. Skinheads, including skins from Chicago and Detroit, have often attended the semi-annual conferences he organized for hate groups held in privacy at his farm from the mid-1980s. He also made a special point to praise the Detroit skins' publication *Hail Victory!* (*Hate Groups in America* 5; *Extremism on the Right* 130-131; *Shaved for Battle* 3).

Although hate organizations have ordinarily experienced great difficulties at the national group level in working with each other over protracted periods, their memberships reveal considerable overlapping or interpenetration. Miles for example not only led his own Mountain Church, but was Midwest coordinator for Aryan Nations, the white supremacy organization directed by Richard Butler from his home in Lake Butler, Idaho, not far from Coeur d'Alene. Butler also headed *his* church of Jesus Christ Christian, which like Miles's preaches that Jews are the children of Satan and Africans are subhuman. One of Butler's chief aims was to create a "national racist state" for whites in the Northwest. Idaho, Montana, Wyoming, Oregon and Washington have been identified by Butler and other leaders of national hate groups (Christian Identity and some Klans, for example) as a future "Aryan Republic." Miles refers to the establishment of this racially and ethnically exclusive enclave—the White bastion—as the "ten percent solution" or the "ten percent and out" solution (Mayer 3; *Klanwatch*, Aug./Sept. 1989). Whites seeking a purified homeland would move into and settle these states, non-Aryans (including some southern Europeans) would be eased or forced out. The current minority population of this region is only about five percent, mainly (outside of various ethnics in Portland and Seattle) American Indian.

According to the Religious Advisory Council of the Idaho Department of Corrections, Butler employs both old-time appeals to violence and modern technology in his attempts to persuade his followers to "rise up and kill all non-whites." Helped by Louis Beam, an ex-Klan leader in Texas and an Aryan Nations "Ambassador at Large," Butler "established a high-tech system of communication with like-minded phone link-ups" (*Extremism on the Right* 70). Since at least 1986 skinheads have attended meetings Butler hosted at Hayden Lake. In 1987, the skinhead ex-convict Martin Cox was arrested for illegal possession of firearms while driving away from an Aryan Nations conference. Cox was an organizer for Tom Metzger's White Aryan Resistance in California and has appeared with Metzger on his "Race and Reason" tapes distributed by followers and shown on cable stations around the country (*Shaved for Battle* 4). He was also part of the uproar on the Oprah Winfrey television show. In February 1990, he was arrested by police in California for threatening the life of a Jewish man working as a pizza cook (*Klanwatch*, June 1990).

One of Butler's special projects for many years has been an attempt to gain adherents to the white power cause through work in prisons, providing, for example, money and staff to David Lane in 1987 for a "prison outreach letter." Lane was at the time in jail for his illegal activities with The Order, a white power guerilla gang also called the *Bruders Schweigen* (or Silent Brotherhood) whose members were hunted down or jailed 1984-1985 for crimes including "murder, bombings and armed robbery" committed presumably to bring about the new white order (*Extremism* 70, 51). Their activities were fictionalized in the film *Betrayed*. Members of The Order killed by civil or federal agents are considered martyrs by many extremists including skinheads. The death of Robert Mathews, the group's founder, is commemorated each year at Puget Sound, his death place. On December 10, 1988, from 20 to 30 skinheads took part in the ceremony.

Like Miles, Butler has praised the skinheads extensively. In a leaflet issued from Hayden Lake, Idaho, combining the imprimaturs of the Church of Jesus Christ Christian, Aryan Nations, and Teutonic Unity, the skins are lauded as "the new addition...the next generation...called 'skins' or 'skinheads'." Ecstatically, in language that must have seemed strange and pleasing to them, Butler sermonizes that the skinheads "promise to be a veritable fountain of fire. Oh yes! They are beginning to understand that the sins of their fathers have fallen on them, the sons," welcome news for the young men who although they often inherited racism from their fathers, were frequently also engaged in a generational struggle with them. "These young Aryan youths search through the land, in which their fathers had pride, for their inheritance—their territorial imperative. It is no longer there. Did the fathers squander their rightful inheritance?" The same leaflet features an advertisement for *The Auschwitz Myth*, a Holocaust denial book by Dr. Wilhelm Staglich, and for many "sermons on tape" by Butler including "Skinheads—There's a Calling Out" (ADL archives).

This kind of attention which came to them unsolicited during the last half of the 1980s must have been a heady inspiration to skinheads unused to most kinds of institutional encouragement for their primal ideas and brutal actions. Remarks like those of Butler would further validate their racism and sense of pride in the worth of their violent activities on the street, and feed back articulated concepts into their not very well worked out racist ideology intensifying their hostility through developing what had originally been an occasional fistful of sharp racial, ethnic, and sexual dislikes into substantial and consuming hatred.

Butler's Aryan Nations sponsored a three-day congress of white supremacists at Hayden Lake in July 1988, which about a dozen skinheads attended along with Klan members and other hate group regulars. According to the Southern Poverty Law Center's *Law Report* (July 1988) "more than 20 speakers, including Butler and Miles, addressed the enthusiastic audience with 16 hours of savage racist and anti-Semitic rhetoric. By the end of the conference, about 100 of those attending pledged their loyalty to the Aryan Nations." Butler, who had previously praised the "Skinhead phenomenon as a 'natural biological reaction' of white teenagers banding together after being taught that 'non-white kids are great and white kids are scum' " now claimed "Skinheads would eventually 'clean up the streets' after receiving 'the proper guidance' " presumably he and the other assembled hate leaders could provide them. Butler appeared proud that even so small a contingent of the "front line warriors" showed up for the diatribes (*Young and Violent* 10).

Robert Miles mentioned in his *Mountain* for March-April 1989 a "Skinhead National Seminar" soon to be sponsored by Aryan Nations that would assemble a gathering of hate groups for what sounded like an innocent series of college extension program instructional meetings.

Held on Butler's 15-acre Hayden Lake compound, the conference convened April 20-23 to celebrate Hitler's 100th birthday. Over 1,000 demonstrators protested the event, which attracted fewer than two dozen skinheads rather than the 100 predicted. Those skinheads who did trek to Butler's out of the way retreat (good for relative secrecy and room in which to practice war but poor as a location easy to travel to) heard Butler claim that "today it's Blacks, Crips and Bloods [who] rule the streets...But in the future, it's going to be our white young who rule the streets, not with drugs, but with truth." David Cooper, a 21-year-old skinhead, delivered a talk that would have pleased either Butler's or Miles's congregations. While admitting that blacks and other people of color were "creatures of God" just as animals were, they were "not welcome" in America. Cooper's skinhead gang, he proclaimed, would be pleased to "build the ships" returning them to their homelands. The Jews would have to be considered separately, however, since they were agents "of Satan, just as it says in our Bible" (*Bruce Buursma* [sic], *Chicago Tribune*, 21 April 1989).

This Hitler Centennial conference was Butler's idea but was implemented by Kim Badyinski, a Klan leader originally from Chicago but more recently based in Spokane, Washington, one of those according to the Anti-Defamation League "involved in efforts to raise money for Butler's defense" against his seditious conspiracy charge. He and Butler insured that skinheads were featured at the meeting, and even had them attend a press briefing before the event itself began. Reporters were told that the skinheads would be trained over the weekend as "shock troops" for the movement. Badyinski added that they would be taught "how to stay out of jail, because they don't do us any good in jail." At the "Seminar's" opening ceremony "Skinheads held flags of various 'Aryan' countries" just like young Nazis had been so frequently and flatteringly filmed doing in Third Reich documentaries. They were also "encouraged" by Butler to "unite under a single umbrella," but their small numerical participation in the celebration suggested an exotic drink miniature parasol might have been more appropriate. Butler and Badyinski were "privately bitter" and particularly scorned the "interference of Tom Metzger" who "had sent out letters urging his followers not to attend." According to an Anti-Defamation League report, "The consensus of those skinheads who were present at Hayden Lake" (not necessarily a nationally representative sample—and it is difficult to establish what would comprise such a sample) "was that their movement should remain decentralized" (*Skinheads Target the Schools* 11).

Courted by WAR: The Metzgers Attack

Perhaps the two racists who during the 1980s most assiduously and successfully forged links with the skinheads were Tom Metzger and his son, John. Tom Metzger has had a long and dishonorable career in extreme right wing and hate groups, having been at various times a member of Robert Welch's John Birch Society, David Duke's Knights of the Ku Klux Klan, James K. Warner's anti-Semitic New Christian Crusade Church, and his own California Knights of the Ku Klux Klan (a split-off from Duke's original organization). In 1980 he won the California Democratic Congressional 45th District primary campaign but lost overwhelmingly in the final election to incumbent Clair Burgener. He then created the White American Political Association, which preceded his White Aryan Resistance (WAR) movement. He has encouraged paramilitary training for his followers and when he ran for the House of Representatives declared his support for teaching marksmanship classes in public schools. Metzger likes to brag that he is an everyday guy who earns his living as a television repairman. For many years he has offered a slim but widely distributed hate magazine, *WAR*, to subscribers several times a year for $20—single copies available at selected newsstands and bookstores. Apparently, *WAR* was a money making enterprise and one in which Metzger could hawk a variety of hate commodities for sale. In the civil case ultimately launched against him and his son for damages relating to Mulegeta Seraw's death, prosecuting attorney Morris Dees of the Southern Poverty Law Center proved that John Metzger diverted funds to his own private use that he accumulated through selling *WAR* and other hate items. He paid for his toupee from his *WAR* chest. He also helped distribute books instructing in terrorism and guerilla warfare such as *The Anarchist's Cookbook*. When ten members of The Order were convicted in Seattle in 1986 for "various crimes including killings and bombings," Tom Metzger stood on the courthouse steps and declared "They have given us ten martyrs. A new day is dawning for white people in this country" (*Extremism* 128-129).

Metzger proselytized for his different hate groups in high schools and colleges, but he seemed especially fixed on recruiting skinheads to more organized political action groups. Though he has been quoted saying that "skinheads are more a symbol than anything else. They are an energized generation of people who see the writing on the wall: that their future is in danger," (*St. Louis Post Dispatch*, 8 January, 1989), it is clear that they are of more than symbolic value to him. He is especially attracted to them because of their willingness to act violently, a quality he greatly admires. Often he defends skinheads from imputations of wrongdoing, either by declaring that their violent acts are correct and justified, or by proclaiming that official powers are falsely charging them with crimes they have not committed. A WAR hate message telephone transcription on November 28, 1988 asserted that an alleged assault by three skinheads that took place on a subway platform was not carried out by skinheads at all. One "so-called skinhead" according to Metzger "was a Jew, one a Puerto Rican and one [was] unidentified by race." Skinhead Ken Mieske's admitted murder of the Ethiopian Mulegeta Seraw was termed a "civic duty" on another telephone transcript.

Metzger is quite capable of sympathetically reinterpreting what any ordinary person would consider evidence absolutely damning skinheads or hate group members. He does not ignore attacks as much as he appears to assimilate them and invert charges which he then recycles as proof of his peculiar vision of racist life. On his transcripts he has even offered praise for the film *Betrayed,* which is a slightly veiled and openly critical account of the notorious "Order's" criminal activities which included armed robberies and murder. He endorsed the film and advocated its viewing since, he stated, despite its "obvious silly parts" the movie's "thrust is great." One of the film's sequences depicts a group of men and one woman (played by Debra Winger), covertly an FBI agent, hunting down and killing a black man who has been let loose in the woods, partly for their sport but supposedly more for paramilitary practice. Many would see this as one of the film's overstated "silly parts," but it is quite possible the action demonstrates for Metzger part of the movie's powerful "thrust." Sometimes on his hate telephone transcripts Metzger resembles a character from *Betrayed.* After urging his telephone listeners to see this production, which anti-fascist director Costa Gavras certainly intended as an assault upon the extremist right wing mentality, Metzger intones ominously, "We are on the move and it is too late to stop us. Our friends in sensitive positions should remain in increasingly low profile for the foreseeable future."

Tom Metzger's son John ordinarily presents a much milder image than his father. He talks like a member of the Young Republicans or Young Democrats most of the time, not in the specific ideas he expresses but with the same seeming openness and glib tolerance. In his public appearances he is anything but a rabble-rouser, though if his messages are listened to carefully or scrutinized for their underlying themes, his ideological links to Tom Metzger's brand of violent racism are apparent. He has been president of the Aryan Youth Movement, formerly the White Student Union, since 1987, when he was 19. The name change, he has claimed, represents his search for a broader-based youth constituency which would include non-students such as skinheads. John Metzger often sounds relatively temperate on the subject of race, seeming to accept other organizations who express an interest in various racial, ethnic, or religious heritages. "Our main goal is we feel that white people, just like any other racial group, or even religious or economic group, have a right to be determinists in the sense of deciding their own future. What we want to do, since we figure there's the NAACP and various black organizations, strictly for black people,...and you have your Indian organizations, and Israel is mainly for Jews, and so on and so forth, we feel that there shouldn't really be a problem for white people who are really interested in their culture and their heritage, who want to be around themselves, and not integrate with other cultures...and that's the main thing we're pushing now, basically for an area, who knows, somewhere, somehow, but we do want an area for racially-conscious white people who want to take an alternate route. [We want] instead of integration, separation" (Roger Adams interview, March 15, 1988).

John Metzger sounds harmless at first, as though he were advocating merely some more broadly European counterpart to the Knights of Columbus, unviolent as Laurel and Hardy's "Sons of the Desert." The territory he is actually calling for, however, is like the "White Bastion" in the current United States of America, from which non-whites (among others) could be forcibly expelled. To help achieve this utopia, skinheads would have to be, according to Metzger, "intelligently racial, but [ready and able to] kick ass physically, no exceptions." If resisted and attacked, they had license, he felt, to "go for the gusto. Destroy 'em. Anything you have to do. Poke the eyeballs out. Beat the hell out of 'em...When they come down to that level we fight and we win and we brawl and we have fun" (Metzger in *WAR* and on hate-message tape, December 2, 1988, reported in *Klanwatch*, October 1990).

And while he contends that "the days of going out and burning crosses is fine, as a ceremony, but it shouldn't be done just for the hell of it, or wearing sheets, or wearing a swastika," his opposition to these symbolic statements stems from his feeling they are no longer effective as recruiting devices. "Things like that are not turning on working people out there [and] we're trying to appeal especially to the working people." Though the swastika he says holds no particular fascination for him, "I like the symbol in the sense that it's a sunwheel, and it's very ancient and very old and was used in the 1912 election, and it means good luck." So it is clear there is considerable subterfuge in his remarks. Obviously people who wear swastikas in America now are neither demonstrating their allegiance to candidates Wilson, Taft or Teddy Roosevelt in the 1912 election nor wishing anybody good luck, but are declaring at the very least their willingness to exhibit a sign under which the mass murder of Jews was accepted or sought by a twentieth century state.

John Metzger admits that in some other "groups, like the Klan and National Socialists...there are segments...that are hateful, and there are a few people in our group that are hateful, [but] we try to keep it under control...People who strictly go around hating somebody because the first fight they got into happened to be with a black man...is ridiculous. It's just ridiculous. Our main goal, and the thing we strive for, is to recruit people who are intelligent, who want a healthy atmosphere, who don't want to go and fight in some war that doesn't benefit white people, [that is] just commie-bashing...We want to end abortion, we want to get drugs off the street—we don't allow drugs at all in our organization—as a matter of fact, I'm glad to see Louis Farrakhan, in a certain segment of his pretty much all black group, goes out and starts raiding some of these houses that sell crack...The people should get together and take care of themselves, and not rely so much on the police" (Roger Adams interview).

It is presumably to attain this cleaner, purer white society that leads John Metzger to seek among skinheads for adherents to his cause. He is proud that he can "pat myself on the back a little bit for organizing" them, for being "able to have an influence and fine tune their perceptions. We're filling a void in their lives" (*Klanwatch*, October 1990). For him, the skinheads originated when "a lot of the Middle Eastern people" entered England, "Turkish people and Pakistanis," and took jobs from white working families. Then bands like Skrewdriver "popped up" singing lyrics the young working class whites "wanted to hear." For Metzger, "the media is to blame" for the idea that "all skinheads are hateful and they're all Nazis...A lot of them aren't; a lot of them are real patriotic...A lot of them want to clean up America.... When they come in, we try to tell them that we're not just a hateful group." Metzger says he tries to discourage recruits who think once they are allied with the Aryan Youth Movement "we can go out and get in a fight and have twenty guys on our side and beat up some poor black guy." In fact, he claims, black people are not the main difficulty AYM faces. "The biggest problem that we have, that we're fighting constantly, is white people in power who are not caring about white people at all. They don't try to protect white people; they don't care [about] affirmative action or forced busing, or abortion, or other things that greatly affect white people..."

Supposedly, the Aryan Youth Movement did not actively seek out skinheads to persuade them to join their ranks. "There's a misconception that we go out to every bar and drag some skinhead in and start preaching racialism to him, or her. That is not the case. They come to us. And when they do, we say, 'Look, this is what we're about. We're not going to go out and start bashing homosexuals. We don't like 'em, but we're not going to go and bash 'em for no reason.' And if they can't handle that, then they're just going to have to go to some other organization. We have to have a few rules...We want people who are genuinely interested in preserving their own, white heritage, and their culture, who want [not just] to segregate, but separate" (Roger Adams interview).

But much of what Metzger says is belied by the history of violent actions his organization and the people in it have either engaged in or condoned that is in no way connected to bettering society. Evidence made public during the Metzgers' trial establishing their complicity in the murder of Mulegeta Seraw demonstrates that they did purposefully send WAR representatives to Portland to work with and ultimately incite local skinheads (*New York Times*, 26 October 1990, "Law" section). And

John Metzger's obsession with ideas of racial purification, though usually unaccompanied by the kind of thunder and lightning rhetoric of apocalypse often associated with demagogues, strongly suggests he is not the moderate live-and-let-live (but not close to him) lover of simple cultural self-determination he seeks to disguise himself as. When Dave Mazzella traveled to Portland to organize skinheads he took with him a newspaper publication of John Metzger's Aryan Youth Movement titled "Operation Warlord," containing an article by Metzger about the new sport "Clash and Bash" which whites can win by breaking the bones of non-whites (*Klanwatch*, December 1990).

So John Metzger does not always seem like a demagogue. He seems physically indistinguishable from hundreds of thousands if not millions of other young white Americans, only he is straighter looking than many. His utterances whether written or spoken lack style. He has about him the quality of a minor committee member. He seems to anticipate sharp, angry objections, and muffle them beforehand in his seeming reasonableness. But he is very strongly committed to his cause of national white purification through separation and either isolation or expulsion of others, the impure ones. Astutely enough, what he fears most about the skinheads is that he anticipates a lack of long term commitment from them. "All I can say to the skinheads is, don't make it a fad. Don't make it into something that is just a passing phase, or something that's just gonna take care of your personal needs for a few years. [Some of them] go from punk rock to heavy metal to skinheads. People like that, I don't know what they're looking for...I think the reason the skinhead scene started is because [of] frustration from the working kids. They wanted change. And I don't want to see it degenerate into just a strictly music kind of a rebellious attitude" (Roger Adams interview).

In describing the strong identity of racist skinheads, a feature that makes them easy to target as a group, John Metzger recognized that much of their group self-image stems from the "music involved" in their scene. Tom Metzger also, though generationally not nearly as close to the skinheads as his son, recognizes the importance of music in attempting to draw skinheads into his white power movement. Although it is difficult to accept that he truly appreciates Oi! music or the persistent clang of most skinhead bands, whose sound is raw and unmelodic and frequently approximates the timbre of a loud, angry, monotonous accusation, he frequently praises groups such as Skrewdriver or the Tulsa Mid-Town Boot Boys, whose tapes he peddled in his *WAR* magazine and through blurbs broadcast over his telephone hate line. Doubtless the lyrics of these groups appeal to him, though he would probably need a song sheet or interpreter to inform him of their words, for they are extremely difficult to grasp in recorded or live performance. Like many new music lyrics, their meaning is known to initiates but hidden to outsiders who only hear a verbal blur. Metzger seems one of the uninitiated. He appears hopelessly square in voicing his enjoyment. "This is a hot tape" he declares like an aging Saturday Night Live hipster on one of his September 20, 1988 telephone messages hawking the Boot Boys, "they are great! Don't be cheap, let's make sure this red-hot band has some traveling money so they can come visit our Aryan festivals."

The Music Problem, A Twisted Woodstock, and Other WAR Cries

Music is so much a part of the skinhead world and the punk world from which skinheads in America emerged as a group dominated by racist ideology, that it has become a matter of importance to extremist organizations not otherwise focused on popular music who wish to attract skinhead allegiance. Often there is a note of muted lament or a defensiveness about recent popular music in the extremist press, because so much of it is derived from African-American roots, a source of annoyance sometimes explained away by labeling rock and roll degenerate, and establishing it as another instance of commercial exploitation engineered by the imagined covert Jewish conspiracy. Thus, the hate publication *Front Line* (March 1987) praised bands like Skrewdriver which it claimed "describe the decadence of our times and point the way to regeneration," and supplied addresses for Romantic Violence in Chicago and the White Noise Club in Croyden, England, where these bands' tapes can be purchased. This popular music for youth is highly politically acceptable. Otherwise, according to *Front Line*, "Many people in the National Liberation Movement automatically identify today's rock and roll with the deracinated pop culture in our age which promotes drug use, mindless violence [as opposed to the presumably thoughtful violence committed by skinheads] and supreme individualism. At the hands of the big record corporations which are almost completely Jewish-controlled, modern music is dominated by Negro and mulatto singers." As if this predicament were not bad enough, "In addition, many White stars gladly imitate the screeching jungle rhythms of Black music and adopt multi-racial and anti-national themes in their lyrics, and they are rewarded with contracts when they do."

Most of the skinhead bands or the bands skinheads admire, produce sounds that seem indistinguishable from the music of typical punk or new wave or heavy metal bands. The problem for right wing extremist organizations who seek to appeal to dissident youth groups is how to accommodate this music which has its roots—some of its roots anyway—in black arts and folkways. Rejecting the music might turn away potential followers attracted and committed to the music scene the particular rock sound inhabits. It is sometimes difficult for older onlookers to accept the vigorous disagreements adherents of one musical style or group can engage in with contrary advocates. Who seriously debated decades ago the merits of Tony Bennett's variety of crooning opposed to Guy Mitchell's, or Patti Page's style against Jo Stafford's? But popular music preferences are now much more a matter of personal and group identity, causing sharp disputes which sometimes are affected by the increased violence that seems part of the world of the young and their elders as well.

Tom Metzger's strategy has been to embrace and publicize the music skinheads produce and enjoy, and to attack the idea that skinhead music is tainted with black strains. His *WAR* magazine openly expresses Metzger's racist ideology and his keen interest in skinheads, including their music which he tries to demonstrate is thoroughly white and not black music. Published by his White Point Publishing company and edited by himself, *WAR* in the 1980s typically contained in any one issue a fairly full display of Metzger's broad range of hatreds in articles written sometimes by himself or by associates; cartoons, and wide-ranging letters from white power believers who contributed praise for Metzger's efforts along with their own thoughts on the topics his magazine has dealt with; and scraps of information for fellow far right extremists: "We will lead this country back to purity once again. Then we will hunt down the race traitors, like the two women displayed on page 7 of your latest newsletter." "If you walk around downtown San Francisco or New York for ten minutes, you will see a black man strutting along with a White girl on his arm. You'll also see his brothers giving him all kinds of winks and nods, behind her back, cause they know he's got a feather in his cap!" "Did you know that during the Vietnam war, the South Vietnamese owned the third largest air force in the world?....The only time they flew was to escape to American carriers in their helicopters which they ditched in the ocean...What a lowly, disgusting, degenerate crowd of human trash!"

The 1989 issue from which these letters are quoted (8:2) is worth extended study since item after item in it announces Metzger's admiration for the skinheads and displays his recognition that music is important to their scene, an opportunity to gather them into his fold. Concurrently, he and his followers and associates deliver venomous hate messages to a standard array of enemies common to his organization and the skinheads he seeks to win over. In one article he distinguishes between "priests" who don't "plan on being in the trenches but build...power based on word manipulation" and true "warriors" (like the skinheads) who "are always in the thick of the struggle against the enemies of our race." One cartoon shows a gay white man holding hands with a black man being yanked into an open grave on whose tombstone is written, "Adios Infected Demented Sodomites [AIDS]." The dying men are encouraged to "Keep up the Good Work You Pathetic Queers!" Another cartoon depicts a stereotypical street Negro who raps, "I blames de white man for my plight...It's him what makes me smoke dis crack, He push my kind to burn and loot, An sends de po-lice dat we shoot...But inch by inch we takin' hold, Like when de white bread starts to mold." In the cartoon "Introducing 'Aids Raids'," two booted, helmeted soldiers wearing gas masks burst into what resembles a hospital room with a "Gay Pride" poster on one of its walls, shooting either flame or bullets at a skeletal patient who feebly holds a book titled, *Rock Hudson*.

The magazine throughout this issue presents a blend of materials appealing to skinheads and to a more generalized, extremist audience. A cartoon by "Kris," age 12, captioned "WHITE MEN AND WOMEN WORKING TOGETHER IS THE WAY OF W.A.R." shows a skinhead with a swastika on his shirt holding hands with a young, white, female warrior wearing a "Skullhead" t-shirt. Kris may also be Kristina who contributed the poem "Being White Is Not A Crime": "White and proud, That's what I am, Storming the streets, Getting rid of the trash." Readers are encouraged to write jailed "P.O.W.s" such as convicted skinhead murderer Dean McKee whose prison address is provided, and under the heading "Aryan Entertainment" (the "nation's largest white separatist library") videotapes offered for sale include "Undercover Kosher Expose," "Geraldo [Rivera] Brawlers—The True Story," "Students Against Race Mixers," "Skinheads of America," "A.Y.M. [Aryan Youth Movement] and Skinheads," "Ian Stuart and Skrewdriver," "Tulsa Boot Boys," and "D.[ave] Mazella on A.Y.M. and Skinheads." Skrewdriver's concert scheduled for West London on May 27, 1989, is advertised, replete with fascist symbols. Mention is also made of the supporting bands Frontal Attack, Sudden Impact, No Remorse, Squadron, Vengeance, and Bunker 84. Ian Stuart is interviewed in a separate article in which he claims that the American skinhead scene is "gaining strength all the time."

He defines a skinhead as "A clean, patriotic man or woman who is proud to be White, proud of their country, and is not afraid to show it." Stuart praises American skinhead bands he has heard (without naming any) because they "sound well produced and gutsy," admits that he would classify himself as a Nazi, and lists among his political heroes Hitler, Mussolini, Sepp Dietrich, Rudolph Hess, Henry VIII, and Robert E. Lee! Tom Metzger is not in this pantheon but Stuart thanks him for his help on the jacket of Skrewdriver's "White Rider" album.

Politically oriented articles about skinhead music dominate the issue. John Jewell's lengthy and seemingly learned (at least to uninitiated readers not highly expert in popular music history) "Skinhead Rock and Roll" appears under a fascist "solar wheel" logo upon which are crossed an electric guitar and a pistol, establishing a connection between the skinhead's racist ideology, their violence, and their music. The colorful Jewell, who was according to Tom Metzger "on the executive board of the IWW [Industrial Workers of the World] and fought in the streets as a flaming left-winger during the Vietnam War" (Ridgeway 174) energetically attacks the concept that "Rock music is the precious gift of soulful Blacks to soulless Whites. Of sexual Negroids to sexless Caucasoids." This idea he says may appeal to "middle-class White-Zombies" but "White working-class youth know better—or should know better. (And better know better.)" The idea is a " 'black propaganda' lie put out by the insidious Anglo-Jewish Establishment." Skinhead music according to Jewell comes from "Cockney Oi!" which "incorporated into it several British working-class musical forms" including "Cockney street-singing and Old London music-hall audience-chorusing; football-club and patriotic-military male surge chanting"; and "White American 'rockabilly' elements preserved in Britain by the White working class 'Teddy Boys' and 'Rockers'." Jewell minimizes or totally erases the role of "amateurish N.Y. area" punk and rude-boy or Reggae music in establishing skinhead music. Rock 'n roll itself Jewell declares stems from rockabilly—which is white—and black rhythm and blues, which in a lengthy harangue filled with eclectic musical folklore references that perhaps only a popular musicology student would be qualified to disagree with, he claims also derives from white music. His argument seems fairly sophisticated and gains intensity (and complexity) from its highly compressed (and usually unsubstantiated) development.

While Jewell admits that certain "styles" that helped create the basis for rock 'n roll are African, such as syncopation, mojo-voodoo, juba dancing, cornshucking chants, and "nigger" field hollers, he admonishes his (white) readers to remember these are just styles, and that "ALL of the Black American musical FORMS" whether "Pentecostal ecstatic improvisations," the Anglo-Scottish "lament ballads," or the Anglo-Irish "jigs" were "copied" by black folk performers. The " 'bandore' or 'bandoor' " of the sailors was also "borrowed as the 'banjo' by Black slaves." Later, the "White 'polka,' the military 'march' (brass band), and White 'Cajun' (French) 'bougalie' (fiddle reel and accordion)" musical forms were "stylized by Blacks into 'ragtime,' 'jug-band,' 'spasm band,' 'Dixieland,' 'jazz,' [and] 'boogie-woogie'." According to Jewell, musical influences from all over Europe and white America (including the Hispanic "fandango guitar flourish" played first along the "Tex-Mex border") converged to produce rock 'n roll, which to whites meant "a rollicking good time" and to blacks (in line with the hyper-sexuality attributed to them in Metzger's magazine and racist literature generally) meant simply to "fornicate." Along the route of this cultural journey into the past establishing the white source of most modern popular music, Jewell generally inverts much of the revisionist musicological research of the past half century, which has generally produced evidence to establish the primacy of the black community in creating the basis for modern popular music in America. For example, he denigrates the black music Stephen Foster based many of his best known melodies upon, claiming Foster "elevated these songs to folk-tunes," suggesting that the songs became generally known and performed among black folk only *after* Foster successfully modified them.

Details supposedly demonstrating the white foundations of rock 'n roll cascade in Jewell's essay into a forceful but wandering torrent of accusations, assumptions, assertions, analyses, and claims attacking both white liberalism and traditional conservatism as part of a "CONSPIRACY" perversely dedicated apparently to the dethronement of pure white supremacy. Jewell sprays comments interpreting events from Reconstruction, turn-of-the-century, World Wars I and II, the Cold War, and recent days into the stream of his polemic in a manner that would make rational contemplation or factual investigation of his argument difficult. "Black 'spirituals'…were heavily propagandized by Radical Republicans to push race-mixing after the Civil War. 'Dixieland' was spread from the brothels…of New Orleans by the White Race-traitors who frequented the 'high-yaller' mulatto-whores…Black troops ran amok in Parisian brothels" during World War I, " 'blues jazz' was spread to Northern cities by Southern Black 'scabs'…to break the White strike-waves of 1917 and 1919-20." Occasional fact and mostly trite fantasy are mixed here in a fashion that would dismay most professional students of history but would doubtless please conspiracy-minded white supremacists by providing them with a rich soup of distortion to feed their paranoia. Yes, black laborers were used to break white union strikes sometimes. The phenomena is a complicated one in American labor and race relations. But while black scabs were temporarily "protected by police & troops" as Jewell states, the protection was short-lived— usually until the strike was settled to the satisfaction of management and sometimes to the agreement of the predominately white unions—and accompanied by standard white attitudes of disdain and ultimately by the exploitation of black scab labor also. And of course, ample evidence now exists of the courageous, and under the circumstances noble performance of black soldiers in Europe during World War I.

Another trick of Jewell's is to string together in rapid-fire progression culturally significant detail but to distort the legitimate significance of the detail by slotting it exactly into his wall of evidence, supposedly proving the liberal and orthodox-conservative connivance to destroy the rightfully white society he and Metzger and (his diatribe assumes) the skinheads long to reestablish. "A Jew-composer [Gershwin] would put blues-jazz into a symphonic form…The first 'talkie' was a 'blackface' Jew [Jolson]." And constantly in his narration he returns to the illegitimacy of black claims to cultural importance. Even the blues are not black. The word itself used to describe a mournful mood is a "centuries-old English [white] expression...Likewise, the word 'juke,' as in 'juke-joint'...is not Black in origin...but another old English term" meaning to "leap about, jerk, jiggle, dance the 'jig'."

After chronicling more recent years of cynical manipulation of music history "by the liberal establishment," pointing out that "We Shall Overcome" was first a "17th century Sicilian fisherman's tune," Jewell describes the co-optation and corruption of punk and heavy metal caused by the Establishment's fear of "both as spontaneous revolts of the White lower classes." Co-optation is a favorite theme of hate music advocates. *The Nationalist* in 1987 repeated what was already a standard claim by charging that "the big record corporations...are almost completely Jewish-controlled" and "dominated by Negro and mulatto singers" assisted by "many White stars" who "gladly imitate the screeching jungle rhythms of Black music." These performers are "rewarded with contracts" when they "adopt multiracial and anti-national themes" ("Nationalist Youth Create New Rock Movement" 14-16).

David Bowie is according to *The Nationalist* a good example of the co-opted white performer. The magazine states that having previously been a member of the National Front and telling *Playboy* magazine in an interview that he was a fascist, Bowie was given "a choice" by "the Jews" who said he could either "cavort on stage with blacks and sing the 'proper' lyrics' " or say farewell to his career. Bowie allegedly "betray[ed] his race" and "immediately became a big star." This bit of purported musical history concludes with the unacademic warning that "David, and his kind, had better pray that the National Revolutionaries never take power because no mercy will be shown to such people."

Jewell's critique reinforces many of the ideas cursorily advanced in *The Nationalist* analysis though he seems less heavy handed and almost temperate by comparison. He concludes his survey of the white foundations of rock by listing decadent spin-offs from the true source that has been contaminated as part of a program to weaken society by promoting integration: "transvestite 'hard rock,' faggot 'punk,' lobotomy 'disco,' coon 'ska,' monkey-mimic 'rap' (see how fast Black 'protest rap' was replaced by nigger-idiocy)...jack-off cover versions of any 'spunky' tunes from the past; and 'big chill' nostalgia garbage from the '60s for balding, baby-boomer yuppies. Meanwhile, Nashville 'country music' (sic) had been cemented to a bar-stool of booze, pills, hookers, and sordid adultery-betrayal" [the "(sic)" is Jewell's].

Jewell's vigorous style adds power to his argument by making his invective-filled disquisition entertaining to readers who would not find his claims thoroughly odious. His prose is in the violent bang-bang gonzo style of many new journalists and rock music analysts for periodicals such as the early *Rolling Stone* or more recently *Spin*, making his idiom more acceptable to the young audience he is attempting to reach and convince. And though his analysis seems often historically flawed, particularly in asserting consequences of corrupt liberal rule, sometimes his claims echo interpretations that are fashionable among factions of left-oriented youth who also inhabit the popular new music scene. Thus, while his message would automatically appeal to skinheads who feared black or Jewish domination, he occasionally employs proof that would not be thought so wild on the scene, because already stated by trendily acceptable sources. Drug infestation for example he perceives as part of a government policy to neutralize youth and blacks, an analysis some white liberals and blacks subscribe to. And he shows proper respect for some militant blacks. "When the liberals & Zionists finally decided to scuttle the Vietnam fiasco...Psychedelic music and drugs were rammed into the 'youth-gap' already opened up by the 'British Invasion' of 1963-66...Even sooner than expected, the 'Love Generation'"'went 'helter-skelter' on LSD. Meanwhile, the niggers were sent back to their 'soul' and dope in rotting, Hymie-owned slums. (At least the Black Panthers went down shooting)," heroically. Here his language would be objectionable to these liberal and black commentators, but quite possibly not all of his analysis.

The lesson Jewell wants skinheads and new music fans to learn from his essay is stated at the conclusion to his article more clearly than it had been presented in the body of his argument. The "System" will permit young people to "come up with" any kind of music they desire "so long as the System is never really threatened." The System would even prefer that the young fans "suicide out" rather than adopt a music or an outlook that would challenge its power. Jewell implies (and this is not so clear) that the System in its conspiracy to weaken dissent has adopted a racial policy of toleration toward non-whites. Since the System itself is overwhelmingly white, why this toleration is to its advantage Jewell never illuminates, nor why it is to the advantage of Jews who presumably are powerful in the System. What is clear, however, is that the acceptance of black origins for modern popular music is part of the System's plan to tolerate if not in some ways uplift blacks in America. "They are trying to race-mix and destroy the only totally genuine race-threat ever [to] emerge: White separatist Skinheads."

This is heady praise indeed for the skinheads, not all of whom would have been intellectually capable of following Jewell's argument, which would however have provided in its detail and general concepts ammunition to reinforce them in already held beliefs, or to persuade others that skinhead ideas were not so outrageous after all. If skinheadism were to become a movement and not just a collection of largely fragmented and isolated scenes, it would need a basic ideology to rely on beyond the philosophy of brute force. Jewell's essay, in which his racist ideas are embedded in an analysis of popular music, seems calculated to appeal to skinhead tastes and passions. It tells them that the music they love is white, and that they are the hope of the future in achieving a new order of pure white rule. Jewell begins his article by writing about this music, but he ends his cultural analysis with a political declaration. His audience is urged to resist the race-mixing System that seeks to destroy skinhead heroes. "Don't let 'em" he says. "ALL WAR." The music of his message is distinctly martial.

Tom and John Metzger along with Robert Heick, a young skinhead and leader of the extremist American Front, showed their support for skinheads and recognition of their music's importance in exhibiting skinhead style and demonstrating skinhead ideology by sponsoring a "racial-political music gathering" they advertised in 1988 as an "Aryan Woodstock" to be held in early March on farmland in Napa County, north of San Francisco. Metzger's *WAR* newsletter boosted the event which also received wide publicity across the nation in mainstream newspapers partly because at the time skinheads were a focus of media attention and partly because 1989 was the twentieth anniversary of Woodstock. The juxtaposition of events would be theatrically ironic. The Metzgers featured groups like the Tulsa Boot Boys, *Haken Kreuz* (German for Hitler's twisted cross) and Wisconsin's Hammer Heads. These seemed an unlikely contrast to groups such as Country Joe and the Fish, Crosby, Stills, Nash and Young, and The Who, bands who appeared at the original outdoor concert which attracted an attendance of perhaps 300,000 blissful listeners.

The greatly ballyhooed Aryan revival seemed a dud to outsiders, almost farcical. A UPI release noted that Heick (*Tampa Tribune*, 5 March 1989) "leased the undeveloped grazing site" from Howard Lonsdale, "a Jew born in Berlin who fled Nazi Germany in 1937" and became a citizen in 1944. Lonsdale claimed "he did not know Heick was the leader of" an anti-Semitic, white supremacist group. One day before the celebration was to begin, Napa Superior Court Judge W. Scott Snowden ruled the concert's sponsors did not have proper permits or facilities for live music. The highest police estimate of the crowd inside Lonsdale's barricaded property was 100 skinheads, with another 90 to 100 arriving too late to join their brothers inside. Miserable weather may have partly accounted for the poor turnout. Cold rain mixed with sleet pelted skinheads, about 450 police in riot gear, and approximately 400 anti-skinhead counter-demonstrators. Metzger "called three riot alerts" which allowed the outnumbered skinheads to imagine they were under military siege, though much of the group's time according to one infiltrator was spent "drinking beer, swearing at each other, and trying to figure out what to do." The event seemed a paradigm of much skinhead activity: poorly carried out and attended, filled with latent (and some actual) violence, and generating much publicity cranked out by both Tom Metzger and standard media sources, mainly newspapers, news magazines, and network television. Though the gloomy affair had originally been planned for two days, it ended after one. But this brief time in the shine of public attention enabled John Metzger, who knows how to manipulate reporters by exploiting his own and the skinheads' notoriety, to declare Aryan Woodstock a success against all odds. Tom Metzger also spoke to the assembled, music-less skinheads, bragging that "we, the Aryan movement" had defeated ZOG simply through holding the event for even one day. Furthermore the skinheads had helped him show that the "Jew police" were afraid of the greater Aryan movement. He concluded by declaiming with words echoing the Nazi's Holocaust rhetoric that "the final solution is White revolution" (ADL booklet *Skinheads Target the Schools* 10-11).

At day's end the skinheads, protected by police, vacated the wooded area they had so drearily occupied. About five miles from their enclave "about 75 law enforcement officers with guns drawn surprised a six-vehicle caravan of about 30 departing skinheads...ordered them out of the vehicles, handcuffed them, photographed them and then released them after searching the vehicles." One reporter described the interception as "an ambush" complete with helicopters circling overhead and participation by US Department of Justice officials (*Tampa Tribune*, 5 March 1989, 12A). Although the attack may have been thought justified by state and national law enforcement officials because of the skinheads' record of violence, the tactics could also be viewed as reflecting techniques the skinheads themselves would embrace were they in power, and questionable in terms of civil rights procedures.

Tom Metzger satirized police and judicial actions in *WAR* (8:2, 7) in order to turn the Aryan Woodstock fiasco into triumph for true believers. In one of two connected panels, a blossom-spotted cartoon captioned "A 60's FLOWER CHILD JOINS THE RIGHT WING SYSTEM" depicts a pig-faced, drooling judge speaking to a bearded, long-haired, barechested hippie wearing a vest inscribed with a peace sign: "This court declares you to be a dangerous nigger-loving Jew commie faggot...therefore you are forbidden to sing or play your music in this country." A policeman and a businessman with a dollar sign emblazoned on his suit jacket stand behind the judge, twin pillars of government and enterprise in "NAPA 1971." A connected panel underneath is labeled "NAPA 1989" in clear reference to the recent abortive concert. Now the head-banded hippie stands between the policeman and the businessman, showing that the old rebel has been tamed and is now part of the establishment's ruling powers. The same pig-faced judge, still drooling, now sentences a clean-cut looking skinhead who wears a tie and sports a solar wheel on his pressed shirt, looking like a model of correct deportment. The judge tells him: "This court declares you to be a dangerous anti-Semitic racist homophobic bigot...therefore you are forbidden to sing or play your music in this country." The cartoon suggests that today's skinheads are treated as rebels as the hippies were, that the hippies have sold out and joined the pig enemy, and that compared to the hippies, skinheads are more acceptably neat and orderly. Elsewhere in the issue the solar wheel is described as symbolizing "spiritual power, law, order, contained religious force, holiness." Also, of course, the cartoon suggests that as in the sixties the state acted illegally in banning hippie music, it has acted illegally to ban skinhead music at Napa.

Several other supporting articles in the magazine reinforce the idea that skinheads are integral to the white power movement and that the Aryan Woodstock proved their strength and courage. Stephen Wayne Foster in "The New Barbarism" quotes Herman Melville (who substituted the word "snivelized" for "civilized") and William Blake ("Sooner murder an infant in its cradle than nurse unsatisfied desires") in a rather esoteric argument declaring "what we need is not weekend masculinity and video-game barbarism, but the real thing...We need to perform Nietzsche's 'transvaluation of all values,' to turn all condemnations of masculinity on their head and advocate the very things that are most harshly tabooed in our effete society...Skinheads should therefore see themselves as the vanguard of a realization of the true nature of mankind, which is warriorhood, defending their Aryan tribes against all other tribes and against the tyranny of industrialism." Skinheads might not easily grapple with how to defeat "the tyranny of industrialism," but they would have no difficulty understanding the iconography of *WAR*'s page one photograph showing an elderly man in glasses, wearing the kind of old codger hat Henry Fonda affected in "On Golden Pond," looking sternly at a younger mustached man who waves his fist at him. The old man's lips are tightly set. A caption announces that he is "88 YEAR OLD VIKING WARRIOR BILL HERRELL" who is "STAND[ING] UP AGAINST HOMOSEXUAL COWARDS IN NAPA COUNTY." Aryan Woodstock counter-demonstrators are also pictured as weak and ineffectual in a brief note purportedly by one of the event's security guards, "Baxter the Pagan," who sounds a little like Teddy Roosevelt or Spiro Agnew in calling the demonstrators "milksops of pantywaisted mollycoddles" who "did not even strike our forward observers as even a minor threat." If the "chickenshit homos and Zombies" who were numerically superior to the skinheads really "plan to stop radical racists," Baxter suggests they "start killing all the White Zombies and limpwristed White homos and bearded White lesbians." This would "help us both in finding the correct enemy to engage." Here, the security guard supports the idea occasionally stated by Metzger's followers that white liberals and conservatives are greater enemies than blacks such as Muslims who also encourage a belief in separatism.

Monique Wolfing, titled "Aryan Woman's League Director," similarly mocks the demonstrators who "when 6 brave skinheads from Concord, California tried to break through their numbers to try and get

124 Skinheads Shaved for Battle

up to the rally, they didn't have a word to say, but when Tom Metzger's 88-year-old friend tried to tell the media the right side of the story, the protestors were sure out for blood." Wolfing also contends that Howard Lonsdale and his wife were "eager and willing to have a White Power rally on their land because they wanted to get involved in the movement" and that she and (her husband) the security guard Baxter the Pagan "spent many a night" prior to Woodstock "rocking out to the Mid-Town Boot Boys" and telling "quite a few nigger jokes." Contending that at the concert-turned-rally, "We proceeded to make new friends, have beers, laughs and speeches despite the rain and 'squat-team' hiding in the hills shakedly [sic] pointing their big guns at us all day," Wolfing regrets only that the police "didn't let the scum on the bottom of the hill [the protestors] come up to the top—hopefully next time!" *WAR* managing editor Wyatt Kaldenburg, another Aryan Woodstock security guard, refers to police action as "about 30 FBI queers goosing each other and photographing us…Three times the pigs told us that they had scopes on us and if we made the wrong moves, they would shoot to kill. [When] Tom Metzger asked one of the pigs if he would really kill teenage boys and girls for playing rock music, a barnyard grunt was the pig's only reply." Kaldenberg's recasting of Aryan Woodstock into a sixties confrontation between pig police and innocent new music fans underscores the importance of music to the skinhead scene. He claims "the great lesson learned from our first Aryan Woodstock is that Rock 'n Roll is the way to go. Our enemies have taught this by the way they over re-acted. Anything that scares the creeps this bad has to be good."

John Metzger's comments in *WAR* are essentially quieter in tone than the other writers in the issue, milder in language, completely serious and non-threatening. He is formally complimentary to all the workers who helped put Aryan Woodstock together, and pleased that the event enabled *WAR* and the skinheads to gain so much publicity in reports that he contends circled the globe. The meat of his prose seems macerated or marinated for easy, non-abrasive digestion, like the language of a political candidate who does not wish to offend his listeners, and again he projects himself as a kinder, gentler racist. He attacks the "courts and their lackeys" in relatively even-tempered prose, deploring that the festival's organizers were "ramroded" by them, but spends more time praising the "great legal staff" who "worked feverishly against all odds" to prove the planned concert was a "private gathering."

Typically, John Metzger's bland delivery muffles the potential for violence flimsily caged within the event's structure. He describes the " 'Iron-Guard' Aryan Security team" for example, simply as "White youths who were very professional and knew how to handle problems," who worked "tremendous hours and got no sleep whatsoever, but...still kept their cool."

Metzger's voice, unlike his father's kick-ass drill-sergeant's bellow, sounds almost prissy, with no rough core. He avoids rhetorical intensity and builds to no climax when he concludes the Aryan guards (skinhead toughs) "must have made an impression because when they said no fighting, there was no fighting!" Sometimes he sounds like a mild man trying to sound tough and failing, like an ordinarily timid teacher berating a class of hoodlums. He even compliments the media, usually excoriated vigorously in *WAR*'s pages. Metzger claims the Woodstock organizers "did not return continual calls from the media because obviously they would do us no good" and that "this really made the media mad." But "the press actually helped us in a sense. They were the recruiters of the month for *WAR* by their blatant reporting! Do you realize that *WAR* has again reached into every home in the US? You'd have to work for years to get the kind of play we got!" John Metzger naturally praises the "300 plus" (his estimate) skinheads who braved "cruel and unusual conditions" to attend the concert that never took place and once more sounds like a religious young people's team leader in gushing that "the unity was one of the most incredible and uplifting things I've seen in a while. Very aggressive and hardcore youths mixing together fine." Though he claims "pulling off this event...worked...and we again proved that WAR is by far on the extreme cutting-edge of racialism," his words are unarousing compared to the other reports about Aryan Woodstock in *WAR*: "I'm glad everyone got a fresh taste of what we are up against, it just proves that our fight is real and our strength and determination is gaining momentum." He clearly lacks the natural virulence and gut-ripping assertiveness of his father, who overshadows him greatly.

Since neither of the Metzgers has been successful in gathering large numbers of skinheads into their extremist organizations, it is not clear whether the rough guy/mild guy combination they present is effective, nor if Tom Metzger's truculence is more or less effective in attracting adherents than his son's comparative moderation. Perhaps Tom Metzger is stuck with a dud son who often seems almost meek in his appeals and actions. Perhaps the duo has consciously divided between them the roles of Super-racist and an organization man Clark Kent to entrap a wide range of followers and financial supporters, some of whom might favor revolution now! while others wish to pursue more cautious, prudent approaches to the final solution in America. John Metzger would seem to be the problematic member of the two, but perhaps his less severe appeal, though it might never attract hardcore skinheads, is necessary to construct a broad based organization needing warriors and bureaucrats and clerks. Many racists do not want another Hitler. They do not long for another Holocaust, but they do desire what they imagine to be a more traditional, less liberal society which to them means one less directed toward redressing old civil grievances, less sensitive to what they perceive as the illegitimate or outrageous demands of newly recognized minorities, the new Hispanics or Latinos, Asians, the "new" Native Americans. These blander, generic racists might find John Metzger reassuring when he says, "Well, I'm always for sitting down, working things out, coming to a kind of agreement...I'm all for listening...I'm not close-minded; I'm open-minded. I talk to Mexicans and Blacks all the time—all different racial groups just to see where they're coming from, and what they think about things. I'm not just an idiot who's ignorant out there, just [saying] White people, wake up in the morning, put on my swastika, and say I'm white I'm white I'm white. I really do want to better America. I really do want to bring down the tension between racial groups. There's a lot of things in my life that don't have anything to do with race: I work, I do other things, so it's not a fetish." So often he sounds reasonable, almost mild as Mr. Rogers. Perhaps he is the racist of the future (Roger Adams interview).

The liberal interviewer Roger Adams who elicited the just-quoted response from John Metzger admitted to him, "It's a little bit surprising to talk to you because quite frankly I was expecting a more, what I would expect of an Aryan...." He meant, though he never completed his thought, that he expected a more violent person, a brutish person, a man more like the man his father appears to be in his thoughts and actions. But that is not how John Metzger presents himself. Still, what he wants is for skinheads to commit themselves to his father's organization, what he wants is a land free of blacks and people of other "mud" races. And he has never disavowed the final revolutionary means his father called for in every issue of *WAR* and most of his public utterances. The Aryan Woodstock was planned to celebrate those ideas, which John Metzger has never separated himself from. WAR is not merely an acronym for White Aryan Resistance, it represents a goal, a promise, a strategy of overturning an American society based on racial and ethnic and sexual acceptance, it stands for a willingness to engage in destruction to achieve a new order that could not possibly endure the United States Constitution. John Metzger may be his father's shadow, but whether that means he is a less powerful reflection of him, or simply another murkier, dark version of him, is not clear. What is far more certain is that no matter how moderately he speaks, he fully believes in WAR.

Aryan Woodstock was important as a public event for both white supremacists and skinheads, and those who would combat them. What seems the small number of skinheads who came to it, including those inside the gates and who arrived too late to be allowed entrance, might be ascribable to the bad weather, or to the small number of skinheads available, or to the lack of skinhead interest in events—even musical events—staged by the larger, organized extremist groups; to causes as wide apart as the inability of skinheads in America to organize their lives sufficiently to get to this kind of event or even the good sense of skinheads in avoiding what might easily be viewed as a potential disaster for them, guzzling beer in a drizzle without any live music and only fatuous harangues to listen to. More media reporters rushed to the area than skinheads. Nationally distributed reports stressed the gathering's failure, the legal defeat, the low attendance, the strutting absurdity of skinhead posturing. Some few libertarians might conceivably have deplored police actions when the day was over and skinheads were leaving the area, but actually no representative of the standard organizations monitoring civil rights questioned publicly the skinhead caravan's reported "ambush," the car and body searches, the photographing of skinheads presumably for identification purposes in the future. But for the manipulative Metzgers, every knock is a boost, and all the attention added up to a substantiation of skinhead power.

Throughout 1988 and 1989 news about skinheads was frequently reported in papers and magazines especially because of their intriguing image. Their acts of violence became sensational news because as a group they were sensational items. The press is particularly sensitive to clear examples of racism, especially incidents that contain easily exploitable elements—Al Campanis the baseball coach, once Jackie Robinson's teammate and one of his strongest supporters when Robinson broke in with the Montreal Canadians' baseball team, was treated as though he were John Wilkes Booth for clumsily and confusedly mouthing on national television the kind of backyard racial remark many whites, *even reporters*, might toss off during the day. But he did so on national television speaking to a widely known interviewer, Ted Koppel. Skinheads increasingly were perceived as a threat, or reporters subscribed to the belief—adopted the posture—that they were a dangerous threat to the egalitarian American dream. Therefore in theory observing and documenting their activities would become a way of exposing them, an eminently exposable, inherently sensational group. Media exposure supposedly constitutes a way to kill off substances—organizations, beliefs, activities—harmful to the body politic, as sunlight is held to destroy certain harmful germs. But exposure can also place groups in the spotlight, and so the paradox exists that events such as the Aryan Woodstock could also affirm its organizers' and supporters' beliefs that they are growing in their impact on the American scene, that they are succeeding in dramatizing the supposed plight of white people forced to live in a racially contaminated society. The treatment Aryan Woodstock received in the press and to a lesser extent over television (where skinheads had been given greater attention on talk shows hungry for titillating debate) was used in the pages of *WAR* to reaffirm their sense of victimization and importance. Skinheads feed on the tepid, not totally committed opposition they can assimilate and perhaps actually grow upon, though their history in different areas of the country shows they can be greatly weakened for a time if not completely rooted out, by thoughtful, legal, continued, and coordinated community action.

But like many true believers, skinheads and their supporters are adept at turning evidence against them into testimonials on their behalf. When skinheads in Milwaukee were arrested late in the summer of 1988 for shooting at the passengers in a car that had trashed their property, the five felony counts filed against them—"enough to get them thirty years!"—were converted by a publication of the local "Euro-American Alliance" into proof that "the White race in America is a pitiful example of a humiliated people. ZOG gives orders and the whites obey...No charges were laid against the trash punks who had attacked the house...Racial garbage that attacks the skins is acceptable to the good Milwaukee *Burghers*, but strong Aryan fighters should be driven from the town...We support the Skinheads. They are proven warriors" (*The Talon*, ADL archives). Both police and media response to racist skinheadism should therefore, ideally, be carefully calibrated. Unfortunately, measured and coordinated and communally broad-based opposition to racist skinheads is difficult to sustain. The other side of the media coin of exposure is legitimization or even glorification. Police overreaction or constitutionally questionable reaction could ultimately shift focus from the racist skinheads' folly to authoritarian ineptitude. Tom Metzger was pleased to allege that police coverage for Aryan Woodstock cost perhaps $400,000 ($4,000 per skinhead in attendance, by his calculation) and gloated over the report that police refused to permit his daughter to return to the Aryan Woodstock compound carrying $100 worth of pizza (ADL archives).

When the WAR Music Stops:
The Murder of Mulegeta Seraw

Reports concerning the Aryan Woodstock in both Tom Metzger's *WAR* and on his prerecorded telephone hate-line, and in nationally distributed news articles, saw the event partly in comic terms: Metzger satirized the absurdity of the media, police, and counter-demonstrator response, while newspapers could ridicule the foul-weathered, sparsely attended non-concert by tacitly comparing it to the joyous if muddy gathering of hippie tribes it was intended to emulate. But Metzger's link to the skinheads has not always been so harmless, and Metzger's support and court-confirmed instigation of skinhead violence was cruelly displayed in the skinhead murder of Mulegeta Seraw early in the morning of November 13, 1988. The civil trial that became a positive element of the terrible crime's aftermath also revealed a new and promising weapon in the organized assault upon hate groups.

As I have previously stated, the Anti-Defamation League, the Southern Poverty Law Center, and the Center for Democratic Renewal are three of the more prominent organizations who have monitored crimes committed by skinheads since about 1985, as part of their broader interest in the activities of hate groups in America. They have collected and frequently disseminated to the government and public in various ways documented evidence of violent, often racist, ethnocentric or homophobic crimes committed by skinheads as individuals and as isolated groups during the eighties decade, crimes such as defacing or destroying Jewish property; disturbing rightfully assembled congregations of people; harassing or assaulting blacks, Jews, gays, and ex-skinheads; and murder.

As the skinheads have grown at least slightly each year through the 1980s in number and been targeted increasingly by other guardian organizations as a dangerous hate group, the number of criminal incidents and acts of violence skinheads have been reported committing has also risen annually, far more dramatically than their membership. The violence performed collectively by skinheads was more and more publicized in local and national news reports through the 1980s. However, no single incident of violence captivated as much national interest as the celebrated scuffle on Geraldo Rivera's show, or outbursts during Oprah Winfrey's investigation of skinheadism, both shortly to be discussed. Even subcelebrity Morton Downey Jr.'s alleged assault by chimerical skinheads received more national exposure than most hostile acts by various local skinheads or groups. A great number of Americans are apparently still more intrigued with skinheads on the level of entertainment than as an actual danger to society, or as a symptom of dysfunction or sickness in American life.

The brutal murder of Seraw, a 27-year-old Ethiopian, received more extended attention than most skinhead crimes for a variety of reasons. Seraw's age was invariably mentioned in news releases about his death and its aftermath though his occupation (he drove a shuttle bus for Avis Rent-A-Car) was not. Apparently his youth made his killing seem more tragic or newsworthy than his bland, unglamorous occupation in one of those common jobs that fills up the spaces of American life while remaining absolutely indistinctive (there have been sitcoms and movies about the lives of cab drivers but not shuttle bus operators). He was black and his murderers white, but he was exotically enough Ethiopian (which may have suggested to some he was an escapee from civil war and starvation) in Portland, odd habitat for an African. At least one of his killers was an all-American boy, a high school homecoming king, and the city of his death was distant and arcane to many Americans who however may have thought of it—when they thought of it at all, and Portland is not a city of the imagination like New Orleans or San

Francisco—as itself a candidate for all-American status. Was it not swept by bay breezes and ocean winds?

Actually, the predominately white city was experiencing a period of unrest and a rise in racial crimes. The *Klanwatch* (February 1989) noted that four skinhead gangs operated in Portland, where police in 1988 attributed at least 40 serious crimes to skinheads, including 30 major assaults. Skinheads had first appeared on Portland's punk scene in 1982, but according to local reporter Christopher Phelps (6), "the characteristic skinhead style and ideology" of white supremacy did not become apparent until 1984, the same year Robert Mathews, who founded The Order, escaped the FBI from a Portland motel room prior to his immolation in Washington state. Typically, the punk scene itself prior to the emergence of organized skinhead groups from it, possessed its own violent, racist elements. One of the early hardcore punk bands in Portland called Lockjaw had a guitarist who Phelps says "idolized mass murderers like Ted Bundy, penned racist lyrics and cultivated contacts with prominent white supremacists like Richard Butler's Aryan Nations in Idaho."[2] In 1986, however, some 50 skinheads with homestyle arms (knives, baseball bats) attacked a concert featuring three leftist punk bands.

Seraw's three killers were also young: Kyle Brewster was 19 and Steven Strasser 20. The parents of one of the murderers were well-to-do property owners, the father a lawyer and the mother a businesswoman. Ken Mieske, the 23-year-old who was chief among Seraw's assailants, was also known as "Ken Death." His life and manner made him weirdly notorious, evilly glamorous, like Ted Bundy or Gary Gilmore. Mieske had even starred in the three-minute movie "Ken Death Gets Out Of Jail," made by local filmmaker Gus Van Sant, who would soon become nationally known for directing teen idol Matt Dillon in the acclaimed *Drugstore Cowboy*, itself a sometimes violent, mordant, quirkily funny movie about young addicts who steal drugs. The film was adapted from an unpublished novel by a jailed, habitual, life-long criminal. Mieske's story is the variety that becomes more terrible and fascinating and culturally revealing the more it and its spinoffs are pursued. His crazy life reveals a crazy world (see Redden 1-7). He acquired the name Mieske when his birth mother's best friend, Sharon Mieske, adopted him after his mother abandoned him as a very young child. His father was according to Mieske "screwed up and long gone." Mieske lived on the streets of Seattle much like the real children and young people in Martin Bell's 1984 documentary shot in Seattle, *Streetwise*. Raised vagrantly and often in trouble with the police for theft and cocaine possession, Mieske learned some but certainly not all of his racism during an eight-month jail term from followers of Tom Metzger, whose conceptual seeds sometimes fell on previously fallow ground in the area's jails. Mieske seemed like a sick soul waiting for someone like Metzger to direct his pathologies. Hooked already on death-metal and hate-metal music—among his favorites were MegaDeath, Slayer, and an anti-gay group called Machine—he was for a brief time lead singer in a heavy metal band that featured racist lyrics. He was primed for the violent, racist skinhead scene he entered so easily. He belonged.

Dave Mazzella had been early in his career as an extremist a member of the Pennsylvania-based Warskins. His marriage, officiated by a former Klan leader, recently granted him some notoriety back East.[3] Mazzella, more recently Vice President of John Metzger's California centered Aryan Youth Movement, became friendly with Mieske/Death while acting as a roving skinhead ambassador sent to Portland by the Metzgers. Mieske had written in "A Skinhead's Song":

> Victims all around me
> I feel nothing but hate
> Bashing their brains in
> Is my only trade
> Senseless violence is the only thing I know....

Mieske was Mazzella's man. About 1:30 a.m. Sunday morning, November 13, 1988, Mulegeta Seraw was dropped off in front of his apartment by two Ethiopian friends. He was saying goodbye to them when Mieske, Brewster, and Strasser—all members of Portland's East Side White Pride gang—began yelling at them and then assaulted them. Seraw's friends were able to run away but the battered Seraw himself was trapped and savagely beaten and killed, while girlfriends of the skinheads watched with apparent approval. His skull was cracked so hard with a baseball bat that the bat split. All three assailants pleaded guilty and their trials were brief and perfunctory. Mieske received a 20-years-to-life sentence, Strasser 9 years to 20, and Brewster 10 years to 20. Seraw's murder and his assailants' arrests did nothing immediately to slow down skinhead activity in Portland. In just one month following the crime, according to *Klanwatch* (February, 1989), "Skinheads were implicated in 13 crimes in Portland, including robbery at gunpoint, assaults, and car break-ins."

The Southern Poverty Law Center together with the Anti-Defamation League successfully instituted a $12.2 million lawsuit in 1990 accusing Tom and John Metzger of inciting Mieske, Strasser and Brewster to murder Seraw. At this trial Seraw was shown to be also a student at Portland Community College who had dreamed of a better life in America than he had ever known in his homeland, a "gentle man" who "when he knocked someone down while playing" soccer, "would always stop to pick them up" (*Klanwatch*, November 1990). Prior to the trial, Morris Dees, Executive Director of the SPLC, noted that "the evidence will show Seraw's death resulted from Tom and John Metzger's efforts to win impressionable, young converts to WAR and its white supremacist cause" (*Klanwatch*, January 1990). The lawsuit stated that the Metzgers "established communications in 1988 with members of East Side White Pride" and "that John Metzger—acting on behalf of WAR and his father—contacted the East Side White Pride and sent agents to Portland to organize the Skinheads in pursuing the policies of WAR."

The agents were skinheads Dave Mazzella (who became a key witness for the prosecution) and Mike Barrett. Further, "WAR provided the members of East Side White Pride with racist materials that incited violence against blacks and Jews" and "specifically encouraged the Skinheads to use baseball bats, steel-toed boots, and other weapons [that Mazzella had brought with him]. At a meeting [the evening] prior to Seraw's death, the agents of WAR encouraged members of East Side White Pride to commit violent acts against blacks and others to promote white supremacy." Evidence against the Metzgers was plentiful. John Metzger sent a letter to Mieske introducing Dave Mazzella to him and saying that Mazzella would teach him what the Metzgers wanted him to know and would show him "how we operate." Mazzella was able to report back to his leaders that his very first night in Portland he had beaten a black man while Mieske and a skinhead friend watched. Mieske's first telephone call after his arrest was to Tom Metzger, who taped in turn a telephone hate message praising Seraw's killers for having "done a civic duty."

Morris Dees was able to reveal a great deal of damaging information about the Metzgers in presenting the suit against them, including a videotape of Tom Metzger training skinheads in weapons usage and the previously mentioned details of how he used funds sent to WAR for his own private needs. The trial itself was a dramatic revelation. Dees is perhaps never eloquent but ever steady, never wavering, never intimidated, always boring in like a precisely driven drill through the Metzgers' attempts at defense (claiming poverty and harassment, the two had only themselves as lawyers, and at least once in a masturbatory dialogue, Tom Metzger asked questions of himself in the witness stand). Dees embodied the implacable power of truth as he piled up damning bits and chunks of evidence the team of watchdog forces undergirding him had accumulated, until the Metzgers were submerged in an avalanche of testimony.

The trial judge, Ancer L. Haggerty, was African American—one of two the state of Oregon could provide. Dees showed Tom Metzger a cartoon depicting a stereotypical black man challenging a well-drawn skinhead to "skin my motherfucking ass." In the next panel the skinhead is portrayed doing just that—skinning the black man. Dees asked Metzger if this cartoon appeared in Metzger's *WAR*, and Metzger smiled. Judge Ancer simply twitched his head up and looked over toward Metzger for a clear half a heartbeat of time. The effect of the tableau is devastating.

Tom Metzger was often directly combative toward Dees, biting and sarcastic. His defense was often an offense. He contended that Mieske's trial was a legal hanging, that if Mieske and his friends had been black, the trial "never would have happened." He claimed that some African Americans themselves felt as he did (about supposedly lazy or criminal blacks, for example), that his venomous remarks only addressed those blacks who deserved his attacks, not necessarily all blacks. Once he looked at Dees and sneered "some of my worst enemies are white people," paused like a comedian for effect, then added "like you." Dees simply ignored him. Tom Metzger has a definite though definitely warped sense of humor, but his pronouncement after the verdict against him and his son was rendered, that "we will put blood on the streets like you've never seen" (*Klanwatch*, June 1991) shows his stone coldness at heart.

John Metzger's typical strategy was to look neat and try to side-step, duck, deny, wheedle out of, shrug off, reformulate incoherently, waffle around, slither away from, swallow and reduce to a gluey pulp the sharply pointed accusations Dees targeted at him that hit dead center time and again. Dees must have felt that he was slapping liquid mercury or pounding dough, but ultimately he contained Tom Metzger's son to the shape he wanted, that of a guilty bigot with perhaps as much violence and hate in him as his father.

The combined forces arrayed against the Metzgers in their trial functioned impressively. The Southern Poverty Law Center has been particularly successful in past cases in obtaining financial reparations from hate organizations it has proven in court were responsible for violent actions. The strategy seems effective in dismantling specific hate groups. A local Klan organization in Alabama was bankrupted when forced to comply with a legal judgment ordering it to pay reparations in a case involving the lynching of a young black man. In fact, Klan property had to be deeded to the mother of the Klan victim in an ironic maneuver to satisfy the court's judgment. This kind of legal action should be very damaging to the Metzgers' attempt to attract future skinhead "front-line warriors" since it appears to have destroyed the financial base from which they operate. Whether successful prosecution will "help bring about a marked reduction in racist violence committed by Skinheads," as the SPLC suggests, is problematic though certainly worth the effort. The extent of the Metzgers' real influence among skinhead groups is difficult to gauge. Tom Metzger seems less a center of force or inspiration away from the Pacific coast, though his *WAR* publication does receive fairly wide distribution. But there is little he can offer skinheads in Florida or New York, for example, in terms of direct aid or help in organization. What Metzger appears to provide ordinary skinheads, beyond the twisted arguments a publication such as *WAR* can supply with which to persuade or win over the unenlightened, is a sense of mission and focus. Like would-be skinhead organizers such as various Klan groups, or Richard Butler, it is possible that someone outside such as Tom Metzger could help establish an increased and more intensely targeted political identity among individual skinheads and the groups or gangs they develop locally among themselves.

Hate Against Hate: Skinheads Against Skinheads

All too clearly, hostility is an element of skinhead style, an attitude skinheads have seemed determined to project, through their dress and behavior since their early days in America at musical events. The skinhead look is a hostile look, the skinhead manner a hostile manner. Skinhead music is not a music of love or beauty or environmental harmony but a music of hostility. Skinhead dancing inevitably leads to hostile interaction unless others totally avoid it, which itself is a response to feared hostility. Someone like Metzger might be able to direct the flow of this hostility and perhaps adjust its force for greater or lesser power depending upon strategic needs, the way the spray from a simple garden hose can be directed in a concentrated jet or diffused mist. But neither the Metzgers nor Richard Butler nor the Klan developed—though they might nurture—the hostility and violence within individual skinheads.

Nor does a national leader or extremist organization seem necessary to develop local skinhead groups into more militant, racist warriors. In Milwaukee the loose congregation of largely non-racist skinheads known as SHAM, meaning simply Skinheads Around Milwaukee, was turned in 1988 into the more aggressive and clearly racist Skinhead Army of Milwaukee largely through the leadership of young Pat O'Malley, one-time member of a band called " 'One Way'…. The Right Way…The White Way." Police alleged that the charismatic O'Malley instituted plans to escalate the random violence skinheads had previously been associated with in the city, and to direct it more against racial enemies. I have already noted that with the help of a young woman named Jane Rhodes, O'Malley had letters sent to other groups in the region, for example in Kenosha, Wisconsin, in an attempt to link SHAM to a "network of Midwest skin groups called the Northern Hammer Skins" (Romenesko 3-7).

After SHAM goose-stepped at a Milwaukee ethnic street festival, precipitating a fight, SHAM gained increased notoriety. A newspaper printed a map to the house where O'Malley, Rhodes, and SHAM members hung out, sometimes reading skinhead literature and drinking a cheap local beer called Huber which they termed "skinhead war beer." The Brew City Skins, who identified themselves as anti-Nazi skinheads, circled the house in a car shouting epithets such as "Nazi fags!" but elicited no response from SHAM members inside. On July 14, a car with Hispanics in it allegedly fired at SHAM's house and SHAM returned their fire. O'Malley now set up a firing range where his Skinhead Army could practice. People in other cars supposedly hassled SHAM members in their house and threw bottles and refuse on their lawn. One of these cars was fired upon from inside the house and a passenger hit by a bullet. O'Malley and some others were arrested.

The interlude demonstrates that local leadership can greatly change the nature of the skinhead scene within a community without much recourse to personal intervention from larger extremist groups, that skinheads themselves sometimes oppose the racism of skinheads, but that this opposition itself can reveal unwise, confrontational aggression and ("Nazi fags"!) anti-social hostilities. Anti-racist skinheads often speak of "fighting" white power skinheads, and their strategy frequently includes street brawling. "We are violent," one member of The Baldies, a skinhead gang with black, Latino, and Asian skinheads, "proudly" told a reporter interviewing him at an anti-racist skinhead gathering. "We believe in direct action" (*Tampa Tribune*, 15 January, 1989). And although many of the anti-racist skins are sincerely opposed to white power ideologies—newspapers for example reported a sprinkling of black skinheads at the January 1989 meeting of non-racist skinheads in Minneapolis—the deeper feelings of some are suspect and sometimes blatantly racist. Dennis Criner, one of several supposedly anti-racist skinheads interviewed in the *Omaha World Herald* January 8, 1989, told a reporter "Everyone should think their race is the best. If you don't think your race is supreme, you're scum." Another demonstrated his supposed lack of prejudice by declaring, "I'd give a black or Hispanic a chance to gain my respect...I don't really feel so much superior. I just feel like whites genetically have more intelligence than others." Frequently relying on force to combat racist brethren they may thus resemble, making themselves another vigilante organization seeking to impose social judgments from outside the law, the various anti-racist skinheads however often seem sincere in their disavowal of racist skinheads' ideology.

The advice a group circulated in 1988 on a leaflet in Minneapolis is sound: "Don't become a Clockwork Skinhead....Learn to think for yourself" (ADL archives). Sometimes bands the skinheads like, but who do not admire the skinheads' racism, speak up. The lead singer of Murphy's Law, a hardcore band, introduced the group's set March 17, 1990, at Jannus Landing, a new music performance space in St. Petersburg, Florida, by declaring, "We wanna celebrate all you skinheads out there, the American ones, not the Nazi ones. We fought a war: we fought the Nazis and we beat 'em. We did it for a reason. Don't forget it!" But another leaflet distributed by SCAR (Skins Committed

Against Racism—the violent acronym is itself revealing of the non-racist skinhead stance) at the January 14-15, 1989 meeting in Minneapolis of anti-racist skins demonstrates both their good intentions and shaky attitudes—belligerent, historically idealistic, and mannicheeistic: under a drawing of black and white hands shaking each other is the message, "Now we're starting to fight back in the media and on the streets. The line has been clearly drawn, you are either a sucker for the racist scum or you are true to what being a skinhead is all about: the racial harmony of Ska, the working class solidarity of Oi! and the scene unity of Hardcore."

Some media accounts about anti-racist skinheads are misleading, such as the CNN News feature aired several times May 22, 1992. CNN reported the good news that a racist skinhead had quit his gang to join anti-racist SHARP (Skinheads Against Racial Prejudice). But CNN failed to add that SHARP itself had a history of violence fighting against racist skinheads. Following the 1988 murder of Mulegeta Seraw, battles between SHARP members and various racist skinhead factions were frequent as SHARP angrily tried to crush the racists they claimed had corrupted the originally non-racist skinhead culture (historically, a questionable assertion) and the racist groups fought to maintain their power, protect themselves, and as usual eliminate their enemies (*Klanwatch*, "Violence Among Rival Skins Turns Deadly," December 1990, 7-8).

In April 1990, The Portland Anti-Racist Action, the Coalition for Human Dignity, and the Center for Democratic Renewal convened a conference of "young people including skinheads, punks, whites, blacks, Latinos, and Asian-Americans...to learn from each other and build an anti-racist youth movement" (*Monitor*, May 1990 3). Members from SHARP attended, including at least one black skinhead. This meeting was a praiseworthy attempt at mediation that laid plans for future enterprises to defeat the strongly entrenched bigotry poisoning life for so many in the region. But the disparate groups attending it could not be expected to defeat the social virulence the racist skinheads represented to them overnight, particularly when some of the anti-racists were violent and intensely anti-social themselves.

Fights between racist and SHARP skinheads continued and possibly escalated in the next months with each group claiming publicly,

according to *Klanwatch*, that they used "violence only in self defense."
Yet both groups "demonstrated an eagerness to do battle." Some of the
non-racist skins also saw the police as their enemies, and in May 1990,
police who were attempting "to arrest SHARP skins during a gang fight
were struck with rocks, bottles, and pieces of pipe." In California,
SHARP and racist skins also clashed frequently and sometimes
murderously. Certainly the racist skins were not generally innocent of
originating these beer-hall confrontations, but neither were the anti-racist
skins always guiltless. One Anti-Racist Action skinhead admitted after a
rock concert fight in Petaluma, California that took police an hour to
stop, that "we indirectly antagonized them." The Southern Poverty Law
Center has concluded that while "many anti-racist Skins are genuinely
opposed to violence and have worked to change the Skinhead image
through nonviolent means...the primary distinction between racist Skins
and anti-racist Skins is one of ideology, not tactics" (*Klanwatch*,
December 1990). And in Portland, police claim that by the middle of
1991, racist skinheads were "stronger and better organized" and better
armed than they were when Mulegeta Seraw was killed—and more
politically oriented (*Klanwatch*, August, 1991).

Skinheads at Home

The activities of anti-racist skinheads underscore the paradoxical
complexity and simplicity of the skinhead scene which was in the 1980s
distinguished by uniformity of appearance and taste in music, a
willingness to commit or to accommodate violence, highly limited in age
range, and actively identified its own society as outside or even counter
to what it perceived as mainstream America. And yet within the scene
are adherents of racist ideologies, those who wish to fight this racism,
and (decreasingly) those who are apolitical, who attach themselves to the
scene because of its excitement and the energy of its music, who are
intrigued by its dangerous behavior, but who wish only to skirt the
fringes of its wildness. Many skinheads are school drop-outs or students
who somehow stagger through the public school system, some (who
seem fewer in number) compartmentalize their lives, appear on the scene
weekends but do their homework nightly and succeed at school. They
may ultimately attend college where almost invariably they apparently
are no longer skinheads though they may return to the skinhead scene
periodically for its music and vitality at concerts.

In San Diego there was Mike, whose father was a fundamentalist preacher adamantly opposed to abortion at least for whites. Mike became a War Skin (allied with John Metzger's Aryan Youth Movement and San Francisco's American Front) only after passing a series of interviews and a polygraph test. Then if he wanted to continue as a War Skin he would have to agree with the group's strongly avowed stand against drug use, particularly crystal meth (popular among other area skins). In San Diego there was also Anthony, a Boot Boy kicked out of the War Skins for drug use after he failed a urine test, who has trouble finishing sentences, whose father, a fisherman, was away from home frequently; Sheri, a "baldie," a "wannabe" (want-to-be), who says she is into white pride, not white power, who is "living in America and I'm white and I'm glad" (San Diego newspaper article written probably late 1988-early 1989 by Brae Canlen, in ADL archives).

Around Clearwater Dean McKee and his brother Scott lived, before Dean was convicted of murder in 1988 and sent to jail—where he was moved around a good bit because he was so young, and because his life could have been in danger from black prisoners who might know his conviction was for a racial killing. Dean and Scott's maternal grandmother was from a very good Southern family, a lovely woman who moved to Florida after her trial for shooting to death her unfaithful husband, according to Dean's mother. The grandmother drank too much and when Dean's mother was very young police took the child away. Until she married young, she lived mostly in a great number of foster homes where sometimes she was abused. Dean and Scott did not know their biological father very well because their mother left him when they were virtual infants: he was unreliable, a drug and alcohol abuser, she said. They knew him best when he came back to the Clearwater-St. Petersburg area to die of cancer.

By that time their mother was married to an older man, and for a time the boys seemed to have a stable, fairly well-to-do middle class suburban home, and they did things as a family like participating in bike rallies, where Dean especially was very successful. But at the outset of adolescence the boys began getting into a lot of trouble, Dean in particular. After a while it was clear to their stepfather (who had adopted them) that the boys were out of control, but neither his authority nor the inadequate resources of the community could prevent the boys, still in their early teens, Dean two years the younger, from "acting out"—the common counselling term for their destructive and self-destructive behavior, their truancy, drug and alcohol ingestion, their fighting, their crazy acts of rebellion like Scott's execution by hanging of a favorite stuffed animal. Dean seemed suicidal. The parents' marriage shreaded around this time with the usual charges and countercharges of an acrimonious couple who were in concert at least in thinking the boys were heading along a dangerous route, though not always in agreement about what to do to get them headed again in an acceptable direction.

Both boys loved the crazy local new music scene and were notorious in it for their wild humor, drunkenness, and violence. Scott became a skinhead following a trip he made to the Los Angeles area in the mid 1980s, and Dean, who worshiped him, followed soon after though he had previously claimed to his mother that he did not like their kind of music. They bounced back and forth from one parent to another, Dean always a little weirder, less in control, a sadder case than Scott. In June 1987, Dean at 15 was featured in two newspaper articles about skinheads, claiming he had been a skin since he was 13 (*St. Petersburg Times*, 21 June 1987, 1B; *Clearwater Sun*, 22 June 1987 1A). His depiction as a skinhead lout identified his white supremacist views (which his mother said he had never possessed growing up: one of his earliest friends had been a little black boy). Scott and Dean were members of a loose gathering of skinheads from the region known as the Saints. The brothers loved the punk and post punk crazy concerts, though they often fought at them and broke at least one of them up. In December 1987, on a night when they were both murderously drunk, they beat up a black man, and eventually Dean, his hair grown out so he would look less menacing to his jury, was sent to jail for 25 years minimum for his apparently primary role in the victim's death. Scott, who plea-bargained, was in jail only briefly, in time to be charged by an angry father for impairing the morals of an under-age girl after his release. He also no longer shaved his hair.[4]

In Tampa there was Ray, who lived with his parents in a lovely suburban home on a quiet subdivision street where almost all the homes have pools. His house is filled with books, many of them popular histories and biographies. His living room (or his parents' living room) possesses a small, neatly stocked bar and a good compact disc player. When Ray was a skinhead many of his suburban friends were skinheads too. This was several years ago, when the scene was not quite so violent and less political, or not so greatly publicized as violent and political. He knew the Saints, the only skinhead gang in the Tampa Bay area (not including Orlando) cohesive enough to have a name, though they possessed no real organization. Dean McKee from the Saints had helped him at a concert once to kick the shit out of a guy who had pinched his girlfriend's ass, but he didn't like to be too close to Dean for too long a time—he was too crazy, too violent. Ray didn't like a lot of "niggers"; for one thing he didn't like their lapping up so much welfare money. He said he had seen in Mississippi once "a Negro lady" buy about $60 worth of groceries and pay for them with food stamps he knew very well he could never get, and then purchase a six-pack of beer with a hundred dollar bill. He'd started *Mein Kampf* but found it incredibly dull and boring. He also read *The Rise and Fall of the Third Reich* and that was much more interesting and he thought, accurate. He didn't buy any of that Hitler final solution crap he heard some of the racists around spouting. He had no use for Hitler. He didn't know "hardly any Jews" so he couldn't subscribe to the anti-Semitism he knew some skinheads stood for: "It was a tragedy what happened to the Jews." Homosexuals were another matter. One had once put the make on him when he was doing yard work for the man, and he didn't like that, so he'd later egged the guy's house and thrown fertilizer at it. He still liked some of the music the skinheads liked, but he stopped shaving his head after he discovered a few things about himself, that he was destroying his life fooling around as he was, and that he could be his own person without dressing wild or acting crazy, without having to shave his hair, or letting it grow down to his shoulders.

Ray "left rock 'n roll," he says, around the time when he was 13 or 14. His father had been regular army for over 20 years so his family moved around a good bit, every three years or so, until they came to Tampa. When Ray was quite small, four or five maybe, they had lived overseas in Germany, but he remembered little of that. Toward the end of his father's army career and coinciding with his own developing adolescence, Ray's mother began dying of cancer. Her sickness shocked him. It seemed as if one moment she was fine and then as though one evening he came home and she was wasted. He remembered his father not being around a great deal of the time, and that he was no disciplinarian. That was the time Ray's life exploded. He felt the classic symptoms of a child who is losing his parent for whatever reason, anger and confusion. He had listened to bands like Flock of Seagulls but then moved into punk and heard JFA (Jody Foster's Army), Agnostic Front, Triple X Girls—a local Tampa group comprised of four men affecting lipstick, rouge, and eye make-up on stage—Belching Penguins, and Jehovah's Sicknesses, the band that shot out Nazi salutes before they played. As his mother was dying and then afterward, he became he said angrier and more confused. Then one day he shaved his hair and was recognized at concerts as a skinhead. He was never a Saint, but he knew the Saints and sided with Saints sometimes when they punched out people. They accepted him—he said he needed acceptance almost more than anything else then—and they provided a scene that permitted him to release his anger. There were not too many skinheads in Tampa then, maybe only 20, and he says they were not "totally rowdy" then, though they did get into a lot of fights and beat up people, they drank a lot of beer and got drunk a lot, and yes they did do drugs, cheap stuff, a lot of glue sniffing. The feeling the skins exuded was "We are invincible!"

Ray's father was annoyed the first time he saw Ray had shaved his head, but not appalled, because he realized the act was designed in part to irritate him and fit into a pattern of rebellious behavior. He had so much to worry about concerning Ray that his baldness in itself seemed a minor matter. There were just so many other issues to deal with he could not concentrate on that one. He knew no more of skinheads than he read randomly in the papers, which then did not feature them (around 1985) so much as they would later. He knew they were on the fringes of the punk music scene, and troublesome, but he had no awareness that here, as Ray said, was a bunch of neo-Nazis beating up queers and throwing rocks at niggers while speeding through the public housing projects, here were local school kids rolling drunks. What did shock Ray's father about Ray's skinhead was that it made him resemble the father's wife when she was dying and ravaged by both cancer and chemotherapy. Ray, who was quite thin, greatly resembled her in her final stages approaching death. That was agonizing to his father.

The other skins accepted Ray and gave him a sense of power. The first concert he attended after shaving his hair he spotted an "art fag" dancing in the pit where skagging would soon begin and he walked up to him and said, "Get the fuck out of the way!" right in his face, and the art fag stopped dancing. One of the older skins came up to him and said, "Hey, you're good." And he felt good. In school when he had been an even younger kid he had received good grades and had always been recognized for his superior intelligence. He was obviously very bright and witty. But the older skins made him feel really good when they recognized his confrontation with the art fag. Ray never moved as deeply into the skinhead scene as some of the others whose parents seemed to have lost track of them. But he was definitely a skin. He knew about tricks like luring gays from El Goya, a nightclub in Ybor City for homosexuals, and then beating them up and maybe taking their money, though that wasn't the point of the beating. And he listened to Oi! music and bought Oi! records, English groups mainly though Belching Penguins had an Oi! song they often played. Now, he didn't own any Oi! records. All that stuff got thrown out a few years back, during his rehabilitation.

Is Ray a typical skinhead? It is questionable that any very fully developed profile could provide the outline for a typical skinhead. None seem extremely wealthy—children of millionaires—but some are from affluent families and others from homes where a small pension provides all the family's income. Skinheads themselves work part time, full time at jobs providing adequate income, and don't work at all—just bum about. Many are from broken homes, but so are other American children who don't become skinheads. The so-called broken home or the single parent home are standard working models of family life in our time. Being from one of them is an increasingly common experience. Ray's father knew little of the skinheads but was not precisely thrilled that his son had become one, though his objections were muted since that negative act of his son's was simply another in a long line. That the adolescent was rebelling against his father hardly distinguishes Ray from millions of other adolescents. His mother's death was sharply disturbing to Ray at a critical time of his life, and his response was extreme but hardly extraordinary. His early adolescent years seem very unsettled and perhaps that is something he had more in common with other skinheads than with his former straight friends who simply hung around the new music or punk scene on weekends and during the week did the work and lived the lives they felt they were supposed to, or that they wanted to.

Some parents are more accepting of their childrens' adoption of the skinhead style. Around the period Ray was watching gays being beat up outside El Goya, the father of another local skin was quoted in a local newspaper (*St. Petersburg Times*, 21 June 1987) declaring his lack of interest in the scene which he considered just another teenage fad for which he was in some ways grateful. It meant his son did not bring drugs or beer into his house since he was a skinhead. Another father hearing that his son had said "Homosexuals just make me sick to my stomach," replied, "I don't have any trouble with it [the remark]. I'm not a big fan of gay people."

Some parents claim ignorance of the activities their skinhead children are engaging in. This could reflect the skill and duplicity of skinhead kids in keeping their way of life hidden from parental observation or interference, a tenuous possibility but not one that is totally impossible, given the long history of kids keeping their lives private or of parents not knowing what their offspring are up to. Parental innocence or ignorance is, then, not out of the question. But considering the extremity of skinhead appearance and behavior, it seems more probable that many parents of skinheads (again like parents in general) are practicing denial in maintaining lack of awareness concerning the lives their children lead. Perhaps nearly all parents would be appalled to discover exactly what possible troubles their children were exposing themselves to, but sometimes the stated ignorance of skinhead parents seems disingenuous, a sign of indifference or perhaps, in some few instances, a mask for approval.

In 1987 police arrested members of a skinhead gang in Los Angeles called the Reich Skins, including their leader Michael Casey "Peanut" Martin, an 18-year-old high school dropout. Martin had led the gang in six months of racial terrorism. The middle-class teenage Reich Skins placed Nazi swastikas along three blocks of light poles in their home suburb of Chatsworth and once threatened the family of a Latino boy from a nearby development by wearing weapons and shouting "white power" at his house. Martin kicked open an apartment door and displayed a .380 automatic to aroused neighbors as he and his followers escaped (Caplan 62). The parents of these skinheads were surprised to learn about their actions. "None of the parents of these kids realized what their kids were into," a police officer stated. "They just thought their kids were trying to be cool" (*Los Angeles Times*, 1 November 1987). Newspaper accounts claimed Peanuts "Martin's mother was as astonished by what her son was accused of as the parents of other Reich Skins members and some school officials were." Martin shared a two-bedroom house with his mother. Police discovered in Martin's room "a gang photo album and newsletters" advocating "white supremacy and racial violence." The photo album contained pictures "of young men wearing Nazi armbands, posing in [the] sieg-heil salute." On Martin's walls hung a Confederate flag and next to it the flag of the Federal Republic of (East) Germany. Adjacent to Martin's bed on his nightstand was a copy of *Mein Kampf*, and "another book in the room, *Auschwitz, The True Story*, argues that the Holocaust never took place." Police also confiscated from Martin's room "a 9-millimeter handgun and a .22-caliber rifle, a membership roster and a book that described gang rules, dress and tactics." Since Martin's mother is described as neither totally deaf nor blind, it is difficult to accept—unless her son denied her entrance absolutely to his room and life—her complete surprise at his behavior.

Notes

[1] It is my impression that in the early 1980s, the average age of skinheads was older than it would be later in the decade, but that in the early 1990s the average age again increased.

[2] See Elinor Langer's excellent "The American Neo-Nazi Movement Today," in *The Nation*, July 16/23, 1990, pp. 82-107, for further details surrounding Seraw's murder.

[3] See "Skinheads" by Dan Mayers in *Inside* magazine, Fall 1988, in ADL archives.

[4] Details of this case are discussed in my forthcoming *Skinhead Murder: Another American Tragedy*.

Klansmen and Skinheads march together September 5, 1992, at a racist Labor Day celebration in Gainesville, Georgia. Courtesy of the Southern Poverty Law Center. Photograph by Danny Welch.

Skinheads form a Nazi brigade in this June 13, 1992 march to a confederate memorial in Birmingham, Alabama. Courtesy of the Southern Poverty Law Center. Photograph by Danny Welch.

Aryan Nations Skinheads sing white power songs, January 11, 1992, at the annual celebration of the Ku Klux Klan's birthday at Pulaski, Georgia. Courtesy of the Southern Poverty Law Center. Photograph by Danny Welch

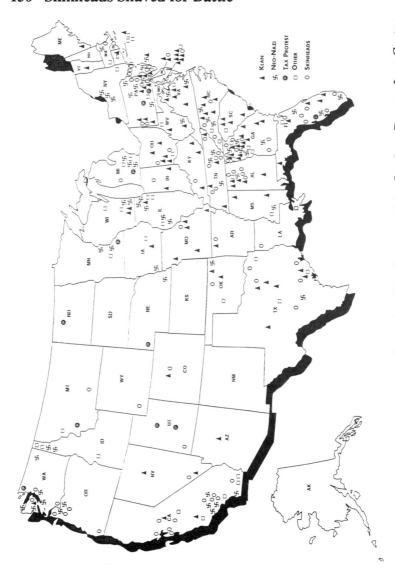

White supremacist group in the United States in 1992. Courtesy of the Southern Poverty Law Center. Map provided by Danny Welch.

Chapter Four
Skinhead Images:
From Hatemongers to Someone to Hug

Though some articles about local skinhead groups from Los Angeles and San Francisco and Washington state to New York City and Atlanta and Orlando and Tampa appeared commonly in local newspapers by 1986, national publicity on the skinhead movement was generally infrequent before 1987 except in watchdog literature and may have peaked in 1989. Therefore it is highly possible that in a nation not known for the all-consuming voraciousness of its television and print news audiences (some read newspapers thoroughly and large numbers watch a great deal of television but many are faintly concerned with news in detail) the general populace might not in those early years have known what it meant for an adolescent boy or girl to be a racist skinhead. By the end of the decade, however, the mass media had presented a clear if not finely drawn portrait of hostile, brawling youth. Occasionally, reporters would offer mitigating circumstances for skinhead violence, but rarely would they be described as vulnerable teenagers worth rescuing.

One of the earliest appearances of skinheads on national television came when Sally Jessie Raphael moved her syndicated talk show from St. Louis to New Haven in mid-June 1987. Teenaged members of extremist organizations such as the Ku Klux Klan and White Aryan Resistance, some skinheads, and a few parents of the participants were questioned about their beliefs. *USA Today* (Roush 4D) reported June 16, 1987 that from 70 to 100 protestors picketed against the extremists and the attention given them on Raphael's show. Those non-extremists who were admitted to the audience sang "We Shall Overcome."

A greater and more publicized confrontation occurred early in February 1988, when, as one headline stated, "Skinheads Disrupt Oprah Winfrey Show" (Persky-Hooper 5 February). Winfrey or her producers had arranged a show featuring skinheads, but no one realized two factions—racist and non-racist (mostly punkers from Chicago)—existed.

151

The two hostile groups constantly interrupted and threatened each other, and Martin Cox, a member of Aryan Youth Movement flown in with four other skinhead "panelists" from San Fernando, California, called a black woman in Winfrey's audience a "monkey." Winfrey replied, "You think because she is black and because I'm black we're monkeys?" and Cox asserted, "It's a proven fact." When he grew angry with another hostile member of the audience and gestured threateningly and cursed, Cox was ejected. His four fellow skins then began chanting Nazi slogans and goose-stepped off the program like Nazis, shooting their right arms out stiffly as though they were stormtroopers on parade.

After the Winfrey furor groups monitoring skinheads began questioning the value of permitting skinheads time for appearances on national or local radio and television shows. Generally these groups recognized skinheads' right of free speech, but wondered, particularly when they were so difficult to control in the studio, if talk show managers in their search for higher ratings clearly realized the difficulties they would face presenting them. Talk show hosts could insist they had the right and responsibility to air variant, even extremist views, and argue that exposing such groups would actually demonstrate their viciousness and irrationality to a wider audience. But the suspicion remained that frequently the motives of those involved with introducing skinheads to the public through mass-media appearances were a mixture of right thinking ("show up the goons for what they are") and show business opportunism ("OK, let's have a show of hands now, how many of you people in the audience agree these guys deserve a right to be heard?"). Hate group leaders claimed increased interest in membership after skinhead appearances on television. Court documents released in the civil trial against the Metzgers showed that WAR deposits increased five hundred per cent in three weeks after the Winfrey show. (*Klanwatch*, December 1990). Tom Metzger was particularly gleeful about the fiasco on Geraldo Rivera's show.

On November 3, 1988, Rivera was taping a future broadcast whose title sounded like a bad drive-in movie, "Teen Hatemongers." Rivera, who prides himself on his aggressive and flamboyant investigative television journalism, would air that same day a previously taped show in which he sparred with a woman prizefighter who knocked him down in their studio fight. In Rivera's audience for the "hatemongers" taping were a number of skinheads and on the stage with him were John

Metzger, two other young extremists, and Roy Innis, black civil rights activist and national chairman of the Congress of Racial Equality. According to Rivera, the suddenly belligerent Metzger called a member of the audience a "kike," and then said to Innis, "I'm sick and tired of Uncle Tom here, sucking up and trying to be a white man" (*New York Times*, 4 November 1989; *National Enquirer*, 17 November 1989). Innis stood from his chair and began choking Metzger—in Rivera's words "put his hands around his neck"—and suddenly skinheads in the audience and others began a wild fight, "hurling chairs, throwing punches and shouting epithets." Innis said later he was "trying to cool things down quickly and end the verbal assault against me. I wanted to avoid a Sharpton-like confrontation." Several months previously, on a Morton Downey, Jr. show discussing Tawanna Brawley's claims that she had been assaulted by white racists including a police officer in New York City, Innis had shoved the Rev. Al Sharpton into his chair, which fell backwards tumbling Sharpton to the floor.

While thrashing about in the battle royale his studio had turned into, Rivera was hit by a chair and punched in the nose possibly from behind. His producer told reporters Rivera's nose had been broken but that he would not go the hospital right away because he had two more shows to tape that day. The melee was widely reported in the national press, usually with tongue-in-cheek possibly because of Rivera's reputation as a newsmonger who exploited sensational stories shamelessly in order to advance his television ratings. The *National Enquirer* published a blow-by-blow account of "Geraldo's Bloody TV Brawl" supplied according to the magazine by Rivera himself. In the *New York Times* Rivera called the skinheads "racist thugs [who] are like roaches who scurry in the light of exposure." In the *Enquirer* he stated, "Sure, I have a broken nose and I'm pretty bruised up. But it's worth it to know we stood up to them."

When he first saw skinheads rushing the stage Rivera says he thought, "I can't let these mindless thugs hurt anybody." But one of Metzger's bodyguards, quite possibly Wyatt Kaldenberg (*Klanwatch*, December 1990), "threw a chair through the air and hit me in the bridge of the nose. Searing pain shot through me as I felt the bone in my nose cave in." An accompanying picture in the *Enquirer* shows Rivera looking like a parody of Jack Nicholson in *Chinatown*, his face criss-crossed with bandages that leave the swaddled, ruddy tip of his nose shining through white tape. He says the blow from the chair made him woozy but then "rage surged through me and I thought, 'These punks are ruining my show and I'm not going to let that happen. Now's the time to fight these Nazi Hoodlums!' "

Rivera tried to rise from the floor where he lay crumpled, but he says Metzger's 200-pound bodyguard fell on him. Somehow, "I managed to fight my way to my feet and we began to rain blows on each other." Rivera's first-person account—if it is his, for the source in which it appeared is notorious for the shoddiness of its reporting—continues for several paragraphs, making his struggle sound like several rounds of Tony Zale against Rocky Graziano, or Dempsey versus Firpo, combined with the heartiest minutes of fabled wrestler Ed "Strangler" Lewis against anybody. The whole squabble, ultimately shown on Rivera's cable program, cheapened as it was by the guffaws implicit in nearly every account of it, remains possibly the single most publicized action involving skinheads in America. Portions of the show cropped up as an image of sensationalized, commercialized news-making in Steven Seagal's popular 1990 film *Hard to Kill*. Even the *Enquirer* seemed to sense the odiousness of Rivera's farcical Laurel and Hardy pie fight against his skinhead antagonists. As bottom-of-the-page filler underneath the account assembled by three of their reporters they printed the accidentally relevant, didactic message, "It ain't how much book learning you've stuffed in your head that counts. What does count is how you use all the stuff you've stuffed."

In *WAR*, Tom Metzger attempted to manipulate the affair into a victory of brave skinheads by focusing on Rivera as essentially ridiculous. Metzger offers a videotape of "Geraldo Brawlers—The True Story," and has published a number of satiric accounts and cartoon depictions about the event underscoring its absurdity. Some of these cartoons may be reprinted from strips appearing in mainstream newspapers, such as (8:2 5) one showing a small boy in front of a television set from which emanate the words "OH YEAH, GERALDO?! WELL, TAKE THIS," followed next panel by a thrown chair that narrowly misses the boy, who in panel three sprawls on his back saying, " 'Reality Television' is definitely getting out of hand!" Another cartoon in *WAR*, by A. Wyatt Moon, whose drawing style and content are usually more like standard obscene or racist underground drawings (one shows a skeletal death anally copulating with a "queer" he is killing), depicts a man sleeping fitfully at the "Betty Boop Clinic" when an apparition appears swathed in bandages like a mummy. "Who are you?" a frightened man asks the fearsome creature, "Freddy from Elm Street?" "No," the figure answers, "It's me, Geraldo Rivera." Had Rivera made the skinheads an object of derision his fight with them might have been an effective form of exposure, but if this was his goal he appears to have failed. He demonstrates the danger of exposing the skinheads to greater public view without the ability to control the form in which they are presented. Similarly, TV harangue show host Morton Downey Jr.'s attempt to implicate skinheads in an alleged attack on him during which a swastika was cut backwards (or drawn by himself, some alleged) on his face, a story that seemed at first even more laughable than Rivera's documented fracas, eventually was viewed as a pitiful attention-grabbing ploy. Such exposure only trivializes the conflict with skinheads.

Jeff Coplon's article in the December 1, 1988 *Rolling Stone* is written sometimes so feverishly in accepted rock 'n roll gonzo style it becomes glib: "Britain's National Front...is what you get when you cross a parliamentary party with a race riot" (54). Tom Metzger's repackaging of antiquated racist lies about Jews is pouring "old whine...into a shinier, sleeker bottle" (58). But his account presents a far better expose of skinheads than either Winfrey's or Rivera's television shows. Focusing on American Front leader Bob Heick, whose commitment to white racism Coplan suggests is symbolized by the 16 tattoos including swastikas and German eagles on his body—"SKINHEADS" is imprinted on his chest and inside his lips—the article recaptures the evil the skins sometimes project that Coplan remarks is "all the more evil for its surface normality, for the illusion that here is a bunch of kids like any other. They like to drink, they like to dance—and they'd like to deport or exterminate the non-Aryan half of this country" (56).

Some of the pictures accompanying this article, however, depict Heick and his friends as clowns posing stupidly and grimacing foolishly in crypto-Nazi regalia. One full-page photograph of Heick posed before a racist flag and sneering bug-eyed while apparently trying to show the SKINHEAD tattooed inside his mouth turns him into a ridiculous lout or class dork. The banality of evil can be ludicrous and laughable as the naked emperor, but the violence Heick represents and has committed is not simply the work of some young, good old boy prankster. The smaller and less dramatically posed photographs of Dave Mazzella displaying a White Aryan Resistance tattoo on his back and sieg heiling with three other Nazi skinheads are more chilling. The dumbass picture of Heick, however, is the image that has been most reprinted and displayed in other periodicals.

Generally the article treats skinheads as an increasing and definite threat to civil harmony in the United States, noting their numerical growth to possibly 3500 according to a Center for Democratic Renewal estimate (56). Heick's love of violence is made clear by his own description of the "bitchin' summer" of 1985 when he and some other skinheads emerged as a brawling street gang in the Haight-Ashbury section of San Francisco that was once an Oz of Peace and Love land, then became by turns a druggie's paradise and nightmare, then a "mellow model of gentrification" (65) that suddenly the skinheads seemed to take over, carving swastikas "on patches of pink sidewalk" and "punching out longhairs and interracial couples." It was like shooting fish in a barrel for Heick and his skins, "a big party. And any time anyone gave us any lip, we just bashed 'em." Or so he claims.

The article also relates some debatable myths about skinheads, elements of their social history that are often repeated as gospel but that need further verification or qualification: that they originally in England mixed freely and amiably with West Indian black "rude boys" (92); that they mostly come from broken homes and were abused as children (56); they are "creatures of a Burger King economy with no room at the top" in Coplon's trendy phrase echoing CDR's Leonard Zeskind's more simple, "They're the first generation of white kids who don't expect to live better than their parents." This idea was probably most eloquently stated by Christopher Phelps in his *Portland Alliance* article (6) when he claims that the skinhead rebellion in America has been "fueled by...vacuity and despondence of contemporary middle-class life, and an uncertain economy.... Many...hold down dead-end service-sector jobs, and cannot look forward to a significantly better future, given America's declining industrial base." The interesting variety of assertions is compelling, though like similar, earlier contentions by some of the English commentators about the causes of skinhead postures, it glides sometimes a little too easily over its chosen villains. Before the analysis is fully accepted, some questions should be pursued. Is middle class life typically or especially vacuous? Is it uniquely despondent, or more so than non-middle class life? What makes a job— or who makes a job—a dead-end job? How was it that the skinhead scene in America gained some momentum during both good and declining economic times?

Other frequently reprinted claims Coplon reinforces are that the skinheads are products of the age of Ronald Reagan with its reactionary civil rights stand, and that skinheads, like the Nazis before them (or the Japanese or Italians in World War II for that matter, or generally any enemies of America's wars) are cowardly bullies. Coplon concludes a short and accurate history of brutal skinhead crimes by stating that "the typical skinhead victim is unarmed, outnumbered and often defenseless.... Offer some 'bootboys' a fair fight or catch one alone, say people on the street, and they'll scurry as fast as their Doc Martens can carry them." Coplon also quotes a former skinhead turned anti-racist activist who declared, "These guys are for the most part wimps."

Skinheads frequently act as bullies and exploit their numbers to terrorize adversaries who often are virtually defenseless or weaponless. They behave like most boys or men in gangs whether on the street or in pitched warfare in seeking to take advantage whenever possible of their enemy's weaknesses. But there is little evidence to support the notion that they are significantly more cowardly than most men who fight. Some skinheads are very cowardly, some are not. Dean McKee, for example, whose stabbing of Isaiah Walker is mentioned in Coplon's article, often took part with other skinheads in acts of personal violence against other people—as he did the night Walker was killed. But he also engaged in many other brawls one on one, sometimes with older or bigger adversaries. Clearly German or Japanese soldiers in World War II were no more or less cowardly than their Allied counterparts. The myth of the wicked enemy coward is captivating and reassuring, but seems determined, as so many other historical interpretations, by which side writes history. If the message of the myth is we should prepare ourselves to combat this evil force and stand up against it so we will triumph, then the myth may have some value even though the "evil force" may be employing the same myth against us, whom it perceives as we perceive it. If the message is all we have to do is isolate these wimpish scum and squash them, then the myth is dangerous. Coplon tells of a storeowner in Haight-Ashbury who induced his Hell's Angels friends to "approach...the head skinhead—the tallest, meanest wimp of them all"—and order "him to get out of Dodge. Since then they...haven't really hassled anybody." The solution seems like a slightly different version of *Death Wish* or perhaps *Gunfight at the O.K. Corral* with biker Peter Fonda and scruffy Jack Nicholson in the Wyatt Earp and Doc Holliday roles. The shoot-out at high noon is always an engaging cinematic and popular solution, but not necessarily realistic in dealing with a complex, deeply rooted phenomenon such as the skinheads, who are anyway only one of many branches, many manifestations of anti-minority violence and hate in America.

Another branch of the same root, Tom Metzger, is accurately depicted in the article attempting to create links with the skinheads. Like the skins themselves, he is ridiculed (for being bald and thus "a closet skinhead" [58]) but also identified by the comments of hate group monitors as "a vicious hater" who behaves like "a schizophrenic genius.... He could be as gentle as a Sunday School teacher, but the other side is a neo-Nazi who believes he'll overthrow the government. He's a dangerous man" (62). Metzger's doubleness may be an aid to him in attracting converts, as Coplon notes, but also in advocating his "third way" or "third position" which expresses contempt for both communism and capitalism. Coplon also emphasizes that the skinheads are a growing menace whose movement is becoming larger, better organized, more widespread, whose individual groups are more frequently than ever before linking with each other. He claims that half the "core" of John Metzger's AYM is skinhead and that "Three California WAR skin chapters...work directly with WAR. Heick's American Front and [Clark] Martells' CASH [Chicago Area SkinHeads], as well as major gangs in Cincinnati, Detroit and Dallas, are unconditional allies, while Tulsa and Portland are drawing closer" (58). Further, "CASH is now tight with the Detroit Area Skinheads and the Confederate Hammer Skins of Dallas; the Dallas gang is organizing in Wisconsin and has links to Oklahoma City" (94). That skinheadism is becoming more and more political, and that individual skinheads are increasingly aware of their political expectations, is clear.

That skinheads individually and in groups are connecting more and more with extremist hate organizations is also clear. Unquestionably, skinheads do travel. One of Robert Heick's subordinates in American Front may have recruited nearly 20 teenagers during a journey he made to high schools in Newburgh, New York; Terence Georges of Atlanta's Old Glory Skins relocated to Orlando to contact local skins. Chattanooga Area Confederate Hammer Skins are in some fashion aligned with

Memphis Area Skin Heads and the Dallas Confederate Hammer Skins (*Skinheads Target the Schools*; *Klanwatch*, February 1989). Affluent high school students in the suburbs of Detroit have been recruited by skinheads from the city: music is no longer the primary lure in all these attempts to bring new members to the skinhead scene, racism is (Detroit *News*, 5 August 1990 1C). Whether or not the skinhead scene is being transformed into a national movement with tight organization between groups in a network of cities, and whether skinheads en masse are being drawn into national organizations, the way netted fish are drawn up into tanks by fishermen, is more difficult to ascertain. Generalizations about skinhead commitments to links with other skinhead groups are difficult to interpret even (or especially) when made by skinhead leaders or spokesmen, considering the high drop-out and turnover rate in skinhead ranks, and the highly differential degree of meaningful structure among various skinhead clusters. Even within a cluster, since belonging is so often an informal matter, the degree of commitment to specific skinhead political ideals varies greatly.

Coplon does not provide evidence to document all his claims about the institutionalizing of skinheads and skinheadism. His title, "Skinhead Nation," could be an example of moral panic, unjustified as a prediction for the immediate or distant future. There is a rock 'n roll beat to his hip jeremiad that makes its message seem inflated, but his fears sound exactly like those of the established watchdog agencies dedicated to tracking the direction of hate in America.

If Robert Heick is a skinhead for the future, if he is a guide to the path skinheads in larger numbers will take, then organizations such as the Anti-Defamation League are correct in focusing so intently upon the phenomenon. He is violent and racist, politically very committed, and is aware of a need for greater organization among skinheads and between them and other extremist groups. He is relatively articulate and possesses a sardonic sense of humor that coupled with his air of malevolence makes him good newspaper copy, and could enable him to serve as a more physically threatening, primal variation upon smooth John Metzger in his sanitized, surfer's incarnation.

Heick is reminiscent of 1960s dark side counter-culture heroes who seemed willing to commit violence for reform. In one interview he told a reporter, "Yeah. Well, I like the SDS. I thought they were pretty hip. I like the Weathermen. I think the Weathermen were pretty hip" (article in

San Francisco's *Calendar* magazine by Cary Tennis, February 1989, in ADL archives). Ideologically unpredictable, he also expressed support for animal rights, environmental groups, anti-nuclear protesting, and anti-abortion advocates. Heick and his compatriots have also been depicted as "rebels without a cause," with a cause. That is, they have been perceived or presented as sad, attractive embodiments of a more politicized version of James Dean in need of cuddling and saving, the object of adolescent female rescue fantasy.

In the March 1988 *Sassy*, a glossy magazine with many chic advertisements targeted at privileged young females too savvy for *Seventeen* but not quite ready to stalk the singles scene as boldly as *Cosmo* women, skinhead history is related in a more syrupy version than Coplon's account: "A lot of them are poor, and come from broken homes and abusive parents. Many are high school dropouts who can't find work. As working class kids, they've found themselves at the bottom of a capitalist society gone wrong, where all the money is at the top and there's nothing for them to turn to but hate and violence." At some point in her education the journalist who wrote this article had apparently read either in excerpt or resume Karl Marx and Eric Erikson. She had also probably seen *Bonnie and Clyde*. She portrays herself as coyly intimidated at points throughout the interview and seems breathless when rough Bob Heick makes her touch his knife blade (as delighted Faye Dunaway touched Warren Beatty's pistol). Much of her sympathy is directed toward 22-year-old Michael Palasch, who learned his racism when he was 14 and read books such as *The Hoax of the Twentieth Century* which is about the alleged falseness of the Holocaust. She senses "an overwhelming sadness in Michael" who is portrayed as possessing a lonely guy, self-deprecating sense of humor. "Don't write anything positive about us," he tells her, or "you'll get into trouble." In a touching gesture of friendship, perhaps, Michael induces his collie-shepherd pet to stick out his paw in Sieg Heil! fashion for her. "I just want to hug the hate out of" Michael, the writer cries, "hug all the pain he must feel about his mother's death" by cancer according to the story, "about losing his sister" who died in an automobile crash in 1981. The reporter concludes her report with a classy quotation she attributes to Rilke, "Perhaps everything terrible is in its deepest being something helpless that wants help from us" (Gysin 44-49, 102-103).

Skinheads seem to appeal particularly to two kinds of young women, those who share their violence and hostilities, and those who dream softly and hopefully of redeeming them (interviews with young women on skinhead scene, Tampa, 1988-1989). While love or affection should never be eliminated as rehabilitative powers, and while ideally the most abject and terrible should be treated with care, hugging and cuddling have therapeutic limits. The approach to skinheads presented in the *Sassy* article seems like playing the Beatles' "All You Need Is Love" to pacify dangerous animals or sociopaths. Still, the attitude persists at least among a small number of young women—usually teenage girls—who are not themselves skinchicks but who roam on the fringes of skinhead territory. A Tampa Bay area skinhead who does not seem atypical claimed that after he entered the pit for the first time as a skinhead at a punk music concert, some local girls whom he had previously known but who had generally ignored him began squealing delighted cries like "Oh I want to take you home!" (as though he were a bald version of menacing Elvis Presley in his "want to be your Teddy Bear" incarnation). Of course this particular skinhead might be fantasizing, or the young girls whose responses he recollected could have been behaving sarcastically. But the incident was accepted at face value when related to some other skinheads and scene girls.

Certainly not all publications intended primarily for younger audiences presented the skinheads in such a romantic light as *Sassy*. *Read*, "the magazine for reading and English," distributed periodically to public junior high and high school students throughout America, presented a more sober and thoughtful analysis of skinhead violence and hates. Displaying an angry, ugly, unfunny skinhead on its cover, *Read* concludes its unsensational but chilling story with a provocative exploration of whether "people like Tom Metzger and Nazi skinheads should be allowed to present their side of the story through the mass media" ("Our Heads Are Shaved For Battle" 9).

Reports in daily newspapers on local skinhead activities increased considerably during the late 1980s as skinheads became a more common sight in American cities. These reports which typically treated skinheads as violent and dangerous, often included comments from representatives of the non-profit agencies who had by now been recording crimes and other incidents of hate-filled skinhead behavior for several years. Additionally, local newspapers reprinted excerpts from releases distributed by agencies such as the Anti-Defamation League in their own local news items or feature articles about skinheads. Thus, the attitudes and even phrasing of a relatively small number of organizations and experts received broad distribution. By 1987 Nick Knight's book was fairly well known, though the information repeated from it often seemed more second-hand rather than the result of intensive first-hand study. By 1988 few journalists would question Jeff Coplon's use of the term "authoritative" (Coplon 62) to describe Knight's book, though its presentation is unscholarly and its slant highly subjective, at times celebratory and elegiac. That Knight was himself a skinhead when he wrote his book (letter to me from Dick Hebdige, 6 November 1989) or that the scholarly work of Dick Hebdige, Stan Cohen and their British academic colleagues though less accessible was at least an important source of information on the early years of the phenomenon, seemed not at all well known to the American journalists whose depiction of skinheads does not vary greatly. They are violent young boys and young men who hate minorities. "Most had histories of abuse—alcohol, drugs, physical and sexual. They were social and academic washouts," according to a Portland, Oregon juvenile court counselor who had worked with more than a dozen skinheads. "The kids I've seen are real angry, real hostile.... They have a damaged self-image and they receive acceptance from the group. And they receive acceptance for taking out their anger in what we see as a real inappropriate way" (Frolik in ADL archives).

The profile is typical of those sketched in other newspapers in other regions of the country. In Daytona Beach, Florida (*News Journal*, 6 May 1989), skinheads are "middle-class teenagers from single-parent homes. They are likely to be having problems at school, and perhaps with alcohol and drugs. They are likely to be violent." The profile seems valid because it has been so frequently repeated and because it does seem to describe a great number of skinhead youth. Precisely how meaningful it is demands a scrutiny the skinhead phenomenon rarely receives in news articles. The generic characterization "middle class teenager from single parent home who is having problems at school" identifies, for example, a very large number of male (or female) adolescents, only a very small number of whom become skinheads. I have already noted that children with a record of what helping professionals would characterize as some variety of abuse are similarly legion. What proportion of these become skinheads? Very few. Is the profile of skinheads who do *not* end up in court or under police jurisdiction significantly different from those who *do*? Are helping professionals familiar with the family histories of skinheads who do *not* get remanded to them? These are questions thus far uninvestigated by reporters and presumably their sources, that might further illuminate the skinhead scene. One intriguing comment voiced by the mother of an ex-skinhead in Daytona Beach, Florida (*News Journal*, 6 May 1989) describes the skinheads as "tofu kids," because "tofu takes on the flavor of whatever it's cooked with." Her image is arresting. The problem is, so many other children are "cooked" with many of the same "flavors" the skinheads are steeped in, it is difficult to isolate the differentiating ingredients that determine their special identity. An important question is, why *aren't* hundred of thousands of other Americans kids skinheads?

In fact, at the eighties' end, the number of skinheads nationally by most estimates remained very small, at most 3,500, a statistically unimposing figure though one large enough to have accounted for considerable social damage that has received a remarkable amount of publicity. Skinheads and skinhead style seem to have infiltrated the surrounding trendy cultural scene. Doc Marten boots were "The Tops in Town" in New York City according to *New York*'s "Hot Line" (30 January 1989 25). "Skinheads wore them, but these days, the big black shoe is taking a step in more mainstream directions," supposedly because they "are perfect for the slushy days of winter." An "East Village boutique that is popular with skinheads and fashionable downtowners" specialized in "the latest fashion craze" of skinhead costume, "Fred Perry tenniswear, Ben Sherman Oxford shirts, and Dr. Martens boots." The boutique also stocked other popular skinhead apparel such as flight jackets. The actor F. Murray Abraham, "neighborhood skinheads, a lot of college kids and even yuppies come into the store," according to its owner. Even Cher shopped there. The shop's owner describes "most of" the skinheads as "articulate and serious-minded." Pieces of skinhead style were apparently chic. In a widely distributed press release early in 1990, popular singer Sinead O'Connor assured her followers who assumed she was "aggressive and strong and tough" because she was "a woman with short hair and a pair of Doc Marten boots" that she was actually a "good person" with tender feelings (press release in "Quips and Quotes," undated, *Tampa Tribune*, 1990).

In less trendy circles, skinheads were also by decade's end exploited as social misfits in an increasing number of films and television dramas, perhaps because of their greatly threatening image or activities, or because of their immediately identifiable hatefulness. Like characters in bad melodramas, little explication was necessary to advance them as despised deviants. Skinheads are easy enemies. Perhaps they reassure older Americans that this is what the young are really like. In a society that publicly worships youth but allows children to be treated cruelly, skinheads like the wicked devil-spawn of popular films such as *Rosemary's Baby* (1968) and *The Omen* (1976) demonstrate that if the young really are the hope of the future America is in trouble, a thought probably not uncommon to millions of older Americans who have already loathed hippies and long hairs and who are privately sick—in a kind of mass reaction-formation—about their own erosion of power in our almost officially youth-oriented society that openly praises while it sometimes privately decries the "hope of the future." Skinheads were the youth terrors of the eighties. Another explanation for their media popularity might be the shrinking possibilities for group villainy or satire in mass media (roles formerly filled by Indians and Hispanics in Westerns, Italians in crime stories, homosexuals in romantic comedies). They constitute a minority safe to hate, one without an annoying pressure group to back them through protest or legal action. In 1989-1990, Chuck Conners, television's "Rifleman," starred in the frankly titled film *Skinheads, Scourge of the Nation*; and Albert Finney appeared in *The Image* as a network anchorman and investigative reporter working on stories about a possibly innocent black man on death row, a doctor who runs a Medicare con-game, and a gang of skinheads whose leader seems more interested in appearing on television than in racist ideology. David Soul portrayed a white supremacist who leads a group of racist skinheads in *So Proudly We Hail*. "L.A. Law" featured Susan Dey as a recently appointed judge with a docket crammed with cases, the most appalling of which is that of a skinhead accused of racial murder (22 March 1989). *Package*, with Gene Hackman, a Cold War fantasy film about Russian and United States military leaders secretly combining forces to subvert world peace, includes a subplot depicting pro-fascist agitators who use skinheads as enforcers.

In Carl Hiaasen's popular tough guy ex-cop novel *Skin Tight* (1989), skinheads in Miami slam dance to the song "Suck Till You're Sore" and then brawl with a dope-dealing Colombian. On "21 Jump Street" the young, multi-racial undercover police confront their own prejudices while investigating a clash between hate groups and anti-fascist demonstrators that seems to have culminated in a murder. The hate group itself is split between factions, one of which is commanded by a slick, new age David Duke-type leader who opposes old-time Klan violence and masquerading. Here skinheads are presented as hate group "soldiers" or "warriors" only too willing and eager to brawl for white supremacy. Young, violent, tattooed, they whine about not being able to get jobs taken by undesirable mud races, and four of them attack a lone Vietnamese who, however, thrashes them as satisfyingly as Charles Bronson or Clint Eastwood might have, using Bruce Lee's martial arts techniques. Easily urged into battle but lacking discipline (they "will follow anyone who gives them enough beer") the skinheads are depicted as cowardly, lower-middle-class drop-outs stupid enough to complain about missing "Green Acres" on television, and emotionally childish: one skin leader cries in the hospital for his mom. Even the comedy "Cheers" used a joke involving skinheads who were the only friends Sam, the super macho bartender, could find to help him after one of his sleazy misadventures. In what previews hailed as "the most heartwarming comedy of the year," Robert Mitchum as an old homeless vagrant in *A Family for Joe* proved his courage to Home Box Office audiences by standing tall against a band of wild skinheads, showing his gruff commitment toward the very lovable cast of unparented kids who had in desperation selected him as their grandfather to escape foster homes. Skinheads, it seems, were everywhere.

Chapter Five
Skinheads Yesterday, Today & Tomorrow

Publicity about American skinheads increased greatly in the past decade but their growth in numbers has not been similarly impressive. Media interest escalated reflecting the public's view of them as intriguing, fascinating inhabitants of the American scene. They are young, violent, almost bizarre in appearance (it is hard to appear bizarre today when strange is almost a norm), and racist. Skinheads espouse extreme prejudices which can be dramatically and meritoriously attacked. More and more in news stories and entertainment presentations they became targets of anger, a hate group who could make the public feel it was decent to hate, a hard to control force for vicious behavior viewed as bikers once were, when nearly all bikers were lumped together and imaged as Hell's Angels. They seem not yet as occasionally captivating an enemy in the media as the Hell's Angels bikers sometimes became. There has not yet in America been a Marlon Brando or Peter Fonda character to embody compelling maleness within a skinhead or his vulnerable tenderness deep, deep inside.

I have suggested that American reports on skinheads generalized easily from a few English sources about early skinhead history in England, but that a more precise account of the skinhead scene's formation is a trickier job, particularly in establishing the original extent of their racism. Their ties in England to black youth subcultures may have been overstated, at least in terms of implying a general climate of tolerance for blacks as people, separate from occasional friendship with individual, neighborhood blacks or from transitory acceptance of some developing forms of black music. Analysis of skinheadism practiced by those British scholars opposed to the older emphasis upon the deviance of such subcultures seems tinctured by the underlying question, what do these people show us that demonstrates what is wrong with conservative or standard liberal English society? When this occurs the investigations seem almost angrier about the sickness in English life that made the young skinheads rebel against it

166

so, than against the destructive forms the rebellious skinhead way pursued. The longer skinheads remained in the English scene, the less popular this sympathetic attitude grew, as more social analysts began writing about seamier aspects of the style such as drug ingestion, pimping, and tough boy work. Articles such as Ian Walker's 1980 "Skinheads: the Cult of Trouble" described the fascism, racism, and violence that had even early been dominant in skinhead life, without suggesting that these ideals and behaviors were a puritanic young working class response to the morally collapsed, socially callous British political, economic system. Martyn Harris's 1984 "The Doc Martens Angels," portrayed racist skinheads extorting money from tourists around Picadilly Circus or talking about committing random violence like bashing "coons." Their actions seem not only senseless but virtually cut off from environmental causation. A. Burr's 1984 "The Ideologies of Despair," while sympathetically viewing skinheads as children from "disrupted backgrounds" (929) many of whom faced an economically blighted if not hopeless future, mainly focused on them as self-destructive victims of heavy barbiturate usage.

This change could be attributed to a change in the skinhead scene as skinheads no longer lived in neighborhoods where they grew up but concentrated in metropolitan areas where they could congregate more with others of their subculture though not amidst their community roots. They became more ordinarily visible "downtown" and more threatening. Or the shift in critical attitude may have followed the perception that the English skinheads were becoming more closely and formally associated with National Front right wing extremism. Another possibility is that the people viewing the skinheads were changing and were academics and social work professionals not so enamored of the skinheads as snappy, defiant rebels. However, it was the first wave of British commentators along with the ex-skinhead Nick Knight who determined what American commentators passed on as the early history of skinheads.

The skinhead scene was tracked in England fairly early. It was soon big, scrutinized intensely, seemed culturally fascinating. While what was really going on in the scene may have been reported with some distortion, its surface seen at football matches and in the pubs was relatively clear. This would not be so in America. Its beginnings here, when it was finally culturally in place at least a decade after its origination in England, are murky. It seems to have existed on the fringes of the much larger and more culturally attractive (for purposes of observation and analysis anyway) punk scene for a time without establishing a strong sense of cohesive identity. It was like a bad smaller brother no one greatly likes, sometimes tolerated, sometimes cursed, but someone people outside the family do not notice much. Nor could much be found out about this bad brother from those in the family circle he was not central to, that he sometimes rejected or was rejected by. The history of the skinhead scene in America is also murky because the scene is spread out (and how the scene has moved from city to city—or if it moved from city to city in any systematic fashion—is conjectural) just as America is spread out, and because even if the scene were to be examined by region or state or community, a wide range of young men and women of varying social backgrounds and varying degrees of commitment to the scene would be apparent in it. Skinheads in Orlando, Florida, had a reputation for acting in gangs, for traveling to other cities such as Tampa in gangs, looking for trouble. Their constituency seems less middle class than the skinhead scene less than a hundred miles away in Tampa, where suburban kids from expensive homes sometimes shaved their heads and hung around the local skinhead scene and got in fights, but few belonged to anything like an identifiable gang. In Brandon, immediately adjacent to Tampa, for several years the Brandon Boys identified themselves as straight edge skins, inimical to the hard cores in Tampa.

Recognized first from within the punk scene almost as much for their easy to ignite willingness and even desire to engage in violence as by their uniform appearance, the American skinheads' homophobic, anti-Semitic and racist tendencies were early less remarked on as part of their group identity perhaps because these prejudices are so common in America. But by the mid-1980s their brutal extremism became clearly focused upon gays, Jews, Latinos and blacks, and increasingly their attacks upon these groups were observed by American organizations monitoring hate groups. Although many skinhead youths adopted the skinhead identity because of elements of its external style, including its bodily appearance, mode of dress, musical tastes and energetic, aggressive behavior at musical events, in time racist skinhead politics became more codified and some skinhead gangs more organized to carry out attacks against their perceived social and political enemies. Individuals who decided to become skinheads now more clearly were aware of the politics expected of them in the view of the general public and those within the new music scene. By the second half of the 1980s to become or remain a skinhead was ordinarily to be thought a member of a white supremacist group, to be described as such in the media and to be courted by other white supremacists as battle guards for their far more purely political organizations.

Generally, during the 1980s, the number of skinheads increased but not nearly as greatly as the publicity surrounding their activities. More skinhead leaders emerged from the ranks which in the 1970s and very early 1980s had produced few in any politically meaningful sense. Some skinheads during the '80s decade dropped the identifying elements of style because they were tired of automatic hassling by the police or because they weren't themselves as politically committed as the skinheads were becoming in their activities. By political here I do not mean engaging in standard political practices such as registering voters or determining a specific agenda for a variety of local or national issues, but simply acting out or expressing sentiments supporting even a narrow political ideology, in this instance belief in heterosexual white supremacy. Some skinheads dropped away because while they retained their racial prejudices, their biases were not strong enough to justify to themselves extreme physical responses, or, because their racialism was a small part of their own self identity, an element of their character to which they did not desire to commit their lives any more completely. Some skinheads left the scene when they got into trouble with the police, and were jailed for crimes (interviews with skinheads in Tampa, 1988-90). While new young kids were recruited, the skinhead base was constantly eroding: some skinheads simply grew older and drifted away.

Since skinheads are so widely and thinly distributed across the nation, clustering more in the cities of some regions (Georgia, Florida, Texas, Oklahoma, California, for example) than in others (the New England northeast and southern border states), and since in any one local community the degree of commitment to racist skinhead ways and actions varies, it should be no surprise that generalizing about the domestic background of skinheads or even their social demographics would be highly speculative. There are simply too many kinds of young men who are skinheads at some time in their development. Even if the statistical details of all those males who have been skinheads could be tabulated and areas of preponderance established, the childhood or adolescent profile of the typical skinhead would possess only the roughest kind of validity.

Some demographic boundaries may be determined, but their usefulness in establishing who becomes skinheads is limited, and the boundaries may only reflect incomplete information anyway. It seems easier to demark who is not a skinhead. I have observed or seen reports of no really wealthy skinheads, for example, and few with easily visible, significant physical handicaps (for example, the lead singer of Rat Cafeteria, an early skinhead band on the Tampa scene, had a leg brace fitted over his steel-toed boots and walked with a dragging limp). This situation may result from the materially advantaged opportunities for the very wealthy to act out their anti-social aggressions, providing them alternatives inimical to the skinheads' minimalist working class subcultural style, and the perceived diminished mobility or physical prowess in battle of the physically impaired.

High school or college team athletes are extremely rarely (if ever) skinheads. Some shave their heads to symbolize their sense of mission during periods of competition, or to enhance their performance (as swimmers, for example). Black athletes sometimes shave their heads emulating Michael Jordan, and white athletes occasionally emulate this fashion of black athletes. But these players do not identify themselves as skinheads. Though athletes can be racists or homophobes, they typically belong to teams and thus do not require the brotherhood or needed feeling of family the skinhead gang can provide. Most athletes also must be willing to accept discipline from older authority figures like coaches, and such discipline is contrary to skinhead behavior.

Furthermore, as I have already noted, common generalities about the social history of skinheads often hold true for great numbers of non-skinhead youth, that they come from broken homes or single parent homes for example, that they lack a father or a mother. A *Klanwatch Intelligence Report* (February 1992) reported one study by a Texas psychiatrist claiming that of 75 skinheads studied, "only two lived in stable homes with both parents." The idea that skinheads generally emerge from families demonstrating instability (a nebulous concept) seems plausible, but this observation may contain circular elements that weaken its value in determining skinhead causation, since the presence of a skinhead in the family can be viewed as proof of its instability or can greatly intensify family instability. And though many skinheads are the products of families out of control or perversely controlled, filled with alcoholism, infidelity, break-up, lack of affection, lack of cohesion, the standard litany of dysfunction, significant numbers of skinheads stem from single or double-parent families that seem as wholesome and beneficially active as society has any right to expect.

Skinheads who make the news or who reach a psychiatrist's office may constitute a special category of the type, may exhibit the classic outlines of criminally deviant youth in their character and family history, may have experienced in their brief lives an appalling accumulation of familial and social breakdown. Skinhead runaways are runaways after all. They are people who have not connected with the standard systems of achievement, belonging, feeling cared for, being loved, being respected, being accepted, of establishing strong, independent identities in our society. It may be that these systems were withheld from them, were deficient, were unavailable, or it may be that because of their own natures skinheads-to-be were unable to hook on to the systems or grow into being a part of them. They are not cheerleaders but some could have been. They are not class presidents or valedictorians but some could have been. They are not ordinarily homecoming kings but some could have been. One of the boys who murdered Mulegeta Seraw was. Some will reintegrate with their families and will form healthy love relationships. But then they will no longer be skinheads. And it is doubtful that those who were the hardest core skinheads will be among the productive survivors. The more intense and abandoned the thrash dance in the pit, the slimmer are chances of emerging from it unscathed.

The question "Who becomes skinheads?" ordinarily contains within it another unstated question, "What is wrong with these people that they have chosen this recourse?" or "What went wrong in the lives of these people that they have decided to be so ugly and mean?" A more revealing avenue of inquiry might be, "What in the skinhead scene attracts young men (and sometimes young women) to it?" because for some youth—and not just those who become skinheads—it is or seems a powerfully attractive scene on its surface. What is so potent about it?

Clearly those within the skinhead scene feel that it provides them with an immediate, distinct and firm identity, and a sense of belonging to something like an extended family that accepts them. Moreover, the skinhead family usually exists in opposition to other institutions or groups of people. To be a skinhead is to be recognized not only by what you are strongly for, whether it be a variety of music or behavior or race, but to be known for what you are strongly or even violently against.

172 Skinheads Shaved for Battle

Skinheads live in an oppositional world: they seek opposition and this stance can be a lure for adolescents who either naturally or through learned expectations frequently assert themselves through their vigorous opposition to other persons, ideas, and institutions.

Though the skinhead scene or the larger new music youth scene in which it was embedded in the 1970s and 1980s (when skinheads increasingly experienced the resentment of non-skinheads) has its own rules and ways, it is perceived by its inhabitants as an alternative world to that in which parents and conventional grown-ups live, that schools would enforce, that the work world demands adherence to. The skinhead world is perceived by those who inhabit it as freer, more open, less inhibited. In some ways it is (skinheads openly express what some other whites covertly feel) and in some ways it is not. Skinheads have limited social and cultural mobility: only the tribe's ways are acceptable, no attending symphony concerts, no lingering over coffee after an art film. These would be ludicrous, unimaginable activities for a skinhead. But a whole range of more ordinary situations would similarly be forbidden that are standard for the young, like open displays of tenderness, or commitments to conventional, straight world fulfillment. Still, the skinheads are perceived as unrestrained and therefore free, and that grants them, to some youth, further attractiveness.

Although much in the skinhead life apes adulthood (excessive drinking, infidelity) it is also a way of prolonging youth in a society that has viciously truncated it. Leaving or not committing themselves fully to school is irresponsible but it also keeps skinheads off the treadmill into the adult world, endowing those among them who select that route (or fall upon it without volition) a seductive marginality. Not all skinheads are thus irresponsible, but even those on the fringes can share the aura.

The sexual lure of the skinhead scene is a tangled matter. As a sexual image the skinhead seems incredibly old fashioned but this may be its appeal in a society that if it has not yet arrived anywhere near androgyny is in a murky transitional stage at least publicly reevaluating and redesigning its concepts of male and female. Skinheads project an image that travels farther back in conceptual time than moody, virile Heathcliffs and Rochesters, those progenitors of forceful, egotistic virtuosi in perfume ads that half embrace, half rape their swooning, yielding, enamored mistresses. Skinheads are cavemen with clubs. Bludgeoning inferiors and competitive predators is their main business, quick, uninvolved sex a momentary leisure to chuckle over with the other Neanderthals about the fire. The scene seems more parody than act, particularly in its focus upon male bonding. Filmed for television, the skinhead/caveman advertisement could conclude with one brawny comrade swigging his prehistoric, cheap beer and grunting some linguistic equivalent of, "Man, it doesn't get any better than this!" There is glamour in this scene for many, though it may not depict skinhead life documentarily in its day to day reality.

The sad truth is that nearly all the ideas associated with the skinhead mentality are supported by many Americans. Violent skinhead actions are excessive and aberrant, and are doubtless often performed not as a policy implementing their philosophy but simply for the delight in disruption or destruction. As one skinhead told me, "the violence is better than sex." But to the extent that skinheads express an ideology, nearly all individual issues in their tangle of concepts are supported by a significant constituency of non-skinheads. Their ideology is attractive, then, and while their extreme actions may be publicly deplored they may also be covertly applauded. Their deviance resides in the breadth, extremity and intensity of their prejudices, not in most of the individual positions they adhere to in stating their beliefs.

They are hostile to gays, and certainly few would argue that homophobia is rare in the United States. Not long ago homosexuality was listed in the *Diagnostic and Statistical Manual* employed by mental health technicians and clinics in America to diagnose psychiatric disorders. In American cities legal ordinances guaranteeing equal treatment to gays are still hotly debated and often only very gingerly supported by politicians at all levels of governmental operations, when not opposed outright. Homosexual activity is clearly offensive to the armed forces.

Skinheads have frequently stated their objections to our welfare system, a stance shared by countless Americans. Their rhetoric is often obscene, their characterizations of black welfare recipients viciously and venomously racist, but stripped of some stylistic excess maintains a very common attitude: people on welfare are deadbeats, lazy drones. People on welfare are suspect, they are failures who deserve to fail. Stated more neutrally, most people on welfare should not be on welfare. They are harmed by being on welfare. The glee with which some politicians and bureaucrats pounce upon suspected welfare fraud, the long-lived, widely-repeated legend of the welfare recipient who drives to pick up her check in a Cadillac, or the woman who pays for jelly rolls and fatty chops at the checkout counter with food stamps and then purchases cigarettes, beer, and cheap wine with a fifty or hundred dollar bill, attest to a residual animosity toward the concept of welfare in the country that is only thinly masked by many irrational, punitive "workfare" programs.

The American history of racial and ethnic intolerance is too commonly known to need repetition here. While the legally recognized civil rights of minorities have improved greatly during the past two decades, and while opportunities for a decent life have increased for a significant number of African, Latino, and Asian Americans who have made it into the middle class, in the pecking order of so-called races African Americans are still at the bottom and are still considered inferior by equally significant numbers of individuals in the races supposedly above them in that order, including many whites who still maintain that blacks as a race are as the skinheads consider them: lazy, stupid, hypersexual, criminal.

Skinheads have little to say about equal opportunity. They do not appear to attack it greatly, though they must find it repugnant since they do not believe that African Americans are equal intellectually to whites. Perhaps it is to them a laughable idea based upon fraudulent assumptions, but they do not comment upon it strongly and their cartoons and jokes and public utterances do not ordinarily deal with it. And in fact nationally there seems little organized opposition from mainstream sources to equal opportunity, an idea so ingrained in the myth of America if not its reality, that it would be difficult to oppose openly. The idea that individuals in America should be given fair opportunities for advancement socially and economically is firmly bound up with the most basic premises establishing for Americans the characteristic identity of American life. In practice of course millions of Americans have been denied these equal opportunities because of such incidentals or accidentals as skin color, but that has never disturbed the acceptance of the idea as desired goal. The Social Darwinism that so captivated the political and social thought of white Americans in the late nineteenth century and that is still a powerful if unacknowledged myth operating in our own times, that declares certain advanced races more capable of winning the struggle for existence that produces a higher evolution among peoples, also accepts the tenet that individuals prove their superiority in the combat for success that takes place in daily life.

Particularly blacks in America were never afforded equal opportunities in the fight for advancement, and one of the successes of the Civil Rights Movement has been the generally rapid acceptance of the idea of equal opportunity, which is not now and never was fought as bitterly as, for example, integrated schooling. Affirmative action, closely linked with equal opportunity, is another matter entirely.

The idea that affirmative action constitutes reverse discrimination is relatively common, and to an extent publicly acceptable in America. The famous Bakke case suggested that the Supreme Court as then constituted felt that affirmative action concepts could go too far in their attempts to achieve equal opportunity. Unions of mainly white civil professionals such as firemen and police have instituted court actions to eliminate allegedly unfair elements in previous affirmative action mandates in hiring. More recently, the Supreme Court again has declared that communities have violated the Constitution in appearing to set up special opportunities for minority contractors unavailable to most companies who bid on local or state government jobs. Skinheads have attacked the idea of affirmative action viciously in their publications and in utterances to the media. They have followed general responses to the ideas of equal opportunity and affirmative action in America. The virulence of their antagonism to affirmative action exceeds that of most open mainstream opposition, and their reason for opposition may differ: they are blatant racists and not constitutionalists. For them blacks belong to a scum race. Skinheads are not concerned with the alleged point at which solutions to redress very old and deeply ingrained discrimination become themselves discriminatory. But considering their opposition alone and not their motives, tactics, or actions, skinheads are in acceptable company, strongly questioning affirmative action.

They oppose abortion, at least for whites. The split in America on this issue is apparent daily. Abortion is much more greatly accepted publicly now in America than in decades past, but a significant number of mainstream Americans still oppose it very vigorously. Skinheads do not oppose abortion among the "mud" races. This seeming inconsistency is easily explained by their desire to drastically reduce the number of African Americans in this country. Historically, black attitudes (like white) toward abortion are mixed, with significant numbers both opposing and accepting the idea. A black minority has in the past adopted a stance that reflects in reverse mirror image fashion the skinhead attitude: abortion for blacks is part of white genocidal plans and so is anathema for blacks, though acceptable for white women.

Skinhead hatred for Jews is sharp and murderous and direct, again an extreme form of the generally (though not always) milder anti-Semitism traditionally practiced throughout the nation's history and still practiced today not simply by skinheads and other organized hate groups, as the files and publications of the Anti-Defamation League will attest. White America has traditionally been a source of open and covert antagonism toward Jews. The 1914 lynching of Leo Frank in Georgia though perhaps the best known single act of violence against a Jew in twentieth-century America, is hardly a unique manifestation of white brutality toward Jews. Perhaps more sinister was the country's open refusal—spearheaded by covert chicanery in the State Department—to permit a ship (the *St. Louis*) filled with German-Jewish refugees to dock and unload its doomed passengers in Miami (whose palm trees were clearly visible from shipboard) in 1939, when some of Hitler's homicidal policies toward Jews were known.

Ironically, the black community, itself a major focus of skinhead violence, is a battleground of controversial accusations concerning alleged anti-Semitism. Amiri Baraka in his various incarnations from the time he was LeRoi Jones vituperated against what he termed (in his poem "W.W.") "jooshladies" and seemed to sanction calls for the destruction of entrepreneurs he labeled Jews in black ghettos. Jones/Baraka's poem "Black Art" declares "We want poems/like.../...dagger poems in the slimy bellies/of the owner-jews [sic]" and refers admiringly to "Another bad poem cracking/steel knuckles in a jewlady's mouth." Kattie M. Cumbo's poem "Domestics" from *Nine Black Poets* echoes Jones's anti-Semitism when it asks rhetorically "Damit blackman/what are you going to/do to get your woman/from the kitchen of/the Jew?" Reverend Jesse Jackson referred to New York City derogatorily as "Hymietown," Minister Louis Farrakhan pronounced "Judaism...a gutter religion," and after supposedly "toning down" his public utterances was reported in the *Chronicle of Higher Education* (March 7, 1990, A 21) to have accused Jews in general of having "sucked the blood of the black community." Minor figures such as "Professor Griff" (Richard Griffen), once so-called Minister of Information for the popular rap group Public Enemy, have from time to time added their own ridiculous, dangerously anti-

Semitic prejudices to the public record. Reports in the *Washington Times* and *Village Voice* quoted Professor Griff's claims that Jews caused the "majority of wickedness that goes on across the globe" (Hall 12).

The racial dynamics underlying both the appeal and disrepute of rap groups such as Public Enemy are complex, as Gene Santoro's very good analysis in *The Nation* for June 25, 1990 ("Music" 902-906) demonstrates. White obsession with alleged black anti-Semitism may itself be a diversionary tactic (deflecting attention from bigotry expressed in white rock, for example, Guns N' Roses infamous attack on "Immigrants and Faggots" in their best-selling album "One in a Million") that also exposes strains of anti-black racism. Obviously, not all black rap music is anti-Semitic, and some black rap groups such as Follow for Now attack skinheads (in "White Hood"). Still, anti-Semitism in more popular rap performances such as Ice Cube's 1991 album "Death Certificate" which contains lyrics encouraging violence against Jews (and Koreans) cannot be ignored as part of a greater American if not specifically African American climate of intolerance.

Gus Savage, an African American former member of the House of Representatives from Illinois, has been accused several times of anti-Semitism in his political campaigns, for example in employing inappropriate phrases such as "Jewish money" and "Jewish newspapers" that communicate negative stereotypes (Tolchin, *New York Times*, 30 March 1990). In 1992 Leonard Jeffries was demoted from his position as Chair of City College of New York's African Studies Department, in large part for anti-Semitic pronouncements. An article by Herb Boyd in *Crisis*, an official NAACP publication, for November 1989, asks "Blacks and Jews: Conflict on the Cultural Front. Is there room for healing?" Many black Americans wish to foster the healing process. Benjamin Hooks, Executive Director of the NAACP, often says of blacks and Jews, "We're in the same boat now," suggesting that these two objects of skinhead hatred should not fight each other but should unite against common sources of oppression. His remark also recognizes that Jews, along with African Americans, are ordinary targets of attack still, in the United States. Unfortunately, not all skinhead targets are united in amity with each other, and skinheads can draw ideological support from some of the individual groups they brutally attack, because sometimes these groups attack each other.

Considered as political and social beliefs disconnected from the skinheads and their extremist rhetoric and violence, many of the ideas skinheads generally subscribe to are either legitimately held or popularly accepted by broadly based, mainstream, non-skinhead constituencies across the nation, including but not limited to Presidents, members of the Supreme Court, Republican and Democratic legislators at the state and national levels, Protestant, Catholic, and Jewish clergy, pro-lifers, military leaders, academics, syndicated columnists and ordinary citizens of various racial and ethnic groups holding strong opinions on openly debatable issues such as gay rights, welfare, affirmative action, and abortion. Concerning matters no longer as publicly tolerable as they traditionally were in the far from distant American past, beliefs in the inferiority or deficiencies or the peculiar wickedness of a race or ethnic group or religion, their positions are far from aberrant. This does not demonstrate that skinheads are central to American life nor that most Americans are little different from skinheads, nor should it suggest that the general hatred of skinheads is a form of self-loathing. But it should indicate that skinhead beliefs are not in America weird or strange or hard to account for, and that skinheads emerge from and are not totally counter to the American scene.

Skinheads are exceptional, though. They set themselves apart from large numbers of Americans (though at the same time connecting to a few other splinter ideologies) through the congeries of beliefs they subscribe to: they are anti-gay *and* anti-black *and* anti-Jewish *and* so on. They reach down in their opposition to what seem far more primal, less rational levels of determination. They oppose affirmative action because they consider blacks subhuman. The so-called black race is not simply in a Social Darwinist sense not fully evolved to the supposed level of development of the white race, but is a mud race to be despised if not destroyed. Jews are not simply conspiratorial they are diabolic. Gays are not just deviant they are deadly slime. Abortion is wrong for white women anyway not just because babies have a right to be born but because the white race may be decaying and losing out to other more irresponsibly prolific racial and ethnic groups and we need more white warriors and handmaidens. Welfare causes further deterioration of white society while fattening lazy non-white degenerates. Though not all skinheads would operate at these morally and intellectually subterranean levels, the foundation of skinheadism, what the ideology is deep down in skinhead beliefs, is expressive of radical hatreds, radical opposition, and radical strategies of action inimical to most Americans who are not themselves extremists except perhaps in pressured times of war or fear of war, and that is the kind of world—a world at war—in which many skinheads live or think they live, now in the 1990s. Because America has not dealt successfully with the issues that serve as targets for skinheads' anger, the most political among them and those who will follow the most political, which may include the most psychologically needy among them, will probably continue their violent behavior, though not necessarily as skinheads.

As radicals, their radical actions and rhetoric doubtless please some of those who agree with their various individual social and political attitudes. They dramatize but on a real scene the hatreds of hundreds of thousands of Death Wish Americans who sometimes blast away at each other for making wrong turns on the highway or driving too slowly, who turn wedding parties into deadly clan brawls, who smolder and then punch out as (they think) pushy gays parade with pride and demand the rights of married couples, who mimic Jesse Jackson's rainbow rhetoric and don't like big noisy black girls someone has told them have seized control of their daughter's third floor high school bathroom, who still shudder at imagined Jewish conspiracies. But skinheads may also offer quick, momentary fixes of angry satisfaction to ordinarily milder and more rational Americans who become frustrated when engaged in conflict over legitimate and still arguable social issues such as alleged job or school quotas or supposedly preferred treatment in affirmative action programs, or the deployment of lesbians and gays in the armed forces. Skinheads enact quick, judgmental retaliations (though not solutions) that cut through intricate issues. Reasonable folk in their better thoughts may know controversial matters involving the possibility of change or movement away from traditional approaches are best dealt with as complex problems needing substantial contemplation and quiet debate. But reasonable folk do not always act reasonably on matters close to the heart.

America is ashamed of its skinheads now, and should be, though some skinhead actions reflect American ways of the past that were all right generations ago, like incarcerating Japanese or driving out gays from wherever they were found in society or enslaving blacks or denying them basic constitutional rights or the ability to drink from a water fountain for whites only, or pursuing policies that helped reduce the Indian cultures of North America from flourishing communities to something occasionally resembling poorly constructed roadside zoos or museum displays of a vanishing society. We can see elements of our past in the skinheads who are much like Lost World throwbacks to earlier times in our own primitive heritage. Part scapegoats we can exploit to make ourselves feel better by hating them, part thugs who fully deserve condemnation and reprisal for their collective history of violence and crime, part classic mixed-up ordinary kids, sons and sometimes daughters caught up in a mode of expression of dubious worth, one among many styles young people adopt to search for who they are or ultimately will be, part sad rejects from their own families, skinheads don't add up the way they should, the way Americans would like them to. They count for more in American life than their numbers total.

If skinheads demand that we Americans examine our past, they demand that we confront our present also and make us fear our future if they and what creates them are not controlled, checked, isolated and bounded. I do not write destroyed for two reasons. First, attempts to ensure pure societies, pure even from evil, are destined to commit some of the evil they would eradicate. The purist vision is obsessive, hyper-pietistic. In control it can too easily swerve out of control: we kill devilish Indians, concentrate subversive Japanese-Americans in camps, ban words we decide are obscene or unbearably offensive. Second, a strong element of the irrational exists in skinheads and skinheadism, something that cannot be mastered by rational explanations or deduced through rational study of causes and effects. American skinheads are largely a product of American intolerance, American fragmentation of family life, American inability or unwillingness to commit full resources to deal with manifold social problems no one may know exactly how to treat successfully but that a fool would know how not to treat—by ignorance and neglect which themselves supply evidence of American society's irrationality. Americans are not alone in this irrationality that chooses death over life, struggle over cooperation, combat over help, anger over understanding, profit (individual, communal, racial) over justice. That may bring some consolation: Americans are human too. Skinheads are part of the craziness in our society that has always known craziness (Salem witch trials, slavery, lynching, Henry Ford's acceptable anti-Semitism). The skinheads' own version of madness grew up in a punk counter-culture aimed at liberation for many good and rational reasons, but that carried along with it crazy variations producing a society as messed up as any in our history. I believe this crazy, destructive irrationalism cannot be imaged as a tumor to be surgically scooped out from the otherwise healthy brain of the state, but must be seen as (in most people—perhaps not in some skinheads) a growth within the body itself intertwined about sane brain cells and productive organs, a substance whose filaments striate the body sometimes crippling it but otherwise inhabiting it and occasionally—maybe in all of us—taking over.

This irrationality on the individual or group or social level seems a constant of human history and it is possible that it is an element of human existence so ingrained it cannot be destroyed without totally eliminating what houses it—the individual or society itself. It is best not to try to destroy what cannot be destroyed. Further, this irrationality may be analogous to the spiritual fall from grace humanity underwent paradoxically, according to traditional theory, for its own good. Perhaps this irrationality of which skinheads and skinheadism are in part results, is a necessary complement to the reason and emotions which bring sane benefits to worthy people and communities of peoples.

But even if skinheads are viewed as deviants in spite of themselves, even if their kind is understood as the product of social pressures over which they had little or no control, even if the destruction they perform is perceived as a small reflection of their society's sometimes similar and sometimes greater acts of destruction, what is extreme and vicious in their thinking must be challenged, and what is destructive and criminal in their actions must be fought and overcome. There is no doubt that American ways of life have helped produce the skinheads, but other American ways can battle or convert them. It has become trite and finally unproductive in America to admit that we are all guilty, that none of us is innocent, that we have met the enemy and they are us. Some few Americans have chosen to be skinheads and millions have chosen not to be. Many of these may be bigots too, but they have chosen not to organize and beat up minorities. Many other millions have decided to fight the bigotry skinheads proudly display, realizing that some of that bigotry resides within them too like some malarial infestation in the blood that they take pains to keep down. Whether skinheads choose their way or have it imposed upon them, it is the wrong way. Racist skinheads and American society would be far better off were that way exposed as ill-determined, dangerous, and leading to further cruelty and destruction in the future.

Epilogue

In the history of hate groups in America, the 1980s were "The Skinhead Decade." From obscurity on the fringe of the punk scene, from small-time notoriety for their violent slam or smash or thrash dancing in the pit or for getting drunk fast or sometimes lashing out brutally but still contained within the boundaries of the punk world, from being perceived in America dimly if at all as vague imitators of their vastly better known and far more numerous brethren in England, skinheads became infamous as the country's most publicized and perhaps its most actively vicious hate brigade. Once largely isolated from other organized hate organizations in America and among themselves only accidentally and sporadically linked to kindred shaven-head and booted and suspendered toughs scattered about the nation, they came to be courted by extremists as coveted soldiers in the war for homophobic white supremacy who in turn consciously courted other, younger initiates to join their ranks, not nearly so much in the late eighties basing their appeal upon their swagger, their wild drinking, their bashing enemies at dances or in dark parking lots as upon their political beliefs.

As the eighties progressed, the skinheads increasingly cut away from the punk scene that was shrinking anyway or becoming diffuse beyond meaningful recognition. Or they were cut away from it—and were less and less harmoniously integral to the various new music scenes that replaced punk. Increasingly, skinheads became more politicized, though usually in urban areas where they thrived, they would still lurk about whatever youth culture music scene was available for kids and aging grown-ups who wanted to reject mainstream music and cultural styles. To be a skinhead at eighties' end demanded a political witnessing, not just that your parents were jerks or that you liked beer and wild times and loud, raw music. And as the skinhead scene became more focused and politicized, some skinheads and skinhead groups began acting in a more recognizably political fashion, forging links with their like in other cities and vague allegiances with extremists who admired their potential for brute force.

182

Now in the early 1990s, it appears in America that the time of significant skinhead growth in numbers is over: in fact, though the number increased approximately threefold during the previous decade this meant in absolute totals only an increase to perhaps three and a half thousand skinheads. Even if this number is low, even if it tabulates only hard-core skinheads, the aggregate seems small compared to the total youth population (male and female) from age 12 to 25. But while the inability of skinheads to achieve large numbers can be comforting, the social importance of this failure can be misinterpreted. Certainly national agencies such as the Anti-Defamation League and Southern Poverty Law Center should be praised for their aggressive educative and legal onslaught upon the dangers to society that skinheads embody. Their work together with other watchdog organizations combined with police and community action has—since undertaken around the middle of the decade—consistently checked what might have been the anti-authoritarian appeal of the skinhead style, had skinhead brutality and fascism not been harshly spotlighted and condemned without qualification or glamorizing.

Yet even if skinhead numbers remain low and constant, the phenomenon represents a real threat for several reasons. Youth who cease to become skinheads do not necessarily lose their intensely racist beliefs. Young males (and females) who are for a time skinheads and then depart the scene do not automatically shed their hostilities or goals simply because they no longer wear Doc Martens or shave their heads. Some skinheads leave the scene or style because as skinheads they are under too much pressure, they receive too much attention. Some grow out of the fashions but not the ideology (interviews with ex-skinheads, Tampa, 1989-1990). Some, like Pitbull Boy Shane Fowler, go to college (Mencarelli 1-5) and don't always look like skinheads, but still appear to be racists. Ex-skinhead leader Michael Palasch declared he would try to start a White Student Union chapter at Tulane University, where he was enrolled as a humanities student in 1990. Skinheads and skinhead sympathizers who were students were also active at the University of Arizona (Tucson) in 1990 (*Klanwatch*, August 1990) and at Arizona State (Phoenix). Many of these skinheads and their sympathizers will not be identifiable as skinheads and may no longer inhabit local skinhead scenes or affect skinhead styles, and may not count in skinhead censuses.

If being a skinhead for a time were seen as similar to attending a school, if the skinhead scene and activities were imagined as a college, the continuing danger of skinheadism might be better perceived. A university or training institution that educated at any one time three and a half thousand persons, constantly graduating some to the outside world where they would continue the ways they learned at school, would still be considered an important force and influence in the society its graduates were fed into. Just as there is a tendency for anti-racist skinheads when they change allegiance, to move from a non-racist to a racist gang (*Klanwatch*, August 1990), there is a clear tendency for racist skinheads, when they cease to be active or visible skinhead group members, to retain many of their racist, homophobic outlooks and attitudes (interviews with ex-skinheads, Tampa, 1989-1990). Little good and much evil can stem from a "Harvard of Hate," though its numbers at any one time might be small.

Though the number of skinheads has not increased from peak years during the 1980s, evidence clearly suggests that the acceptance and intensity of ideological hatred among skinheads did increase during the decade: three or four thousand committed skinheads now constitute a more dangerous cadre of extremist foot soldiers than the less political proto-punks of the early 1980s. That is why skinheads continue to be courted by other extremist groups, particularly now that their link to Tom and John Metzger seems weaker.

Almost twice as many skinheads as Klan members attended the annual cross burning at Stone Mountain, Georgia, Labor Day weekend 1991. Overall turnout at this traditional rally was relatively small, but in November 1991, a much larger gathering of skinheads (about 160 of them) and neo-Nazis took place near Fultondale, not far from Birmingham, Alabama, on property owned by former KKK Grand Dragon Roger Handley. This rally was planned by Bill Riccio (a.k.a. William Davidson), formerly a Klan leader and more recently known for directing Aryan National Front and for attempting to organize skinheads. The event was followed by another well-attended meeting in February 1992. In April, Riccio attracted about 75 skinheads to a rally on his own property. One of the skins, Edward Hardeman, 21, would be arrested with his 17-year-old fiance and two other skinheads for the stabbing murder just hours later of a homeless black man. In August 1992, Riccio and six other men considered by Georgia and Alabama state investigators to be fellow white supremacists were arrested for aggravated assault charges and for violating federal firearms and explosives possession laws.

Thom Robb, National Director of the Knights of the Ku Klux Klan, who has been quoted saying "like our great conquering heroes, our people will...drive the enemies of our race...into the grave," is grooming former skinhead Shawn Slater for a leadership role in the Klan. *Klanwatch* has reported that "Slater owns Skrewdriver Services, a mail order business" selling racist items such as t-shirts, tapes, and other commodities of hate.

Aryan Nations sent Floyd Cochran, at one time slated as successor to Richard Butler, to Murphreesboro, Tennessee, to recruit skinheads late in 1991. Butler began seriously seeking out skinheads in 1990 according to *Klanwatch*, and has tailored his yearly Aryan Youth Assembly at Hayden Lake, Idaho, to gain their support. The April 1991 Assembly, held the closest weekend possible to Hitler's birthday, attracted about 100 young supremacists, one-third of whom were women. Approximately 60 skinheads came. Incredibly enough, children played a game called "Pin-the-nose-on-the-Jew." Attendance in 1992 was not as large as usual. Approximately 55 white supremacist youths showed up, many of whom were skinheads. All were treated to demonstrations of survival skills, hand-to-hand combat, and workshops on topics such as security, propaganda, and the police. A highlight of the affair is always the night lighting of a huge swastika.

Ben Klassen, author of *The White Man's Bible* and *Building a Whiter and Brighter World*, and Pontifex Maximus of the racist Church of the Creator, recruits in prisons and among skinheads to gain adherents to his causes. He has titled some skinheads Reverends of his church, and they have performed tasks for him such as distributing his monthly paper *Racial Loyalty*, the "Spearhead of the White Racial Holy War" which declares each issue "IT'S GREAT TO BE WHITE!" Klassen's thought for Black History Month in 1991 was "let's...make sure the only place our children will ever have to encounter a nigger is in a history book." (*Klanwatch* issues for December 1991, and February, April, June 1992).

Generally, however, the media and public at large appear to have lost some of their interest in skinheads in America though there is greater interest than ever before in European skinheads who are aware of their American counterparts and like them sometimes attack using baseball bats. While the sensational impact skinheads made upon American society because of their youth, hostilities, their shocking appearance, their willingness and even desire to perform violence upon their enemies seems to have diminished (in America, far out is never far out enough for long), the brutal ideology that is now a part of their style still operates strongly and dangerously. Reports from the new decade amply reveal a continuing history of hate crimes they instigate, and suggest that increasingly they are behaving like participants in an at least vaguely political movement, and less and less like unruly rock concert fans. Their general attraction toward hate-filled sub-categories of heavy metal music curiously reflects their greater interest in manufactured rather than home made weapons. Their compelling if repugnant image still gains them attention on the youth music scene. The group Unrest has recorded a song "Yes, She is My Skinhead Girl," and more notoriously, Ice-T has fantasized sodomizing skinhead girls in "KKK Bitch." But more and more, music has if not completely vanished from their scene, been drowned out by ideologies and actions of hate.

Skinheads have been cited by a leading gay and lesbian legal protection group as responsible for the "sharply rising number of killings, beatings and other attacks against gay people" in the United States. Their "attacks were by far the most numerous and brutal of all hate groups documented" (undated July 1990 mailing of Lambda Legal Defense and Education Fund).

A mid-year 1990 report issued by the Anti-Defamation League notes that although the skinhead population nationwide remains around 3,000, some local groups have grown significantly and formed alliances with other neo-Nazi skins in their region. The Arizona Hammer Skins based in Phoenix are now affiliated with the Dallas Confederate Hammer Skins and claim over 200 supporters. As more American cities experience movement of whites to the suburbs, these continue to be centers of skinhead focus. The *Atlanta Journal and Constitution* May 20, 1992, noted "More Skinheads Cropping up in Suburbs" and presented evidence that skinheads were recruiting in local junior high schools.

Though some skinheads appear to have abandoned the shaven skull as a sign of their allegiance in an attempt to deflect police and public scrutiny, they still defiantly proclaim their racism to advertise their beliefs, and speak out to other skinheads in other areas to gain new adherents to their cause. In New Jersey, the Anti-Defamation League has identified *White Power Skinzine, Fire and Ice,* and *Bulldog Breed* as "skinzines"—skinhead magazines (*Neo-Nazi Skinheads: A 1990 Status Report*).

Klanwatch's *Intelligence Report* continues to chronicle the struggle against skinheads in which from time to time there are clear victories such as the so far crippling suit won (appeals are expected) against the Metzgers for their role in Mulegeta Seraw's murder; the indictment of Nashville Area Confederate Hammerskins on several obstruction of justice and witness tampering charges; and the sentencing of five Dallas Confederate Hammerskins to federal prison for planning to "pump cyanide gas into a Dallas area synagogue" (October 1990 report, 1, 5). Six skinheads in Tulsa were indicted and convicted for 1990 hate crimes by the United States Department of Justice. Two skinheads in Reno, Nevada were finally sentenced to life terms on December 20, 1991 for the racial murder they committed in 1988.

But along with these victories *Klanwatch* continues to indicate that skinheads have not relented in what seems a war against minorities if not the state itself, which is comprised largely of minorities and whose laws are designed to protect minorities. When Klansmen marched in two small north Georgia towns in September 1990, about 20 skinheads joined them. *Klanwatch* has called skinheads "the most logical soldiers for a white revolutionary army" (7 October 1990) echoing the words of Tom and John Metzger and other leaders of extremist organizations. Soldiers march and they also train for war. Some skinheads in 1990 continued their basic training in paramilitary camps in California, Oklahoma, and Montana, learning about such matters as first aid, rappeling, and semi-automatic weapons use.

Some skinheads not only march and train, they battle. They engage in discrete acts of violence which as already noted when seen connected by common skinhead ideology if not always direct organizational complicity can be viewed as guerrilla warfare. Their language is often the language of war. Perhaps the chief publication advertising their perverted patriotism was after all named *WAR*, which periodically contained a list of "traitors" to the cause of racial war such as Dean McKee's father who supposedly turned his white warrior son in to the police for murdering an enemy black man. In Nashville, skinhead David Netherly was arrested for attempting to intimidate a former "skinchick" who had informed on local skinheads as a government witness, by threatening to submit her name to Tom Metzger as a traitor. Skinheads consider such backsliders as turncoats who must be punished.

Accounts of victories against skinheads in civil and federal courts are inspiring, and their general defeat in the court of public opinion offers another sign that they are being contained in their battle for bigotry. But most depressing are the casualty lists *Klanwatch* maintains, under the bi-monthly heading "For the Record." Skinheads continue to intimidate, harass, vandalize, assault, and murder their enemies, including their standard black, Jewish, Latino, Asian, and gay victims; people who simply become targets of their often random violence; and non-racist skinheads or skinhead drop-outs who have fallen from the true way. Many of these incidents are unsensational, involve small numbers of participants, and do not evoke nationwide headlines, but they are frequent and widespread.

In Vancouver, Washington, two black teenagers were harassed while waiting for a bus by a gang of skinheads. This occurred on May 19, 1990, just a day after and a whole country distant from the fight precipitated between black and white high school students in Sebring, Florida by skinheads who had published a racist, Satanic, underground newspaper. In Texas a skinhead stabbed a white man he had seen walking with a black friend. In Seattle seven skinheads attacked a white man calling him "cocksucker," "faggot," and "nigger." In Salt Lake City three skinheads were charged for allegedly beating a gay man with nunchaku sticks in a city park.

In Bakersfield, California, four men and a boy, all allegedly skinheads, were arrested for assaulting four other alleged Skinheads Against Racial Prejudice (SHARP) in their apartment. In Sacramento, police arrested a man for murder and assault with a deadly weapon after a fatal stabbing that occurred during a fight involving at least thirty skinheads from several factions including Skinheads Against Racial Prejudice. In Houston, two 18-year-old skinheads were arrested for killing a 15-year-old Asian American. In Pittsburgh, Pennsylvania, a skinhead was convicted of murdering a social worker. The skinhead and his accomplice kicked their victim in the head repeatedly with their combat boots as he lay helpless on the floor of his apartment. Skinheads are learning to use automatic assault weapons in their war for racial and ethnic and sexual purity, but sometimes for them it's back to basics. Where have all the boot boys gone? The answer is they have not yet departed. In a small town in Oregon, one of them banged the head of a black man against a wooden park bench. The logic of simple brute force seems still a significant element of their self-presentational style.

That style is still set forth in literature distributed by skinheads in Montgomery, Alabama, and at a shopping center in San Ramon, California. Skinhead bands No Remorse, Bound For Glory, and War Cry sang the style at a meeting of the Oklahoma White Man's Association and International White Aryan Resistance Movement in Inola, Oklahoma. About 300 guests listened, including Canadian, Australian, and British visitors. Tom and John Metzger applauded the performance (selected items from *Klanwatch Intelligence Report*, August 1990 and October 1990). In Minnesota, the Northern Hammer Skins displayed their style on St. Paul's city cable access Channel 45, running a free, ten-second spot announcement approximately every quarter hour. Cable television is increasingly a medium used for spreading extremist ideas and publicizing skinhead attitudes, as the ADL's special report *Electronic Hate* amply demonstrates. While not at all shedding their early willingness and desire to commit violence as a way of expressing their style, the evolving skinheads seem to be learning more modern methods of communicating who they are and what they stand for and who they stand against.

Skinhead numbers may not have significantly increased, but skinhead organizations have. According to the February, 1992 *Klanwatch*, Klan groups increased from 69 to 97 in 1991, skinhead groups rose from 160 to 203, helping to produce a "Record Number of Hate Groups Active Across" the United States for the year. While expanding as organizations and to a degree modernizing their methods of communication, skinheads in the early 1990s retained their brutality. The first year of the new decade was in fact "The Deadliest Year on Record" (1,19). Twenty murders were either hate crimes or committed by white supremacists, more by skinheads than any other faction. Skinheads continued to be responsible for an extraordinary amount of violence despite their relatively small numbers and new emphasis upon political measures. Accounts of their arrogant and criminal activities seem to tumble around in an endless cycle of repetition.

In San Diego on December 13, 1991, skinheads stabbed to death a white teenager they called "faggot." In February 1992, two skinheads in Port Arthur, Texas, were charged with killing a man in a rite of initiation.

190 Skinheads Shaved for Battle

A dozen skins in Palm Beach Gardens, Florida marched and gave Nazi salutes October 5, 1990 protesting a school ruling that banned Confederate flags. Three skins beat and stabbed in the back a gay Hispanic in Queens, New York, because they wanted to "tune up a homo." A father and son with skinhead links beat up another gay across the country in San Jose, California. Fourteen skinheads were arrested June 27, 1991 at Swarthmore College for disorderly conduct and trespass. They carried baseball bats and chains, the old weapons. In Birmingham, Alabama, three skinheads aged 21 to 17 were charged for the April 1992 murder of a homeless black man. The 17-year-old girlfriend of the youngest skinhead was also charged in the stabbing death. Now the Klanwatch has expanded its categories to include murders, assaults, cross burnings, threats, vandalism, clashes, harassment, intimidation, marches, rallies, demonstrations, meetings, leafletting, intelligence, law enforcement, and legal developments, and all demonstrate significant skinhead activity. Skinheads continue to deface Jewish homes and desecrate synagogues and cemeteries, to distribute hate literature at shopping malls and schools. They attack Asians, Jews, all the "mud races." They try to disrupt Martin Luther King rallies in Colorado and get arrested for carrying concealed weapons in Elkton, Maryland (random newspaper accounts and *Klanwatch* issues from January 1990 through June 1992). Some of them have shaved their heads, some of them have gone underground, but they have not gone away.

***

Attempting to explain "the rising tide of prejudice facing Britain's Jewry" in 1990, an English commentator remarked that "sensitive matters" such as an increasing degree of "parlour anti-Semitism" might "not actually penetrate the thick skull of a lager-befuddled skinhead, but they may provide a climate in which he dimly perceives that Jews are a bad thing and, if he is to beat anyone up, it might as well be Jews" (Appleyard 5). But it is apparent that in America the new skinheads, some of them at least, are no longer to be shrugged away as mixed-up drunken louts nudged into violence by the force of beer and subtle social pressures. Skinheads are still brutal, and many of them are intellectually passive and easily manipulated. Some skinheads, now that their scene is more isolated from protective new music youth subcultural scenes, are responding like political organizers. The group loss in terms of growth may be compensated for by a gain in cohesiveness and clearer direction. What was once a kind of unpleasant and very tenuously connected band of mobs, splinters of a never truly bound together movement, appears now to resemble a bundle of still largely separate chapters—not nearly so isolated from each other—of the same not quite fully formed organization. The word fascist derives from *fasces*, usually imaged as a bundle of tightly gathered sticks. The neo-fascist skinheads can be visualized in this fashion, as separate sticks or clubs, some of which are without doubt linked to each other, all of which are in proximity to each other waiting for final assemblage. Whether they organize themselves tightly together or are given unified shape from without, they will still constitute a dangerous weapon of extremism and hate.

It is always possible that the agencies responsible in the United States for informing Americans about skinhead activities may have overstated their importance and distorted the nature of the threat they embody. Skinheads are few in number, and the crimes they commit are still only a fraction of the hate crimes perpetrated throughout the country. Skinheads in fact commit more standard crimes than they commit hate crimes: sometimes when they smash about they seem to lash out indiscriminately, crazily.

Perhaps too many of them are too anarchic, too intellectually jumpy and emotionally undisciplined to be organizable into an effective force. Perhaps they will wither away as have other extreme youth subcultures, victims of hyper-rapid cultural aging. Perhaps they constituted a momentary unmasking of primal hates too desperate and grotesque to maintain.

But just as a large body of evidence indicates that skinheads were the most disturbing new manifestation of extremist hate to develop during the 1980s, it is clear that, at the start of the 1990s anyway, their continuing presence, their declared intentions, and their visible activities reveal that they remain a social evil that must be watched closely and carefully, and opposed with vigor. Whatever the extent of their real power is, they still think and do what too many Americans who are not skinheads think and would like to do. They could not have been born here and existed for a decade as they have if this were not so. They take into their ranks young Americans whose often unformed prejudices become sharpened by the indoctrination that belonging to such a band of zealots naturally engenders, and they can return to society bigots still whose age or temperamental drift or changed social circumstances may have led them away from membership in the group whose life style is so isolating and in many ways so self-destructively demanding.

Skinheads are a threat in themselves, and a frightening revelation of deadly attitudes that are far from unique to them, that are held by other non-skinheads with varying degrees of intensity and willingness to fight for violently. They are also dangerous because they can feed back into American life young men—and women—who though they are no longer skinheads, may carry through life some of the sharpened hates and willingness to act hatefully the skinhead way has come to encourage. It is not necessary to look like a skinhead, or to claim active membership in a skinhead gang, to be a skinhead in spirit and behavior. It never was.

Works Cited

Alibhai, Yasmin. "Mean Street." *New Statesman and Society* 10 Feb. 1989.

Anscombe, Isabelle, and Dike Blair. *Punk.* New York: Urizen Books, 1978.

Anti-Defamation League of B'nai B'rith. *Audit of Anti-Semitic Incidents.* New York, 1988.

_____. *Electronic Hate: Bigotry Comes To TV.* A report of the Civil Rights Division of the ADL. New York, 1991.

_____. *Extremism on the Right: A Handbook.* A report of the Civil Rights Division of the ADL. Rev. ed. New York, 1988.

_____. *Hate Groups in America: A Record of Bigotry and Violence.* A report of the Civil Rights Division of the ADL. Rev. ed. New York, 1988. (There is also an ADL pamphlet with the same title, issued in 1988.)

_____. *The Hate Movement Today: A Chronicle of Violence and Disarray.* New York, 1988. Pamphlet.

_____. "Louis Farrakhan." New York, 1990. Broadside.

_____. *Neo-Nazi Skinheads: A 1990 Status Report.* New York, 1990.

_____. *Shaved For Battle: Skinheads Target America's Youth.* New York, 1987.

_____. *The Skinheads: An Update on "Shaved For Battle."* New York, 1988.

_____. *Skinheads Target The Schools.* New York, 1989. Pamphlet.

_____. *Skinheads Target The Schools.* Rev. ed. New York, 1989.

_____. "Skinheads Target the Schools." New York, 1989. Broadside.

_____. "Special Edition: Skinheads Target America's Youth." New York, 1988. Broadside.

_____. "Tom Metzger." Special Edition. New York, n.d. Broadside.

_____. *Young and Violent: The Growing Menace of America's Neo-Nazi Skinheads.* New York, 1988. I was fortunate to be allowed to use the ADL's archives, which contain among other items, articles clipped from newspapers and magazines and sent to ADL from various sources. I offer in the text as complete information as I can regarding these items. This holds true for similarly clipped items in my own possession which I have received from various interested respondents.

Appleyard, Brian. "Forum." *The Sunday Times* (London), Oct. 14, 1990, Section 3.

Baker, Glenn A., and Stuart Coupe. *The New Music.* New York: Harmony Books, 1981.

193

194   Skinheads Shaved for Battle

Bangs, Lester. *Psychotic Reactions and Carburetor Dung*. New York: Alfred A. Knopf, 1981.

Belsito, Peter, and Bob Davis. *Hardcore California: A History of Punk and New Wave*. San Francisco: Last Gasp, 1983.

Belz, Carl. *The Story of Rock*. New York: Oxford UP, 1972.

Bergman, Billy, and Richard Horn. *Recombinant Do-Re-Mi: Frontiers of the Rock Era*. New York: Quill, 1985.

Black, Edwin. "Skinheads on a Rampage," *The Jewish Monthly* (Jan. 1988).

Blackmore, John. "Skinheads Are Human." *New Society* 4 June 1981.

Bladow, Janel, and Mark Ivins. *Primal Punk*. New York: Halftone P, 1982.

Bockris, Victor, and Gerard Malanga. *Uptight: The Velvet Underground Story*. London: Omnibus P, 1983.

Boston, Virginia. *Punk Rock*. New York: Penguin Books, 1978.

Brake, Mike. *The Sociology of Youth Culture and Youth Subcultures*. London: Routledge & Kegan Paul, 1980.

_____. "The Skinheads: An English Working Class Subculture." *Youth and Society* 6.2 (1974).

Brown, Mick. "Punk: Something Rotten in England." *Rolling Stone* 11 Aug. 1977.

Burr, A. "The Ideologies of Despair: A Symbolic Interpretation of Punks & Skinheads' Usage of Barbiturates." *Social Sciences & Medicine* 19.9 (1984).

Carson, Tom. *Twisted Kicks*. Glenn Ellen, CA: Entwhistle Books, 1981.

Cash, Tony, ed. *Anatomy of Pop*. London: BBC Publications, 1970.

Cashmore, Ernest. *No Future: Youth and Society*. London: Heinemann, 1984.

Castellini, John. *Rudiments of Music*. New York: W.W. Norton and Co., 1962.

Center for Democratic Renewal. *Skinhead Nazis and Youth Information Packet*. Atlanta: Center for Democratic Renewal n.d.

_____. *Peddling Racist Violence For A New Generation: A Profile of Tom Metzger & The White Aryan Resistance*. Atlanta: Center for Democratic Renewal n.d.

_____. "Jailhouse Rock, 1988," in *Searchlight. Skinhead Nazis and Youth Information Packet*. Atlanta: Center for Democratic Renewal n.d.

Christgau, Robert. "We Have to Deal with It." *Village Voice* 9 Jan. 1978.

Clapton, Diana. *Lou Reed and the Velvet Underground*. New York: Proteus Books, 1982.

Clarke, John. "The Skinheads and The Magical Recovery of Community." *Resistance Through Ritual: Youth Subcultures in Post War Britain*. Eds. Susie Daniel and Pete McGuire. London: Hutchinson, 1976.

Clarke, John, and Tony Jefferson. "Working Class Youth Cultures." *Working Class Youth Culture*. Eds. Geoff Munghum and Geoff Pearson. London: Routledge & Kegan Paul, 1976.

Cohen, Phil. "Subcultural Conflict and Working Class Community." *Working Papers in Cultural Studies* 2 (1972).

Cohen, Phil, and David Robins. *Knuckle Sandwich: Growing Up in the Working Class City.* New York: Penguin Books, 1978.

Cohen, Stanley. *Folk Devils and Moral Panics: The Creation of the Mods and Rockers.* 2nd ed. New York: St. Martin's, 1980.

Coon, Caroline. *1988: The New Wave Punk Rock Explosion.* London: Omnibus P, 1977.

_____. "Anarchy, Venom, Outrage, Fury!" *Melody Maker* 27 Nov. 1976.

Cooper, Mary H. "The Growing Danger of Hate Groups." *Congressional Quarterly's Editorial Research Reports* 1.18 (12 May 1989).

Coplon, Jeff. "Skinhead Nation." *Rolling Stone* 1 Dec. 1988.

Corrigan, Paul. *Schooling the Smash Street Kids.* London: Macmillan Publishing Co., 1979.

Daniel, Susie, and Pete McGuire, eds. *The Paint House: Words From An East End Gang.* Middlesex, England: Penguin Books, Ltd., 1972.

Elson, Howard. *Early Rockers.* New York: Proteus Books, 1982.

Emerson, Ken. "Today's Punks Make the Old Punks Sound Mellow." *New York Times Magazine* 4 Dec. 1977.

Frame, Pete. *Pete Frame's Rock Family Trees.* 2 vols. London: Omnibus P, 1983.

Frith, Simon. *Sound Effects: Youth, Leisure, and the Politics of Rock 'N Roll.* New York: Pantheon Books, 1981.

_____. "Youth in the Eighties." *Marxism Today* 25.11 (1981).

Frolik, Joe. *Cleveland Dealer,* 7 May 1989. ADL archives.

Goldman, Sally. "Skinheads." *New Society* 10 July 1980.

Gossett, Thomas. *Race.* New York: Schocken Books, 1963.

Guccione, Bob. "Topspin." *Spin* 1.9 (1986).

Gunderson, Chris. "Anti-Racist Skinheads Ready to Strike Back at Neo-Nazis." *Utne Reader* May/June 1989.

Gysin, Katherine. "Young White Racists." *Sassy,* Mar. 1989.

Hall, Ken. "Professor Griff, Public Enemy #1." *Music Players Magazine* Mar. 1990.

Hall, Stuart, and Jefferson, Tony, eds. *Resistance Through Ritual: Youth Subcultures in Post War Britain.* London: Hutchinson, 1976.

Harris, Heather. *Rock 'n' Roll: Punk New Wave.* London: Almo Publications, 1978.

Harris, Martyn. "The Doc Martens Angels." *New Society* 24 May 1984.

Harron, Mary. "Punk Is Just Another Word for Nothin' Left to Lose." *Village Voice* 28 Mar. 1977.

Hebdige, Dick. *Cut 'N Mix: Culture Identity and Caribbean Music.* New York: Routledge, Chapman and Hall, 1987.

196   Skinheads Shaved for Battle

_____. *Hiding in the Light: On Images and Things.* New York: Routledge, Chapman and Hall, 1988.

_____. "Reggae, Rastas & Rudies." *Resistance Through Ritual: Youth Subcultures in Post War Britain.* Eds. Susie Daniel and Pete McGuire. London: Hutchinson, 1976.

_____. "Skinheads and the Search for White Working Class Identity." *New Socialist* 1 (1981).

_____. *Subculture: The Meaning of Style.* London and New York: Methuen and Co., 1979.

_____. "This Is England! And They Don't Live Here." *Skinhead.* Nick Knight. London: Omnibus P, 1982.

Hendler, Herb. *Year by Year in the Rock Era.* Westport, CT: Greenwood P, 1983.

Hennessy, Val. *In the Gutter.* London: Quarter Books, 1978.

Henry, Tricia. *Break All Rules! Punk Rock and the Making of a Style.* Ann Arbor: U.M.I. Research P, 1989.

_____. "Punk and Avant-Garde Art." *Journal of Popular Culture.* 17.4 Spring, 1984.

Herman, Gary. *Rock 'n' Roll Babylon.* New York: Perigee Books, 1982.

Hoare, Ian. "Mighty Mighty, Spade and Whitey: Black Lyrics and Soul's Interaction with White Youth." *The Soul Book.* Ed. Ian Hoare. London: Methuen & Co., 1975.

Holmstrom, John. "The History of Punk." *Spin* 1.9 Jan. 1986.

Humphries, Stephen. *Hooligans or Rebels: An Oral History of Working Class Childhood and Youth 1889-1939.* Oxford: Basil Blackwell, 1981.

Ingham, John. "The Sex Pistols." *Sounds* 24 Apr. 1976.

Jewell, John. "Skinhead Rock 'n Roll." *WAR* 8.2 (1989).

Johnson, Garry. *Oi: A View From the Dead-End of the Street.* Manchester: Babylon Books, 1982.

Knight, Nick. *Skinhead.* London: Omnibus P, 1982.

Kozak, Roman. *This Ain't No Disco: The Story of CBGB.* Boston: Faber & Faber, 1988.

Langer, Elinor. "The American Neo-Nazi Movement Today." *The Nation* 25.3 (1990).

Lisanti, Joanna, and Annette Stark. "CBGB's: Sign of the Times." *Spin* 1.9 Jan. 1986.

London, Herbert I. *Closing the Circle: A Cultural History of the Rock Revolution.* Chicago: Nelson-Hall, 1984.

Lutz, Chris. *They Don't All Wear Sheets: A Chronology of Racist and Far Right Violence—1980-1986.* Atlanta: Center for Democratic Renewal 1987.

MacInnes, Colin. *Absolute Beginning*. London: MacGibbon & Kee, 1959.

Malshire, Paul. "Head Games." *Philadelphia* (magazine) Apr. 1989.

Marchbank, Pearce, ed. *Punk Words and Punk Music*. London: Wise Publications, 1982.

Marsh, Dave. *Fortunate Son*. New York: Random House, 1985.

_____. *Rock and Roll Confidential Report*. New York: Pantheon Books, 1985.

Mayer, Marshall. "White Supremacy Groups: Organized, Strategic Racism." *Democratic Left* Nov./Dec. 1989.

McNeil, [Eddie] Legs. "Punk." *Spin* 1.9 (Jan. 1986).

McRobbie, Angela. "Settling Accounts with Subculture: A Feminist Critique." *Screen Education* 34 (1980).

Mencarelli, Jim. "Pitbull Boys Bark, Bite Softly, So Far." *Grand Rapids Press Perspective* 24 July 1988.

Metzger, Tom, ed. *WAR*. Bi-monthly publication of the White Aryan Resistance organization. 8.2 (1989).

The Monitor. A publication of the Center for Democratic Renewal. Atlanta: Center for Democratic Renewal.

_____. "Aryan Nations Hosts Annual Hitler Fest: Many Skins Attend." May 1990.

_____. "Diverse Youth Attend Anti-Racist Conference at Portland State." May 1990.

_____. "Far Right Youth Recruitment Serious Long-Term Threat." Sept. 1987.

_____. "Louisiana Anti-Racist Movement Grows." N.d.

_____. "Montana Activists Plan Two-Day Workshop To Coordinate Strategies." May 1990.

_____. "Nazi Youth Gangs Inspire Alarm." June 1986.

_____. "Neo-Nazi Youth Gang Activity Builds Up." Apr. 1988.

_____. "A Year of Shame As Racist Violence Grows." Annual review. Mar. 1990.

Moore, Jack B. "Antisemitism in a German City." *Midstream* 38.3 (Apr. 1992).

Morlin, Bill. Untitled item, ADL archives. Spokane, Washington *Spokesman Review* 20 (Jan. 1989).

Muncie, John. "Pop Culture, Pop Music and Post War Youth." *Politics, Ideology and Popular Culture*. Milton Keynes, UK: Open UP, 1982.

Munghum, Geoff, and Geoff Pearson, eds. *Working Class Youth Culture*. London: Routledge & Kegan Paul, 1976.

Murdock, Graham, and Troyna Barry. "Recruiting Racists." *Youth in Society* 6 (1981).

Murdock, Graham, and Robin McCron. "Scoobies, Skins and Contemporary Pop." *New Society* (29 Mar. 1973).

"Nationalist Youth Create New Rock Movement." *Frontline* Mar. 1987. (Reprint of article originally printed in *The Nationalist*.)

Nuttal, Jeff. *Bomb Culture*. London: Paladin, 1970.

Orman, John. *The Politics of Rock Music*. Chicago: Nelson-Hall, 1984.

"Our Heads Are Shaved For Battle." *Read* 39.3 (6 Oct. 1989).

Palmer, Myles. *New Wave Explosion*. London: Proteus Books, 1981.

Pareles, Jon, and Patrica Romanowski, eds. *The Rolling Stone Encyclopedia of Rock & Roll*. New York: Rolling Stone P/Summit Books, 1983.

Pearson, Geoff. *Hooligan: A Haunt of Respectable Fears*. London: Macmillan Publishing Co., 1983.

Persky-Hooper, Marci. "Skinheads Disrupt Oprah Winfrey Show." News release distributed by United P International, 5 Feb. 1988.

Phelps, Christopher. "The New Skinhead Assault." *The Portland Alliance* 9.9 (June 1989).

Polhemus, Ted, and Lynn Procter. *Pop Styles*. London: Vermilion & Co., 1984.

Redden, Jim. "The Faces of Death." *Willamette Weekly* (Portland, OR), 1988.

Ridgeway, James. *Blood in the Face*. New York: Thunder's Mouth P, 1990.

Romenesko, James R. "Inside the Skinhead Army Movement." *Milwaukee* Oct. 1988.

"The Roots of Skinhead Violence: Dim Economic Prospects for Young Men." *Utne Reader*. May/June 1989.

Roush, Matt. "Sally Jesse Raphael's Show Raises A Ruckus." *USA Today* 16 June 1987.

Santoro, Gene. "Music, Public Enemy." *The Nation* 25 June 1990.

Santos, Raye, et al. *X-Capees: A San Francisco Punk Photo Documentary*. San Francisco: Last Gasp, 1981.

Saporita, Jay. *Pourin' It All Out*. Secaucus: Citadel P, 1980.

Schaffner, Nicholas. *The British Invasion*. New York: McGraw-Hill Book Co., 1983.

Sears, Eva. "Far-Right Youth Recruitment Serious Long-Term Threat." *The Monitor* Sept. 1987.

_____. "Skinheads: A New Generation of Hate." *USA Today* 1 May 1989.

Smith, David M. "New Movements in the Sociology of Youth." *The British Journal of Sociology* 32.2 (1981).

Sneddon, Bruce. "Skinheads." *New Society* 3 July 1980.

Southern Poverty Law Center. *Hate, Violence, and White Supremacy: A Decade Review, 1980-1990. Klanwatch Intelligence Report*. Montgomery: Southern Poverty Law Center, 1989. I do not list here all issues of *Klanwatch Intelligence Report* that I consulted. In the text I generally use the short form *Klanwatch* unless demands of style suggested otherwise.

_____. "Cookbooks & Combat Boots," *Klanwatch Intelligence Report* 56 (June 1991).

_____. *The Ku Klux Klan: A History of Racism and Violence.* Special issue of *Klanwatch Intelligence Report* 47 (Dec. 1989).

_____. *Law Report.* Montgomery: Southern Poverty Law Center. Periodic publication.

_____. "The Persuasive Sound of Hatred." *Klanwatch Intelligence Report* 54 (Feb. 1991).

_____. "Violence Among Rival Skins Turns Deadly." *Klanwatch Intelligence Report* 53 (Dec. 1990).

"The White Supremacist Movement." *Special Report: The Ku Klux Klan, A History of Racism & Violence.* Montgomery: Southern Poverty Law Center, 1989.

Steele-Perkins, Chris, and Richard Smith. *The Teds.* London: Travelling Light/Exit, 1979.

Stevenson, Ray. *The Sex Pistols File.* London: Omnibus P, 1978.

Stewart, Tony, ed. *25 Years of Rock 'n' Roll Style.* New York: Delilah Books, 1982.

Taylor, Ian, and Dave Wall. "Beyond the Skinheads: Comments on the Emergence and Significance of the Glamrock Cult." Eds. Geoff Mungham and Geoff Pearson. London: Routledge & Kegan Paul, 1976.

Tolchin, Martin. "Savage Presents Rebuttal to Charges of Anti-Semitic Remarks." *New York Times*, 30 Mar. 1990.

Walker, Ian. "Skinheads: The Cult of Trouble." *New Society* 26 June 1980.

Willis, Ellen. "Velvet Underground." *Stranded.* Ed. Griel Marcus. New York: Alfred A. Knopf, 1979.

Wolcott, James. "The Rise of Punk Rock." *Village Voice* 1 Mar. 1976.

Wolfing, Monique. "Aryan Women's League." *WAR* 8.2 (1989).

Working Class Youth Culture. Eds. Geoff Munghum and Geoff Pearson. London: Routledge & Kegan Paul, 1976.

Zeskind, Leonard. *A Profile of Tom Metzger and the White Aryan Resistance.* Atlanta: Center for Democratic Renewal, 1987.

Zia, Helen. "Women in Hate Groups." *Ms.* Mar./Apr. 1991.

Audiotapes

Interview by Roger Adams with skinheads. Mar. 15, 1988.

Interview by Roger Adams with John Metzger. Mar. 15, 1988.

Films

Lowenstein, Richard, producer/director. *Dogs in Space.* (Australian film) 1987.

Parker, Alan, director. *Pink Floyd—The Wall* (release date in U.S.A.) 1982.

Spheeris, Penelope, producer/director. *The Decline of Western Civilization.* 1980.

Interviews

Skinheads David M., David J., Eric T., and Mike M. Copyright 1988 by Steve Burcham.

I conducted interviews with Tampa Bay area skinheads and ex-skinheads, 1988-1990.

Records

"Comin' Blood"/"Hey Hey We're the Gonads." Featuring The Blood and The Gonads. Link Records.

"The Complete Sham 69 Live." Castle Classics.

"Live Slaughter: Rabid Dogs." Featuring Slaughter and The Dogs. Label unknown.

"Oi! Chartbusters." Vols. 2 & 3. Various artists. Link Records.

"Sham 69: Live and Loud." Vols. 1 & 2. Link Records.

"Skins N' Punks." Vol. 3. Featuring The Glory and The Magnificent. Oi! Records.

"The Slaughterhouse Tapes." Featuring Slaughter & The Dogs. Link Records.

"White Rider." Featuring Skrewdriver. Rock-O-Rama Records.

Typescript Reports

Rozanski, Geri. "Skinheads." Blaustein Library, American Jewish Committee Folder. 9 May 1989.

Videotapes

Burcham, Steve. "The Scene" and outtakes from "The Scene." Video about the new music scene. Tampa, 1987.

Raw footage for presentation. Rob North (Channel 8, Tampa) interviewing Dean McKee. Aired 24 Apr. 1990.